and Southern
Womanhood

Faulkner and Southern Womanhood

Diane Roberts

The University of Georgia Press

ATHENS AND LONDON

© 1994 by the University of Georgia Press
Athens, Georgia 30602
All rights reserved
Designed by Mary Mendell
Set in 9.5 on 13 Joanna
by Tseng Information Systems, Inc.
Printed and bound by Thomson-Shore, Inc.
The paper in this book meets the guidelines for
permanence and durability of the Committee on
Production Guidelines for Book Longevity of the
Council on Library Resources.

Printed in the United States of America
98 97 96 95 94   C   5 4 3 2 1
99 98 97 96 95   P   5 4 3 2 1

Library of Congress Cataloging in Publication Data
Roberts, Diane, 1959–
Faulkner and southern womanhood / Diane Roberts.
p.   cm.
Revision of the author's thesis (Ph. D.)—Oxford University.
Includes bibliographical references (p.) and index.
ISBN 0-8203-1567-2 (alk. paper)
ISBN 0-8203-1741-1 (pbk.: alk. paper)
1. Faulkner, William, 1897–1962—Characters—Women.
2. Faulkner, William, 1897–1962—Knowledge—Southern States.
3. Women and literature—Southern States—History—20th century.
4. Stereotype (Psychology) in literature. 5. Southern States in
literature. 6. Women in literature.   I. Title.
PS3511.A86Z9614   1994
813'.52—dc20   93-9957

British Library Cataloging in Publication Data available

An earlier version of the third section of chapter four
appeared in the Faulkner Journal, Faulkner and Feminisms
Issue, 4, nos. 1 and 2 (Fall 1988, Spring 1989).

For Betty Gilbert Roberts

Contents

Acknowledgments

This study began as my D.Phil. thesis at Oxford University: its metamorphosis into a book is the product of much help and generosity in Oxford, London, Tallahassee, and Tuscaloosa. My supervisor, M. L. H. L. Weaver, and Mrs. Dorothy Bednarowska gave me encouragement and seemingly endless time early on. My undergraduate tutors, Bernard Richards and Brian Miller, have always been most supportive of my work. John Rowett of Brasenose College and Ewen Green of Reading University provided historical help; Lyndall Gordon of St. Hilda's and Helen Taylor of Warwick University gave me excellent advice on revising the manuscript; Alan Sinfield of Sussex University shared ideas on cultural materialist ways to read Faulkner. And John Matthews of Boston University provided me with an extremely helpful reading in the later stages of the book.

In Tallahassee I was lucky enough to be taught by—I am still being taught by—Jerome Stern and W. T. Lhamon, Jr., of Florida State University. C. Peter Ripley gave me constant, excellent, patient advice about dealing with the strange world of academic publishing, for which I am grateful. In Tuscaloosa, Elizabeth Meese and Philip Beidler helped with yet another set of revisions and provided much moral support. David Miller let me participate in the wonderful Strode seminar, in which I learned much useful stuff. George Starbuck read a late draft and bestowed much sharp wisdom upon it. And the chair of the University of Alabama Department of English, Claudia Johnson, has been near saintly in her guidance and generosity ever since I arrived in Tuscaloosa.

Finally, I thank my mother and my brother, Betty Gilbert Roberts and Bradford Wayne Roberts, for always coming to fetch me from the airport, and all the friends who have had to listen to me talk about Faulkner when many other things seemed more immediately pressing. In Tuscaloosa: Kathy Starbuck, Mary Finn, Francesca Kazan, Harold Weber, Joe Hornsby, Jillana Enteen, Scarlet Saavedra, and Nanci Kincaid. In Tallahassee: Fita Ferguson, Eileen Drennan, Bob Townsend, Michael Moline, Steve Dollar, Maxine Stern, Moni Basu, Ben Wilcox, and Jane Greenhalgh. And in England: Sarah Jackson, Philip Plowden, Adam Sampson, Alyson Coates, Clare Brant, Hero Chalmers, Emma Holden, Jonathan Hollingdale, Michael Dobson, and Nicola Watson.

Introduction

Everybody knows that William Faulkner was born in the South, lived in the South, wrote in the South, died in the South. Everybody knows about the South. The South is violent, backward, racist, macho, romantic, old, glamorous, gracious. Merely the mention of "the South"—Old South or New South—conjures up a crazy quilt of images, negative and positive, historical, political, or fictional; "the South" is composed of a whole range of responses and representations.

Mention "southern women" and the images become more specific: recognizable characters, stock types, stereotypes. Faulkner has been accused of populating his fiction with mammies and white women who fall into one of two cartoonish categories: "great, sluggish, mindless daughters of peasants, whose fertility and allure are scarcely distinguishable from those of a beast in heat; and the febrile, almost fleshless but sexually insatiable daughters of the aristocracy" (Fiedler, *Love and Death* 321). But Faulkner's fictions are too complex, too contradictory, and too much the product of troubled times in southern culture to be full of such unexamined stereotypes. Recent readings of Faulkner have energetically shown that Faulkner's female characters are so disruptive in the text that a reductive approach cannot tell the whole story.[1]

Yet stereotypes can be useful. As a southerner, Faulkner inherited the images, icons, and demons of his culture. They are part of the matter of the region with which he engages, sometimes accepting, sometimes rejecting. I have found it useful to recover some of these stereotypes, or stock characters, to read Faulkner as a product, as well as a producer, of the multifaceted place (and metaphor) called the South. We "know" these women well; we know them from popular culture—the Confederate Woman, the Mammy, the Belle, the Tragic Mulatta—unexamined, unchallenged, fixed in their race and class positions. Reading them against the Souths that created them for different social purposes, or reinvented them at crucial moments in history, can provide insight into the anxieties and aspirations of the culture. Looking for how Faulkner responds to them, reimagining, revising, recovering, helps us to understand Faulkner as a writer making fiction out of a time and a place.

" 'Woman' must be read as an historically and culturally produced category that is situated within specific material conditions and is interactive with the complicated problems of class and race" (Nussbaum and Brown 15). There are good (or at least explicable) reasons why the South invented the character of the Confederate Woman during Reconstruction when white landowners needed to restore their sense of purity and class prestige, and there are good reasons why the Confederate Woman was reinvented at the turn of the century when the whole Civil War and antebellum past was being reimagined by the Daughters of the Confederacy and other civic organizations dedicated to building monuments to a fictional epic history. There are also reasons why Faulkner reactivated the Confederate Woman in the 1930s, another period of renewing the southern past, when the issues of women's roles and the place of blacks in southern society were the primary cultural concerns of the South.

Bertram Wyatt-Brown, in Southern Honor, says the plantation ideology of the Old South requires "the rejection of the lowly, the alien and the shamed" (365). The small farmer, the "poor white trash," the religious dissenter, the foreigner, and the nonwhite are excluded from power; women are also excluded from power through highly articulated roles or "stories," whether about Angels in the House or punished "fallen women." The southern woman "is a personification, effective only as she works in others' imaginations. Efforts to join person and personification must fail because the idea of Southern womanhood specifically denies the self" (Jones 4).

The effort to fuse "person and personification" betrays the deep fear that women, like blacks, might escape the rule of the patriarchy, that the oppositions of white/black, master/slave, lady/whore, even male/female might collapse into an anarchic conflagration threatening to bring down the symbolic order. Personifications are limited and contained; persons are troubling and volatile.

This book is about representations of women. I do not pretend to present the "history" of black and white women in the South, any more than Faulkner did. His revisions of stock types such as the Confederate Woman and the Mammy tell us more about the South at the time he was writing than about the "truth" of life on an antebellum plantation. What I try to do here is show how the models held up for women to measure themselves against come into play in Faulkner's fiction. Even before the Civil War, the South was highly conscious of itself as distinct from the North. As a slave society in a "free" republic, an agrarian society in a rapidly industrializing nation, southern culture represented itself through binaries. The South demanded definition and categorization: white over black, free over slave, male over female, lady over peasant, angel over whore. From the 1830s on, southern society told itself stories justifying its way of life, insisting on its divisions between classes, genders, and races. The South resisted emancipation, delayed ratification of women's right to vote and concocted laws that designated race according to (in some states) one-thirty-second part of "black blood." The idea of ladyhood had (and still has) a currency and significance in the South beyond its status in the rest of the country. As a society, the South has based its ideology on hierarchies or oppositions where a person is defined by what he or she is not.

The representations of women I look at here are situated in one place or another in the binary. The Confederate Woman is defined by not being the Mammy: one is white, distant, statuelike, and upper-class, while the other is black, warm, physical, and subservient. The other "stereotypes" I interrogate here also occupy a high or low position in the South's defining hierarchies. Faulkner's engagements, reactivations, and reimaginings of these familiar images, however, do not always ratify the binary. On the contrary, Faulkner's attempts to understand these characters for the New South involve destabilizing the binary, showing how the categories, the relentless definitions intended to wall off the white from the black, the upper class from the lower, the free from the slave, are actually precarious. Faulkner's questioning, his attempt to "write the feminine," endangers the categories on which the white South built its power. The extreme ends of the hierarchy tend to move toward each other, undermining the social edifices on which the binary is built, in much of Faulkner's fiction. I agree with Gail Mortimer when she says "the deepest dis-ease in Faulkner's fictive world is a dis-ease with women, a basic conviction of their threatening otherness" (9). Women, along with blacks, are the objects of the South's most careful defining and categorizing. Yet women in Faulkner can dissolve the boundaries. Women can slip toward masculinity, ladies can slip toward whorishness, white can slip toward black. Women are Other precisely because they imperil this symbolic order; Faulkner's fictions often show a culture determined to reassert boundaries and failing, as the class, race, and gender roles on which the South sustains itself collapse.

Each chapter of this book engages a different stereotype or stock image. The first section of each chapter deals with the representation of that type in southern culture, the context in which the type appears, the literature and the popular culture, and the context in which Faulkner reactivates the character in his fiction. The other sections deal directly with Faulkner's texts and the conditions of the South in which he produced that text. Perhaps the most important model I use for reading the different representations of women both in southern culture and in Faulkner's interrogation of it comes from Mikhail Bakhtin's idea of *classical* and *grotesque* bodies. The classical body is elevated, "finished, completed, strictly limited. . . . All orifices of the body are closed" (320). The classical body is nonsexual, cold: "The verbal norms of official and literary language, determined by the canon, prohibit all that is linked with fecundation, pregnancy, childbirth. There is a sharp line of division between familiar speech and 'correct' language" (320). The classical body tidily represents the white upper-class southern woman, estranged from her own physicality, divorced from the "low" by class convention, frequently pictured as standing on a pedestal like the statue from which the classical body derives its imagery. The white lady is prohibited from speaking a vernacular of bodily functions from sex to birth to menstruation to defecation because she is constructed to be "innocent" of such things, chaste, orifices closed, a silent endorsement of the patriarchal representation of her as the designated work of art of southern culture.

The grotesque body, on the other hand, occupies the opposite end of the hierarchy. It partakes of "eating, drinking, defecation and other elimination (sweating, blowing of the nose, sneezing), as well as copulation, pregnancy" (Bakhtin 317). The grotesque body is multiple, not singular, low, not high; it is protuberant and excessive instead of seamless and self-contained. It is useful as a representation of black women as white southern culture understood them. Black women were held to be (in contrast

to white ladies) promiscuous, sensual, earthy. Black women are associated with childbearing and child rearing (the Mammy wet-nursed the
white mistress's children so that the plantation lady would not be associated with such a basic bodily function). The grotesque body is, as Bakhtin reminds us, "a body in the act of becoming . . . it is continually built,
created, and builds another body" (317). The pregnant black woman's
body is present in a way the empedestaled white woman's body is erased.
White southern culture attempted to efface desire, partly because it was
black and partly because sexuality itself endangered the "morality" of
slavery—and later white suprematism—that its power rested on. "The
'grotesque' here designated the marginal, the low and the outside from
the perspective of a classical body situated as high, inside and central by
virtue of its very exclusions" (Stallybrass and White 23).

One of the recurring images Faulkner uses for the female body is the *vase*
or *vessel*. The vessel also stands for *art*. In the introduction to *The Sound and
the Fury*, Faulkner says: "There is a story somewhere about an old Roman
who kept at his bedside a Tyrrhenian vase which he loved and the rim
of which he wore slowly away with kissing it. I had made myself a vase,
but I suppose I knew all the time that I could not live forever inside of
it." Horace Benbow in *Flags in the Dust* makes an amber vase and calls it by
his sister's name; Lena Grove, in *Light in August*, is compared to the nymph
on Keats's Grecian urn, "Thou still unravished bride of quietness"; and
again in *Light in August*, Joe Christmas confronts the fact of menstruation
through a vision of urnlike trees split and flowing with dark fluid.

Faulkner's metaphor for creation is the female body; in his fiction he
writes the feminine, giving birth in language. The urn is the womb, to
which he strives to return, as well as the vagina, the desired space to be
penetrated by male agency. In all his work, the body of the woman and
the body of the fiction are conflated; in his words, he tries to control and
regulate the woman/art into a perfect, seamless vessel, yet the woman/
art sometimes erupts, resists, proves to be cracked, flawed, or a space that
becomes engulfing instead of chaste, "polluted" instead of pure.

As Faulkner confronts the representations of women he inherits from
southern culture, he finds that the distance between high and low is
smaller than the symbolic order can tolerate. And while political and
social forces were trying to reinscribe the binary and tear it apart, Faulkner
makes fiction out of the struggle.

Faulkner
and Southern
Womanhood

We have put her living in the tomb!
—Poe, "The Fall of the House of Usher"

1 The Confederate Woman

The Confederate Woman . . . It took the civilization of an Old South to produce her—a civilization whose exquisite but fallen fabric now belongs to the Dust of Dreams. But we have not lost the blood royal of the ancient line; and in the veins of an infant Southland still ripples the heroic strain. The Confederate Woman, in her silent influence, in her eternal vigil, still bides. Her gentle spirit is the priceless heritage of her daughters. The old queen passes but the young queen lives; and radiant, like the morning, on her brow is Dixie's diadem.—Lucian Lamar Knight, introduction to REPRESENTATIVE WOMEN OF THE SOUTH, by Mrs. Bryan Wells Collier

Steel Magnolias

The Confederate Woman combines the images of belle and warrior, Spartan woman and Roman matron, Joan of Arc and Cathleen Ni Houlihan, Flora MacDonald and Flora MacIvor, embodying the religious, political, and gender discourses of the Civil War:

> The men, the soldiers, were the strong right arm, the mighty body of the Southern Confederacy, as with spirit undaunted they trod, with bleeding feet, the way of the Southern Cross. But as the men were the body, so the women were the soul. The men may forget the uniform they wore—it is faded and moth-eaten today. But the soul, the spirit

our women incarnate, cannot die. It is unchangeable, indestructible, and, under God's providence, for our vindication and justification shall live forever. (Dawson 37)

The lady is the designated work of art of the white plantation South, as many scholars have noted, top of a chain of being that proceeds down through social ranks and races, white to black, plantation owner to slave.[1] She is the heroine of W. J. Cash's compendium of white southern discourses, "the South's Palladium," "a central symbol in the South's idea of itself," the goddess Diana, and the Virgin Mary (Cash 86). Like a blank page, the Confederate Woman is an unfilled space, "pure" so that the ideology of the plantation South may be inscribed on her: she is represented as being what men are not and what blacks are not—soul, not flesh.

Such representations of ladyhood permeated the South in which Faulkner made his fiction. Though he lived in and wrote out of the "New South," the iconography of the Old South was present everywhere. As Faulkner's fiction reexamines southern history and southern race relations, he revises the central representation of the Confederate Woman. She becomes a figure in crisis; she bears the burden of New Southern nostalgia, yet becomes the vehicle for a challenge to it. Faulkner's reactivation of the most cherished of white southern stereotypes, especially in the 1930s, both reinscribes and destabilizes the myth of the plantation South, which had been given a new lease on life by the Depression and such writers as Stark Young and Margaret Mitchell.

To understand the importance of this representation of the white, upper-class southern woman, we should examine the self-conscious construction of the lady: "A lady was not a woman who happened to be more affluent than others. She was a white woman whose privileged position was essential to her identity and social role" (Fox-Genovese 202). The social role of the lady both illustrates and defines an interlocking system of class, gender, and race relations through which the South defines itself. The plantation "aristocracy" and its more subtle survivals in the twentieth century depend on the position of the lady. Black women and poor white women did not have access to the protection and veneration that the mystique of ladyhood supposedly provided. The lady was an objet d'art:

The Old South seems to have firmly assisted its ladies up onto the pedestal, that emblem of chastity and powerlessness, just as surely as it forced black women into the dark corners of the Big House to be used as vessels of sexual pleasure or to breed new property. . . . Since white women were victims of adulation rather than violence, they often internalized stereotypical forms and attempted in great earnestness to become what they were expected to be—faithful standardbearers of the patriarchy and its racial constructs. (Gwin, *Black and White Women* 4–5)

During the Civil War the lady recreated herself to accommodate, even valorize, hardship. With the men away, women had to run plantations and farms, sometimes taking to the fields themselves to bring in the crops. In the southern imagination, they became medieval chatelaines with Crusader husbands abroad fighting the heathen or Trojan women scorning the rude invader. The Confederate Woman image allowed women to take on traditionally masculine roles with no sacrifice of what the culture identifies as *essential* white femininity: maternal feeling, sexual chastity, adherence to a male economy where property (land) is all-important.

The southern lady evolves as well from fiction: the heroine of John Pendleton Kennedy's *Swallow Barn* (1832) is the aptly named Bel Tracy. In a pattern noted by several scholars, she is allowed "masculine" freedom of movement, riding, shooting, even wearing boys' clothes, until her betrothal to a suitable white gentleman. Then she is expected to conform to the shape decreed by her "ladylike" clothing and confine herself in the drawing room: the space decreed by her race and her class.[2] Caroline Gilman's *Recollections of a Southern Matron* (1838) depicts South Carolina aristocratic life as a pastoral ideal identifying the women of the household with the flowers of the garden. The narrator, Cornelia Wilton, describes southern hospitality: "I was early taught to lay fresh roses on the pillows of strangers" (23). In the plantation novel, slavery is benign, the plantation is the new Eden, and the plantation lady is the unfallen Eve, ruling genius of the garden that contrasts exquisitely with the satanic mills of the industrialized North.

Literature from outside the South also influenced the construction of ideal ladyhood. Thomas Moore's *Lalla Rookh* (1817) is full of beautiful, brave, self-sacrificing, and submissive oriental women, confined objects of veneration. Moore's southern readers may have seen his languishing, chaste heroines, contained in luxurious interiors, as an orientalized version of white ladies in the Big House, "protected," belonging to the plantation master as the women of the harem belonged to the sultan.

The subtext of this sanitized version is more disturbing: the white wife and daughters of the plantation owner were isolated in their sexually untouchable domestic sphere, but there was, perhaps, a real harem out back in the Quarters where women did not have the power to refuse the master access to their bodies. This unspoken truth may have contributed to southerners' fascination with *Lalla Rookh*. With no *apparent* sense of irony, Confederate women staged *tableaux vivants* of scenes from *Lalla Rookh* during the war years (Osterweis, *Southern Nationalism* 342). While few publicly discussed the confinement of upper-class white women in sexless ladyhood or the sexual availability of black women confined in slavery, women privately spoke bitterly against the system that created two classes of women celebrated for fidelity, yet conforming to two extreme notions of female sexuality—the elevated chaste and the "natural" fecund. The British abolitionist Harriet Martineau quotes a planter's wife describing herself as "chief slave of the harem" (118), while the slaveholding South Carolina diarist Mary Boykin Chesnut asks, "What do you say to this? A magnate who runs a hideous black harem and its consequences under the same roof with his lovely white wife and his beautiful and accomplished daughters?" (168).[3] At the same time, Chesnut cynically sees upper-class marriage as a state of bondage (29–30, 15). Yet the official version of ladyhood separated white women from black women in a violent hierarchy that defined each as pure/impure, elevated/degraded.

Less exotic works helped anchor the lady on her pedestal. Coventry Patmore's *The Angel in the House*, published between 1854 and 1862, sings woman as domestic deity, simultaneously subservient and superior, a "queen" ruling by courtesy. Ruskin's "Of Queens' Gardens," in *Sesame and Lilies*, sums up the kind of moral sway women were mandated to exercise since men, involved in politics and commerce, would not: "There is no suffering, no injustice, no misery in the earth but the guilt of it lies lastly with you" (178). In the chivalric mode, Ruskin exhorts women to "be no more housewives but queens" and "enduringly, incorruptibly good" (174, 152).

The notion of queenship served the South's representation of white ladyhood. The best-loved novels of the elite classes were often concerned with aristocratic, high-minded women. Scott and Dickens were perhaps the two best-selling British novelists in America; while Dickens provided some affecting, self-sacrificing female models in Esther Summerson, Little Dorrit, and Little Nell, it was Scott and his adventurous heroines who took

firm hold in the South. His popularity has been well documented, sometimes exaggerated to the point of calling the South "Sir Walter Scottland."
Mark Twain in *Life on the Mississippi* blames Scott for the "sham castle" of
the Louisiana state capitol, the southern class system, even the Civil War
itself (332–33). But, as James Hart says: "Scott did not create the tobacco
and cotton crops that made for a plantation system and a wide cleav-
age of classes; and he did not invent the cotton gin that made slavery
profitable. . . . Scott's code of chivalry may have contributed toward the
exaggerated respect for ladies, yet such matters were but the decoration
on a way of life whose foundations were more firmly sunk in economic
realities" (76).

Scott is not solely responsible for the literary edge of southern nationalism, either: Byron's poetry and Jane Porter's novels *Thaddeus of Warsaw*
(1803) and *The Scottish Chiefs* (1809) had popularized sectional piety a few
years earlier. What Scott did was lend a vocabulary to the prevailing southern feudal daydream. The slaveholding ruling class could call itself "the
chivalry," towns and plantations could be named Waverley and Melrose,
dogs and horses called Rob Roy and Grey Bayard. In 1860 the *Richmond
Examiner* compared party politics in Washington to the joust at Ashby-de-
la-Zouche in *Ivanhoe*; indeed, throughout the 1840s and 1850s, there were
jousting tournaments complete with Fields of Honor, Queens of Love
and Beauty, and trophies at Fauquier White Sulphur Springs, Virginia;
Pineville, South Carolina; and even as far into newly settled territory as
Florida (Osterweiss, *Southern Nationalism* 3–5, 98–99). Florida had been a
state for only three years, but the *Tallahassee Floridian* in 1848 informed its
readers that the town's May Tournament was "an ancient custom handed
down from the days of romance and chivalry" (Henry 35–45).

In Scott's *Lady of the Lake* (1810), *Waverley* (1814), *Ivanhoe* (1819), *Rob Roy*
(1817), *The Monastery* (1820), and *Redgauntlet* (1824) are found the images of
women that engaged the mind of the South. Diana Vernon in *Rob Roy* and
Flora MacIvor in *Waverley* are high-hearted, politically astute (but interested in power only for their brothers, fathers, or husbands, not themselves) horsewomen committed to a lost cause; Rose Bradwardine, the
other *Waverley* heroine, and Catherine Seyton in *The Monastery*, are conventionally feminine and maternal, but no less brave; Ellen Douglas in *The Lady
of the Lake*, Lilias Redgauntlet in *Redgauntlet*, and Rebecca in *Ivanhoe* endure
hardship through their dogged adherence to principle. These characters
are grandmothers to 130 years of southern heroines, including Margaret

Mitchell's Scarlett and Melanie, and, to some extent, Faulkner's Drusilla and Granny Millard. Not surprisingly, Scott had his most profound effect both on literature and the popular sensibility once the Civil War broke out. His heroines operate in an atmosphere of crisis: the '45; the arrest of Mary, Queen of Scots; the outlawing of the clans. Similarly, the southern woman as heroine did not blossom fully until the feudal plantation was under attack, indeed, destroyed. The war brought out more of the play-acting medievalism Twain and H. L. Mencken deplored: "America, rationalistic America, progressive America, had given the world the greatest of all chivalrous wars" (Fraser 66).

What did this "chivalric" model mean for the elite southern woman? Her positioning within the political discourse became at once more "elevated" as an aristocratic model placed her in the center of proslavery rhetoric. Thomas R. Dew in his 1832 Pro-slavery Argument says that slavery raises the white woman from an inferior state of domestic drudgery to "directing the society to which she belongs" (339). Slavery allows white women the leisure to be ladies, to help create a southern class along the lines of the British landed gentry, to hold the refinements of culture in trust for their men and their children.

William Howard Russell, correspondent for the Times of London, records in My Diary North and South (1863) how secession-mad southerners did their best to live up to Sir Walter Scott, dueling and affecting aristocratic ways as if they were all Tidewater gentlemen descended from Prince Rupert's cavalry: "A generation or two of family suffice in this new country, if properly supported by the possession of negroes and acres, to give pride of birth" (1:163). The one-time governor of South Carolina and slaveholder, James Henry Hammond, whose family was of lower-middle-class origins, became obsessed in later life with establishing his descent from nobility. He hired a genealogical researcher, then fired him when the search showed nothing but humble folk on Hammond's family tree.[4]

The lady as represented in plantation ideology was a powerless, though significant, player in these class-establishing games, used as a focal point for the virtues of southern society, an image of the virtues endorsed if not necessarily adhered to by the Old South patriarchy, a justification for slavery, an emblem of the wealth and refinement of the region: "the shield-bearing Athena gleaming whitely in the clouds, the standard for its rallying, the mystic symbol of its nationality in the face of the foe, . . . the lily-pure Maid of Astolat" (Cash 86).

The Confederate Woman, the specifically Civil War version of the lady, appeared in print before the war even ended. In 1864 Augusta Jane Evans published a blockade-running success dedicated to the women of the South. In *Macaria; or, Altars of Sacrifice*, heroines Irene and Electra give themselves to the Confederacy, virgin icons of patriotism. Electra declares: "Irene, the women of the South must exercise an important influence on determining our national destiny . . . I am going to true womanly work— in the crowded hospitals to watch faithfully over sick and wounded" (245). Civil War women's diaries and journals were printed by the cartload during and after the war, peopled with real-life Irenes and Electras coping with hardship. One of the earliest published was Rose O'Neal Green-how's dramatic *My Imprisonment and the First Year of Abolition Rule at Washington* (1863). The plot is pure Scott: Rose, smuggling military secrets across the Potomac, is chased and captured. She has an aristocratic sense of injury, comparing her treatment to "the days of the Directory in France" and likening herself to Mary Stuart (7).

Defeat was the site of the Lost Cause aesthetic: "Chivalric romanticism makes the idea of failure insidiously attractive" (Fraser 33). Losing the war devastated the South economically but made it rich with poetic possi-bility, a sort of Scotland-in-exile, a nation of Dixie Jacobites. Southerners were not blind to the literary opportunities afforded by the cataclysmic era, presenting the Confederate Woman as a kind of apologia for the war itself. An industry dedicated to the heroinization of southern women sprang up. Eliza Frances Andrews in her *War-time Journal of a Georgia Girl* (1908) sees material for "future Scotts and Schillers of America" in the em-broidered tales that were already gathering around Confederate life (238). Virginia Tunstall Clay, married to the Confederate senator Clement Clay, writes in her memoirs of a graceful world utterly wrecked. She lingers over details of her "belleship," the glamor of Richmond's war parties, class heroes like Major General J. E. B. Stuart, "conspicuous one night in charades, and the next they brought him in, dying from a ghastly wound received upon the battle-field" (Clay 171). She tells of her harrowing im-prisonment and, like Rose Greenhow, sees the plight of landowners as comparable to that of the French nobles in the *Terreur*: "As we drove away from the station, I felt much as must have felt the poor wretches in the French Revolution as they sat in the tumbrels that bore them to the guil-lotine" (253). The Confederate Woman as heroine rejoices in hardship: as she stands in the wreck of her antebellum garden, Clay declares, "Take these flowers over to Dr. French and say Mrs. Clay sends them with her compliments. Tell him that these camomile blossoms are like the Southern ladies—the more they are bruised and oppressed the sweeter and stronger they grow!" (285).

Virginia Clay's memoirs are consciously "literary," a construction of a construction: the preface says her "rich memories" are a "legacy, not alone to the South, but to all lovers of the romantic and eventful in our national history" (viii). Partisan politics, the war itself, the complexities of Reconstruction, are erased to "write" the South as a fiction full of heroines.[5]

Mary Boykin Chesnut creates a polished, literate, occasionally sardonic picture of the Confederate Woman as belle, as heroine, as remembrancer, as unvanquished, all assembled quite deliberately.[6] Chesnut was a Confederate court lady, widely read, sophisticated, no fashion-obsessed apologist but a serious social critic.[7] She could be skeptical about her culture: "Wonderful how people will grub, fight, bleed and die for a genealogical tree in this democratic republic"; she could be skeptical about the South's chances in the war: "We have élan enough and to spare. If we only had patience and circumspection" (303, 219). She left a brilliant record of what Confederate salons were reading: Goethe, Mary Shelley, Byron, Kingsley, Eliot, Swift, and the inevitable Scott. Yet even this self-possessed social observer subscribed to the image of the Confederate Woman, picturing the invincible lady defying the foe while quoting Seneca: "Medea—when asked: 'Country, wealth, husband, children—all gone. What remains?' 'Medea remains.'" (302).

Mary Chesnut, like so many others, sees the war as a class struggle, southern aristocrats versus the northern bourgeoisie. She compares the plight of the plantation gentry to the French aristocrats' downfall: "They danced and flirted until the tumbrel came for them, too." She assigns literary characters to the ladies of the Confederate elite: Mrs. Robert Barnwell is "Rowena" and Rachel Lyons is "Rebecca" (419). Scott's celebration of nationalism is echoed in her declarations without his mitigating pragmatism: "These Yankees may kill us and lay waste the land for a while, but conquer us? Never!" (88).

Both as moral center of the former plantation Eden and moral mainstay of wartime, the Confederate Woman received her most thorough anatomization in the works of Thomas Nelson Page, the best known of the Lost Cause romancers. His *The Old Dominion: Her Making and Manners* (1908) celebrates the impoverished southern nobility: "Hats were plaited of wheat or oat-straw by the girls; old silk stockings were fashioned into gloves; ball dresses were fashioned from old lace curtains, and ladies' slippers were made from bits of old satin which might have been remnants of ball dresses worn by the fair wearers' great-grandmothers at Lady Washington's levees" (326). Page shows how the construction of ladyhood depends upon aristocracy, history, and various material signs ("bits of old satin" or "old lace curtains") that conjure up a whole world of privilege as well as expectations of race and gender. His "Social Life in Old Virginia Before the War" is a kind of hagiography of the characters of that world from Mammy to Mistress. The illustrated version of 1897 (drawings by "the Misses Cowles") renders southern scenes as cameos, settings for the prelapsarian Eden: "the Plantation House," "Christmas Eve," and "The Sideboard." In the prose Page accords small space to men, the plantation heirs ("given to self-indulgence," "brave") or the Master ("grave and knightly courtesy"), focusing instead on women. The daughters are flowerlike belles: "peach-blossom and snow; languid, delicate, saucy" and "possessed [of] a reserve force which was astounding" (162–63). As for the golden core of the plantation, the Mistress, she had unchallenged moral authority: "What she really was was known only to God. Her life was one long act of devotion—devotion to God, devotion to her husband, devotion to her children, devotion to her servants, to her friends, to the poor, to all humanity. Nothing happened within the range of her knowledge that her sympathy did not reach and her charity and wisdom did not ameliorate. She was the head and front of the church" (155).

Yet despite this devout obeisance to the mistress, she is really praised here for her submissive qualities, for her selflessness; she is both mistress of all and servant to all, Ruskin's queen, secure for a while in her garden but destined, like Job, to be tried.[8]

William Dean Howells said "the wrecks of slavery are fast growing a fungus crop of sentiment" (Hart 202). The southern heroine dominated popular art of the 1880s and remained prominent well beyond the turn of the century. There were a number of plays with southern themes on the New York stage: Shenandoah, Colonel Carter, Alabama, and May Blossom. Such northern periodicals as Scribner's Monthly Magazine and the Century ran essays by Civil War veterans, stories by George Washington Cable, Grace King, and Thomas Nelson Page. The commerce captains of a rapidly urbanizing and industrializing America recognized in southern material an attractive myth of a former agrarian and aristocratic decorum where women (and blacks) behaved in rigidly circumscribed ways; conservative nostalgia for the Old South betrays anxiety over the "New Woman" in Gilded Age America. To construct women in such a way was to attempt to control them, investing them with the enduring strength of the land itself, insisting that their fortunes followed its fortunes: property mirroring the material, if never the moral, decline of the Old South.[9] They would be tested: if their virtue endured, it was somehow validation that the Old South, from which they drew their identity as heroines, could endure. The Confederate Woman as statue (a favorite characterization) is restricted to the limited space of the pedestal, a body of contradictions, a "walking oxymoron, gentle steel, living marble" (Jones 26). She represents what Bakhtin calls the "classical body," closed, elevated, pure and single, given definition by its opposite, the "grotesque body," characterized by open orifices, "lowness," impurity, and multiplicity which, in the southern symbolic order, are all assigned to black (and poor white) women. The black slave woman is a body to be used for the sexual pleasure and property gain of white men, represented as "dirty," the promiscuous "nigger wench"/laborer who spent her time bent over picking cotton or on her knees scrubbing floors or on her back "accommodating" the master. The white woman is the preferred utterance of the plantation class: "The classical statue is the radiant centre of a transcendant individualism, 'put on a pedestal,' raised above the viewer and the commonality and anticipating passive admiration from below. We *gaze up* at the figure and wonder" (Stallybrass and White 21).

As a creation of the South's gender discourses, the Confederate Woman inhabits both literary and popular culture as a solid stereotype of clear outline—set in stone, as it were. Faulkner's fiction takes her into account in his tense negotiations of the southern past. Yet for him she cannot remain the marble goddess, the uninterrogated icon of the Old South. Faulkner's qualifying, destabilizing, of the figure on the pedestal marks his struggle with a past he sometimes finds attractive and frequently finds appalling. The carefully constructed Confederate Woman is readily visible in Faulkner's fictions: she is also deconstructed, demystified, and exposed as Faulkner contests and debates the history he inherits.

Granny Millard and Drusilla Hawk: Clothes and Culture

From the late twenties through the thirties, Faulkner's fiction deals with the dangerous spaces between *ladies* and *women*. *The Sound and the Fury, Sanctuary, Light in August, Pylon, The Unvanquished,* and his greatest novel, *Absa-*

lom, *Absalom!*, all, to varying degrees, question or qualify the Confederate Woman, interrogating the past and its survivals in the present. Faulkner's engagement with Confederate Womanhood in the fiction of this time cannot be reduced to a simple act of piety or of demolition. Certainly he was not the only writer of the time to look to the Old South and the Civil War for material. Stark Young's *So Red the Rose* (1934), published the year Faulkner did the most work on the stories that would become *The Unvanquished*, presents an unexamined vision of the Edenic plantation with stainless belles and uncomplaining slaves easily endorsable by the Sons and Daughters of the Confederacy; some other novels, such as Caroline Gordon's *None Shall Look Back* (1937) and Allen Tate's *The Fathers* (1938) take a more complex, less saccharine view of the Old South. And, of course, Margaret Mitchell's *Gone with the Wind* (1936) became—and still is—the paradigm for the Old South as sentimentally appropriated by the New. *Absalom, Absalom!*, also published in 1936, can be read as, among other things, a bitter rebuke to this arcadianism. But some of his other writings complicate the picture of Faulkner as denigrator of the "hoop skirts and plug hats" of antebellum romances.

I commence my discussion of how Faulkner negotiates the female images he inherits from southern culture in what may seem a peculiar place, both chronologically and thematically. Instead of beginning at the beginning of Faulkner's career in 1926 or with one of the "great" novels, I start with *The Unvanquished*, published in 1938. This sequence of reworked short stories dating from around 1934 to 1938 has never been acclaimed in the way that *The Sound and the Fury* or *Absalom, Absalom!* or *Light in August* have. *The Unvanquished* is seen as everything from a money-making venture to an embarrassing regression into moonlight and magnolias legendizing (Sundquist 33). Appearing in the midst of towering achievements in the thirties and early forties, *The Unvanquished* seems a singularly positive, romantic version of the upper-class southern life Faulkner had savaged in previous work. So what is he doing with the Confederate Woman, apparently represented by Granny Millard and Drusilla Hawk? I suggest that during the 1930s Faulkner was working out a range of responses to one of the most powerful cultural images presented to him. I examine this representation of white women grounded in the specific history of the southern "epic" past. The Confederate Woman troubled Faulkner, and he approached her in a number of various and contradictory ways in his fiction.

Faulkner's range of responses to the Confederate Woman can veer precipitously between adulatory and argumentative. This is not surprising, considering that he was brought up in a Mississippi that still had Confederate veterans and, more important, Confederate widows, a Mississippi that fed itself throughout the uncertainties and the hardships of the thirties on stories of home-grown Rose Greenhows and Virginia Clays. Faulkner's aunt Mary Holland Falkner Wilkins (1872–1946), called "Auntee," and his great-aunt Alabama Falkner McLean (1874–1968) did not live through the Civil War, but their stories often sounded as though they did. The Falkner family had many stories about the "Old Colonel," the "Knight of the Black Plume," Faulkner's great-grandfather (and Alabama Falkner's father). Faulkner must have felt, as Margaret Mitchell (three years younger than he) did growing up: "I heard so much when I was little about the fighting and the hard times after the war that I firmly believed Mother and Father had been through it all instead of being born long afterward" (Pyron 35). Faulkner's younger brother Murry said of Auntee: "We were of the common conviction that had Auntee lived at the time of the War, the South would never (could never) have lost it, seeing that the Yankee had us outnumbered by only three or four to one. Surely Auntee would have made up this trifling difference without half-trying" (M. C. Falkner 8)

Women like Alabama Falkner and Auntee did not need to have experienced war and Reconstruction first hand: between the 1890s and 1930s white (largely middle- and upper-class) southerners began to regain the upper hand in propagandizing the Old South, the Civil War, and Reconstruction. Throughout Faulkner's childhood and young adulthood, organizations such as the United Daughters of the Confederacy revised the past in the manner of Thomas Nelson Page's fiction. The majority of Confederate monuments were put up between 1900 and 1912, including the one in front of the courthouse in Oxford, Mississippi (Foster 273). The Daughters created heroes in their statues and stained-glass windows, memorializing "The Fallen Knight," inscribed with "*Dulce et decorum est pro patria mori*"; but they also created heroines, naming their chapters after women from prominent Confederate families and celebrating the sort of exemplary Confederate Woman found in Faulkner's "Mississippi":

> The major's or colonel's wife or aunt or mother-in-law who had buried the silver in the orchard and still held together a few of the older slaves, fended him [the looter] off and dispersed him, and when necessary even shot him, with the absent husband's or nephew's

or son-in-law's hunting gun or dueling pistols,—the women, the indomitable, the undefeated, who never surrendered, refusing to allow the Yankee minie balls to be dug out of portico column or mantelpiece or lintel, who seventy years later would get up and walk out of *Gone with the Wind* as soon as Sherman's name was mentioned; irreconcilable and enraged and still talking about it long after the weary exhausted men. (*Essays* 15)

Faulkner could exploit Daughters of the Confederacy rhetoric when he wanted to: he had lived around it all his life. There is praise here, but also contempt and trivialization: walking out of *Gone with the Wind* is hardly on the same level as fighting off starvation. These women are keepers of Old South ideology, unfailingly upper class, with big houses and portico columns to monumentalize. Confederate Women rarely speak for themselves; they are spoken for, constructed to serve the ideology that made them into emblems of sexual and racial purity. When, in Faulkner's fiction, they do attempt to speak for themselves, they disrupt the pedestal and contradict the masculine discourses that placed them there.

If the twenties and thirties were a time of southern retrenchment into an heroic and mythic past with a particular place for white women, they were also a time of social change, especially for women. Women were finally enfranchised in 1920 (after much resistance in Congress from southern senators). There was both expansion and retraction in the roles southern culture presented to white women; on one side there was the freedom of career and sexual choice displayed by film heroines in the twenties and thirties from Marlene Dietrich to Katharine Hepburn; on the other side was traditional ladyhood: silent, empedestaled, and always under threat from outside. The fire-eating rhetoric of Reconstruction and Redemption whites depicted white women as perpetually at risk from rape by black men, the most appalling form of "pollution" imaginable in the Jim Crow South. The South betrayed an almost obsessive interest in the limits of the feminine, the play between growing social freedom and hardening traditional values. Faulkner's Confederate Woman of the thirties is an attempt to compensate for and respond to the earthquake upheavals of gender all around him. That his explorations of the territory are so varied testify to the dangerousness of the terrain.

Faulkner was also in a kind of private negotiation with the Old South and the southern lady during the thirties. In 1929 he married Estelle Oldham Franklin, by all accounts a "belle" (in the term of the day), and in

1930 they moved into Rowan Oak, the old Shegog place in Oxford, a near-derelict antebellum house complete with white columns and veranda. Rowan Oak was an emblem of the plantation South, the upper class that Faulkner chose both to overtly ally himself with and to critique. Frederick Karl says "Faulkner spent much of his writing life trying to restore his home, Rowan Oak, to a state of grandeur; and yet he was writing often about a world in which a Rowan Oak—like its name—was a medieval or *Waverley* remnant, and in a language which made no contact with ideas of restoration" (7). Though his writing was frequently at odds with the plantation world, and Faulkner himself was frequently elsewhere (Hollywood, sometimes New York or Europe), in Oxford he had equipped himself with an aristocratic household: columns, chatelaine, and a black butler named Uncle Ned. During the late twenties, thirties, and early forties, when Faulkner was most intently engaged in his spiritual debate with the plantation South, he was buying up as much land as he could to improve the estate. Just as he was having at least one serious affair (with Meta Carpenter) yet refusing to divorce Estelle, his fiction was insisting on the impossibility of marriage. It is no wonder that *The Unvanquished*, among other fictions of this time, is conflicted over the past and the place of the upper-class woman.

In an early short story, "Rose of Lebanon," finished in 1930 and later called "A Return," the life of the upper-class Lewis Randolph is told by two men: her son Randolph Gordon and Gavin Blount. Gavin Blount worships the Confederate Woman; in his eyes—through his *voice*—Lewis Randolph becomes a fantasy Daughter of the Confederacy: beautiful, brave, stoic, enduring. During the war Lewis Randolph's father goes mad (this often happens to plantation masters in novels: *Gone with the Wind* and *The Fathers* are but two examples), her mother gets pneumonia while performing the quintessential Confederate Woman act of burying the family silver, and Lewis herself takes to the fields to bring in food.

Lewis Randolph does not need men, except to make a heroine of her: her soldier husband is shot breaking into a henhouse, an ignoble death similar to Gail Hightower's Confederate grandfather's demise in *Light in August*. She farms her land and raises her child alone. Her life is hard and dignified and solitary, yet Gavin Blount insists on lacquering it with layers of moonlight and magnolias. His sentimentalism threatens to prevail because he speaks where she is silent: he controls the story. He asks her son: "Do you know why I have never married? It's because I was born

too late. All the ladies are dead since 1865. There's nothing left now but
women" (Faulkner, *Uncollected Stories* 567). Blount controls the discourse of
ladyhood, historicizing it, locating it exclusively and nostalgically in the
antebellum South; the women of his own time are modern, lesser, sexually available, and threatening to the "purity" of the Confederate Woman.
Lewis's toughness rebukes his romanticism: she is not allowed to tell her
story, but she does get to throw a plate of soup at him, messily contra-
dicting his insistence on her perfection. Where is Faulkner in this story?
Participating in Gavin Blount's Confederate memorializing or laughing
with Lewis Randolph at it? I think he partakes of both narratives, as *The
Unvanquished*, a better example, shows.

Despite its apparent eccentricity compared to the rest of Faulkner's
oeuvre, *The Unvanquished* is a fruitful place to begin an investigation of
how Faulkner reproduces the white, upper-class male voice creating the
Confederate Woman, celebrating her usefulness to the southern social
order—her placement on the pedestal as the classical body—and punishing her when she encroaches on masculine privilege. Bayard Sartoris
owns the reminiscing voice, but the action is largely to do with women;
as in "A Return," the life of the heroically constructed woman governs
the story while the legendizing man frames the narrative.

The Unvanquished is concerned with the question of a woman's—or a
lady's—proper relation to violence and to power, and the consequences
of usurping "masculinity." Rosa Millard, Granny, appears to be an archetypal Ole Miss out of Thomas Nelson Page by way of Scott's tough old
ladies (like Magdalen Graeme in *The Abbot*), the moral mainstay of the
plantation during the war. While Colonel John Sartoris is away with his
troop, she becomes master, wielder of masculine ownership of children
and slaves. It is understood that this regency is appropriate and in no
way detracts from Granny's ladyhood: at the same time, she is keeper of
"feminine" standards of behavior and religion: lies, swearing, and other
"ungentlemanly" acts call for mouths to be washed out with soap. In "Am-
buscade" she faces down the Yankee captain hunting Bayard and Ringo;
in "Raid" she agitates Union troops into returning her stolen plate and
mules, invoking all at once her race and class privilege, her borrowed
male authority, and her ladyhood: "I want my silver! I'm John Sartoris's
mother-in-law! Send Colonel Dick to me!" (120). Escaped slaves recognize
her command: "Then who are you going to mind from now on?" she asks.
"You, missy," they reply (130).

Granny's adventures are familiar Civil War tall tales: hiding under the lady's hoops, burying the family silver, outwitting the Yankees. Her exploits recall the story of Mrs. Scott of Virginia sitting in her favorite chair, defying northern troops to burn the house around her, or the story in Emma LeConte's diary about the old lady whose house Sherman's soldiers were looting but who refuses to admit she is humbled or frightened even with a pistol pressed to her head (Matthew Page Andrews 205–6, LeConte 52). Granny is part of this sisterhood in a nonlethal Civil War where the Confederate Woman is treated with comic condescension: "I'd rather engage Forrest's whole brigade every morning for six months than spend that same length of time trying to protect United States property from defenseless Southern women and niggers and children" (163).

Gender transgression creates a near-unbearable tension in The Unvanquished: the masculine and feminine spheres of Granny's life collide. Her annexation of power as the plantation master leads her into the political and military world; she steals and lies while her role as feminine moralist forces her to condemn her own actions. She moves dangerously between male and female roles for a while, confessing her swindling of the United States Army before the church congregation—a woman asking pardon for behaving as a man at war, saying she "did not sin for gain or for greed" but for "a holy cause, even though You have seen fit to make it a lost cause" (167).

Eventually, Granny's vertiginous navigation between genders endangers not only her culture's definitions but her own fragile body. Her guerrilla cunning fails to take into account the way the war itself has destroyed old verities of class. Of course, the southern class system was undergoing changes in the twentieth century, with demagogues like Theodore Bilbo rising from the poor whites to take political power from the Bourbons (Faulkner began his first Snopes novel in 1926). Granny miscalculates; while operating in the male realm of violence, she assumes that men will not hurt her because she is a lady. Granny is not, as the hero(in)ic Old South she epitomizes is not, indestructible. She naively assumes "even Yankees do not harm old women" (174). However, the code of sacrosanct ladyhood disintegrates; Granny has been dealing with criminals who have never read Sir Walter Scott. What really kills her is transgression: she has strayed out of bounds, out of the enclosure of Big House and plantation fence, into a masculine territory she cannot regulate, where chivalric values are not paramount. While Lost Cause writers create a reconciled world, embodied by the southern lady, and twentieth-century interpreters of the plantation romance often hold out the verities of Old South female gentry as a corrective relic, Faulkner's fiction explores the wreck of a society through fluid gender and race roles.

Though Granny appropriates the power of the plantation master where needed, she is never *sexually* ambiguous, her *body* does not slip from female to male. She strays dangerously from the pedestal, but she is nonetheless represented by the classical body in her pure, cool integrity. According to the southern image of ladyhood, certainly the one subscribed to by the adolescent Bayard, she is absolved of having any body at all: Bayard and Ringo hide under her hoops as if she had no legs. Her body emerges only when she is killed, and it is still almost absent, just "little sticks" all "collapsed in a quiet heap on the floor, and somebody had spread a clean and faded calico dress over them" (175). As Drusilla Hawk takes over from Granny as the central woman character, a more disruptive kind of transgression threatens definitions of masculine and feminine. In her death Granny's maneuvering between masculine and feminine spheres fails. She becomes fixed in the feminine sphere once she is murdered: a passive, pathetic, victim of a crime that must be avenged by her grandson and his slave Ringo. She is unified, single, and explicable, like the classical body. The dominant story the Old South (and, to some extent, the New) made for itself on the proper relation of family member to family member, of men to women, of young to old—that is, the chivalric model—is restored. Had *The Unvanquished* stopped with "Vendee," we would be justified in reading it as a conservative reinscription of the Confederate Woman and Faulkner as a Bourbon reactionary, responding to social upheaval in the South by affirming the plantation order. But the Drusilla stories, "Skirmish at Sartoris," "Odor of Verbena," and "Raid," complicate the issue. Drusilla, cross-dressed, innocent, masculine, feminine, and violent all at once, represents the other extreme of Faulkner's working out of gender and history in *The Unvanquished*, intersecting with his project in the thirties of negotiating the place of the white woman in the Old South myth.

Granny was associated with the plantation as a closed system; Drusilla is identified with a postplantation landscape, the invaded "world of burned towns and houses and ruined plantations and fields inhabited only by women." Granny died defending the patrimony: Drusilla inherits a diminished world. Her struggle is with purity itself. The body becomes the battleground where the competing constructions of lady, woman, soldier, and boy struggle.

Granny's body was invisible to the child Bayard; as he matures he notices a number of details about Drusilla's body: its athleticism, its "masculinity." The first thing said about Drusilla in "Raid" is that she is "the best woman rider in the country." But in "Skirmish at Sartoris" her mother says Drusilla has tried "to unsex herself," wearing men's clothes. Drusilla herself says she ran off "to hurt Yankees." Drusilla's body bears a number of stories and comes under constant scrutiny and dispute: her mother, the women of the town, John Sartoris, the slave Louvinia, and Bayard compete to define it as female or male, "fallen" or virgin. Drusilla imperils the unity of the classical body by becoming multiple: both boy and girl. Or perhaps neither. She defies the privileged position of *lady*, removing herself from the southern social order and so critiquing it. She cross-dresses, venturing into territory neither masculine nor feminine, forcing what Marjorie Garber calls a "category crisis": "One of the most important aspects of cross-dressing is the way in which it offers a challenge to easy notions of binarity, putting into question the categories of 'female' and 'male,' whether they are considered essential or constructed, biological or cultural" (16, 10). Drusilla becomes the focus for collapsing the binaries of male and female.

However, some types of cross-dressing are not enough to obliterate ladyhood in southern culture; the girl soldier was a popular Civil War figure who in no way gave up her privileged status. Eliza Frances Andrews tells how Roberta Pollock of Virginia was said to have ridden hell-for-leather in breeches through the woods one night with military information for Confederate officers; Emma Sansom went off with Forrest's troop, just like one of the boys (150, 278). The tomboy heroine has a long history from Sir Walter Scott's horsewomen to Bel Tracy to Faulkner's great-grandfather's novel *The Spanish Heroine* (1851), in which a young girl disguises herself as a man to follow her lover into the Mexican war. These heroines retain what is assumed to be an essential femininity even in the guise of another gender: the stories emphasize their devotion to a particular man and to southern nationalism. As the plantation mistress borrows the master's gun, the plantation belle borrows a horse and some trousers: they step outside their prescribed domain to protect his land, his slaves, his house; indeed, his women. Though they risk their precious bodies in the process, they do not turn *into* men; if anything, the cross-dressed heroine's femininity is reinscribed in her uniqueness. But she does, in her effectiveness and her bravery, challenge the conventional division of male and female relations to violence and points up the constructed nature of gender. Drusilla's cross-dressing is more threatening, producing Garber's "category crisis," that "failure of definitional distinction, a borderline that becomes permeable, that permits of border crossings from one (apparently distinct) category to another: black/white, Jew/Christian, noble/bourgeois, master/servant, master/slave" (16)—and female/male. She does not return to femininity at the appropriate time (after the war). She demands a third way, almost a third gender (a "third actor," as Garber has it) disregarding the defining binary of her culture.

Drusilla's cross-dressing challenges both gender and class. "Dress, as a highly regulated semiotic system, became a primary site where a struggle over the mutability of the social order was conducted. . . . when rules of apparel are violated, class distinctions break down" (Howard 422). In her boots and breeches, Drusilla escapes the pedestal, "the highest destiny of a Southern woman—to be the bride-widow of a lost cause"; most shockingly to her mother and the "town ladies" who represent the standard of bourgeois ladyhood, "in the garments not alone of a man but of a common private soldier" (The Unvanquished 220). Doubtless Aunt Louisa would have felt better if Drusilla had worn a uniform of rank, at least paying homage to her class position. But Drusilla's subversion is overtly aimed at her class:

> "Living used to be dull, you see. Stupid. You lived in the same house your father was born in, and your father's sons and daughters had the sons and daughters of the same Negro slaves to nurse and coddle; and then you grew up and you fell in love with your acceptable young man, and in time you would marry him, in your mother's wedding gown, perhaps, and with the same silver for presents she had received. . . . But now you can see for yourself how it is; it's fine now; you don't have to worry now about the house and the silver because they got burned up and carried away . . . and you don't have to worry about getting children to bathe and feed and change, because the young men can ride away and get killed in the fine battles; and you don't even have to sleep alone, you don't even have to sleep at all."
> (114–15)

Drusilla removes herself from a sexual economy she declares now irrelevant, denying that the purpose of her body is to bear children and reinforce the plantation order. The war has freed her as well as the slaves. In placing her body in harm's way as a soldier, she demolishes the edifice of white womanhood: she dismisses the quiescent past as a lost locus of uninterrogated tradition: now there is no more anxiety about beauty and status and especially sexuality. Yet she cannot stop the southern social order from trying to recapture her rebellious body.

During wartime she is a hero/ine; when southern society reasserts the separation of spheres after Appomattox, however, she becomes a monster. In "Skirmish at Sartoris," though the war is officially over, Aunt Louisa's forces battle Drusilla and John Sartoris over ladyhood, reporting that Drusilla has "deliberately tried to unsex herself" (the echo of Lady Macbeth is not accidental) by being a soldier and living with her cousin John unchaperoned. Alternatively, she is a "lost woman and a shame to her father's memory," suspected of being pregnant out of wedlock (217). Drusilla's body is an object of contention between the Sartorises and the middle-class, female-driven social order who charge her with violating the "sacred space" of Confederate Womanhood. Moreover, she has ignored her status as her father's *property* and the symbolic representation of the South; her mother further castigates her as "*a daughter who had deliberately cast away that for which he [her father] had died*" (219). In her refusal to immolate herself on the altar of conventional feminine "virtue" as pictured by postwar nostalgia, Drusilla steps outside all possible Confederate Woman narratives into some unspeakable realm.

What Drusilla does with her body is read differently by the men and the women of the community. The men endorse her bravery; the women, ironically, are scandalized. As Howard remarks, "Women who cross-dressed were less often accused of sexual perversion than of sexual incontinence, of being whores." Drusilla has become a "masterless" woman, and "this threatened overthrow of hierarchy was discursively read as the eruption of uncontrolled sexuality" (Howard 424). Aunt Louisa looks at her and cries, "Lost, lost" (*The Unvanquished* 231). In her freedom Drusilla occupies the position of a "fallen woman," a man, a black person, of perhaps that third gender, *not* a Confederate Woman. Yet her bid to be one of the boys is doomed. She may have temporarily freed herself from the symbolic order, but John Sartoris, still clinging to his position as "gentleman" and planter, has not. Aunt Louisa, the master (mistress?) semiotician, arrives, as Bayard says, "in mourning even to the crepe bow on her umbrella handle, that hadn't worn mourning when we were at Hawkhurst two years ago though Uncle Dennison was just as dead then as he was now," with trunks of Drusilla's dresses to resignify her daughter's class and gender, demanding that John Sartoris rectify her masterless state and marry her (230). Though the dress Aunt Louisa makes her wear does not sit well on Drusilla—at first she tries to hide from John Sartoris in it—it reinstates the hierarchies that had been violated: Bayard says "like in the dress she could neither fight back nor run away" (231). She is seen by the men only at mealtimes, she is no longer allowed to work, and the cabins have been sexually segregated. "They have beat you, Drusilla," says John Sartoris (234).

At the end of "Skirmish at Sartoris," however, Drusilla proves that the reinscription of her as lady, dressed now in the garb most heavily laden with the symbolism of the feminine, the bridal gown and veil, is precarious at best. She asserts her allegiance to violence and Bourbon politics by helping John Sartoris kill the Burdens, two "carpetbaggers" trying to help freed slaves vote. On returning to Sartoris, she confesses to her mother that they "forgot" to get married. Drusilla may try to free herself from the restrictive category of ladyhood, but she aligns herself fully with the reactionary anti-Reconstruction vigilantism that seeks to keep power in the hands of plantation lords. Drusilla's part in murdering the two "Yankees" who try to enforce the federal laws allowing former slaves both to run for elected office and to vote is, perhaps, the most grievous assault on the signs of purity, fragility, and "femininity" contained in the wedding dress and veil. The episode is presented as heroic. But when "Skirmish at Sartoris" is read against some events of southern politics during the time Faulkner was producing the text, it fits ominously into a racist discourse denying blacks equal rights, a discourse that, like the struggle over women's roles, Faulkner at times affirmed, and at times attacked. If the twenties and thirties were a time of both expanding and contracting possibilities for southern women, they were also a time of cultural anxiety over race. Jim Crow laws expanded as groups like the NAACP, the Commission on Interracial Cooperation, and the Southern Conference for Human Welfare attacked segregation and black poverty and powerlessness in the South. In 1868 Mississippi had 86,973 registered black voters (this does not mean, of course, that they all voted), but in 1940 there were 2,000 (McMillen 36). The vast drop-off is only minimally accounted for by the black diaspora to the North: during the thirties under 5 percent of the black voting age population were registered. The numbers are more convincingly accounted for by literacy tests, poll taxes, and a culture of violence intimidating (sometimes lethal) to any black daring to take advantage of the rights guaranteed under the Fifteenth Amendment.

The greatest number of lynchings actually took place during Faulkner's childhood and a little before (1890–1907), but there were still plenty in Mississippi during the thirties: in 1934 a black man was beaten to death near Pelahatchee, and there were lynchings in Oxford itself in 1935 and 1936 (McMillen 29, 206, 230). The Ku Klux Klan had been resurgent since 1915; there was even a women's KKK, organized in 1923 (Blee 28). Drusilla, in her white dress and veil, is halfway to Klan costume.[10]

The violence in which Drusilla participates on her wedding day is designed to keep separate black and white—the one powerless, the other ruling. She may transgress the boundaries of gender, but the racial binary is maintained. Her action becomes more explicable in the context of a strain of southern feminism in the period 1910–40, in which "white womanhood" was to be enfranchised at the expense of blacks. Senator Rebecca Latimer Felton of Georgia and her sister Mary Latimer McLendon argued a feminism that based expansion of white women's rights on a contraction of blacks' rights. Felton insisted it was all right to lynch a thousand blacks a week "if it becomes necessary" to protect white women's bodies (Williamson, *Crucible* 128). Drusilla is not worried about black rape, but she is allied with the hegemony of the plantation patriarchy. Her attempts to partake of "masculine" violence reflect social forces located not only in Reconstruction, when the white South reimagined itself as a wrecked Eden, but in the twenties and thirties, when that reimagining was under strain.

Drusilla's appropriation of masculine values becomes complicated by her forced role as John Sartoris's wife, the lady of the plantation. She has known the freedom of short hair and male attire, her cousin John's calling her "soldier," liberating her from the whole rococo construct of bellehood, but now she wears skirts, she lives not in a tent on the march or a slave cabin next to the fields but in a restored plantation house. Faulkner restored his own plantation house; clearly his position as paterfamilias, as "master," was vexed. It could be that Drusilla reflects the ambivalence Faulkner experienced living as a white aristocrat in Rowan Oak while writing about the collapse of this class, most spectacularly in *Absalom, Absalom!*, published two years before. Drusilla is not a successful reinvention of the plantation mistress on the resurrected plantation. Nor is John Sartoris a successful postwar version of the master. Like the Old Colonel, he is murdered in the street.

The post-Reconstruction South of this story has warily reinscribed its old verities, but without confidence. The simple rawness of the war-wrecked land, the stark ethics of North versus South, the absolute relations of black and white, male and female, are no longer cleanly defined. Roles for upper-class white women, officially returned to the prewar categories of belle and mother, are unstable, a cultural crisis betrayed by Drusilla. She is not a "real woman" any more than she could be a "real man" dressed as a soldier. Her attempt to seduce Bayard creates a dissonance of expectation: the result is to be not sex but violence, not the fulfillment of sexual desire but the demands of "honor." If anything, Drusilla is in drag, still the cross-dresser though now more like a boy in girl's clothes, shifting precariously between feminine and masculine signs in her short hair and ball dress, and between feminine and masculine language, speaking of both "love" and the privilege of killing. She can never really be the Confederate Woman, defined by the unitary classical body— she is multiple, seductive to Bayard both as a woman to a man and as a *man* inciting a *man* to "duty": "Now she was looking at me in a way she never had before. . . . the scent of verbena in her hair seemed to have increased a hundred times . . . 'Kiss me, Bayard' " (261–62). Her body, still a site of dispute and disruption, is only *dressed* feminine, she is "not slender as a woman is but as a youth, a boy, is," simultaneously Eve and the serpent.

Bayard rejects her multiple selves—both her "feminine" seductiveness and her "masculine" violence. She is, to him, intruding in the male sphere of honor. Drusilla may appropriate male dress, weapons, speech, and freedom; she may be more a boy in drag than an angry woman. Still, the direction of Bayard's narrative is to force her to inhabit the classical body of the Confederate Woman, to inhabit a category he recognizes, like that of John Sartoris's sister Jenny—"the bride-widow of a lost cause." Drusilla resists such containment, embodying both Balzac's *femme de trente ans*, "the woman of thirty, the symbol of the ancient and eternal Snake," and, in a sense, the boy Bayard himself once was, prepared to kill to avenge the family's wrong: "the balancing sprig of verbena above each ear, the two arms bent at the elbows, the two hands shoulder high, the two identical duelling pistols lying upon, not clutched in, one to each: the Greek amphora priestess of a succinct and formal violence" (252).

Garlanded with ceremonial verbena, she holds the loaded pistols high: " 'Take them, Bayard,' she said, in the same tone in which she had said 'Kiss me' last summer. . . . 'Do you feel them? the long true barrels true as justice, the triggers (you have fired them) quick as retribution, the two of them slender and invincible and fatal as the physical shape of love?' " (273).

Verbena in classical lore has a double association, Venus and Mars, love and war: it was worn by Roman priests serving as guardians of civic order. Drusilla is herself double, Mars in drag and a calculating Venus who can yet only experience the phallic firing of the guns (two guns, carrying on the duality) vicariously. She must experience empowering violence through Bayard's body in a kind of orgasmic catastrophe: "How beautiful: young, to be permitted to kill, to be permitted vengeance, to take into your bare hands the fire of heaven that cast down Lucifer" (274). To Drusilla, maleness is a cultural license to destroy, whereas femaleness is associated with preservation of manners, "morals," and property. Drusilla's opposite, Jenny Sartoris Du Pre, brings from Carolina the shards of the old plantation, feminine objects—stained glass (with its pietistic suggestion), old sherry, and cuttings of jasmine from the garden. Moreover, Miss Jenny, an exemplary Confederate Woman, reinforces Bayard's commitment to nonviolence, speaking the feminine self. Miss Jenny presents an argument to reduce Drusilla to one gender. In her story of the blockade runner, she argues for rejection of Drusilla's lust for violence, quoting him: "No bloody moon" (282). One reading of this may be that Miss Jenny, exemplar of the masculine ideal of southern womanhood, is telling Bayard to reject the feminine in the form of Drusilla, associating the "bloody moon" with the essential function of the young woman's body: menstruation. No matter how "boyish" Drusilla is, the implication is that she still bleeds every month. In any case, Bayard rejects the multiple selves of Drusilla for the unitary feminine of Miss Jenny.

Drusilla's slipping gender irritates critics. Brooks chastises her for being "an instrument of revenge in defiance of her sex" accusing her of forgetting "pity, compassion, and even her womanhood," "a warped figure, feverish in her pursuit of honor, masculine in her concern for the code and her obsession with the duelling pistols."[11] But Drusilla's real transgression is her semiotic multiplicity. Her transvestite desire is for a third place, between the male/female binary of the symbolic order; she can be both seductress and boy, but this collapsing of hierarchies is intolerable in a cultural narrative that demands her subordination as feminine, as lady. She abjures the true faith of the chaste lady-soldier, the Scott heroine; for this her troubling body is erased from the plantation altogether. She exits laughing like Lady Macbeth (who would, of course, have been originally performed by a boy in drag), reduced to "hysterical" woman in Bayard's revenge against her. The plantation's new mistress is Miss Jenny, the self-sacrificial Confederate Woman, a symbol of affirmation never moved to wear trousers, associated not with the astringent smell of martial verbena but the gentler aroma of jasmine.

Jenny Sartoris Du Pre represents the purity of female heroism, married but immediately widowed, showing her a "true" woman yet absolved from active sexuality. Her heroism reinscribes the uniqueness of the Confederate Woman as she states it in *Flags in the Dust*:

> Do you think a man could sit day after day and month after month in a house miles from anywhere and spend the time between casualty lists tearing up bedclothes and window curtains and table linen to make lint and watching sugar and flour and meat dwindling away and using pine knots for light because there aren't any candles and no candlesticks to put them in, if there were, and hiding in nigger cabins while drunken Yankee generals set fire to the house your great-great-grandfather built and you and all your folks were born in? (46)

Where Drusilla's long speech in "Raid" destroys the circumscriptions of ladyhood, this catalog of affirmations—whiteness, aristocracy, resourcefulness, and patriotism—reinscribes the hierarchies of gender, race, and class. The plantation can be threatened by both "masterless" women and "masterless" blacks, but the southern social order can marshal itself to erase the slips, fissures, and multiplicities of such a challenge as Drusilla mounts. Yet her laughter—and her verbena—fill Sartoris as night falls on the plantation. She makes her mark.

The Ghostly Body in Absalom, Absalom!

Judith Sutpen is a collection of competing and complementary texts "written" by Rosa Coldfield, Jason Compson, Quentin, Shreve, and Faulkner himself, all theorizers of the feminine. Judith herself is nearly silent, always distant: except for a few eruptions we do not hear her voice. She is also nearly invisible: unlike Drusilla, her body is not aggressively present. It is an object of dispute but mostly in the abstract: an *idea* of her culture.

It is possible to read Judith as Confederate Woman; much of the narrative constructs her as the *princesse lointaine* of the big house; the distant belle before the war; the stoic, enduring woman during it; the patient "bride-widow of a lost cause" after it. She is a dutiful daughter, faithful sister, forgiving lover, surrogate mother, and nurse, living and dying on the father's land: a tribute to the plantation patriarchy. Judith's own silence encourages this view. She is drawn by others and contained in the stories of others, an unsentimentalized "Meh Lady" who, like Thomas Nelson Page's heroine, holds the plantation together. In Rosa's, Mr. Compson's, Quentin's, and Shreve's narratives, Judith is usually so still, so passive that she almost seems a statue, the preferred form for the Confederate Woman's body. Albert Guerard finds in her a "marble coldness"; in his reading she is the seamless, single, smooth, sexless, voiceless representation of the classical body (308). A "white lady" (in more senses than one: many of the ghost stories of the antebellum South involve a dead aristocrat who makes filmy appearances in white), Judith haunts the narrative(s) of *Absalom, Absalom!* In the end, she is not a statue, not one of Mr. Compson's tale-telling lady-ghosts but a banshee whose suppressed wailing shakes the bounded spaces of pedestal and plantation house.

Indeed Judith is named for a ghost. Rowan Oak supposedly came stocked with its own spirit, Judith Shegog, a Confederate girl who fell to her death from an upstairs balcony while watching for her Yankee lover. According to Dean Faulkner Wells's version of the story, Judith was buried under the magnolia tree in the front yard (15).[12] Living in a house that, with its white columns and its supernatural belle, signified the upper-class South he critiqued but also partook of, Faulkner made stories about various "Judiths." He began writing *Absalom, Absalom!* in early 1934; it was then called "Dark House" (*Light in August* was also originally called "Dark House").[13] Some time in 1931, perhaps six months after he wrote "Rose of Lebanon," Faulkner finished a story called "Evangeline" a "ghost story," according to its narrator, Don. Like "Rose of Lebanon," it concerns a plantation owner's daughter who marries a soldier-dandy (Charles Bon) and is widowed. Judith, silent, faithful, patient (thus the reference to Longfellow's Acadian heroine) bears much resemblance to Lewis Randolph; both face ruin stoically in a war-crushed world. Judith in "Evangeline," is far less a challenge to Confederate Womanhood than Lewis Randolph; yet she demonstrates Faulkner's fascination with pressing the limits and interrogating the conventions of ladyhood.

Judith in "Evangeline" literally becomes a ghost, haunting the Sutpen house. Fear of "pollution," a major theme in *Absalom, Absalom!* is also important in this story: Henry shoots Charles (not his brother in this version, nor part black) because he has already married a mulatto woman and has a child. Like *The Unvanquished* stories, *Absalom, Absalom!* indicates Faulkner's need to reactivate the great matter of the white South—the plantation, the Civil War, and Reconstruction—in an attempt to work out a range of responses to southern history and to its iconic figures, particularly the lady and the "Tragic Mulatta" (see chapter 3). *Absalom, Absalom!* is, however, a much bleaker rehearsal of the South's story. Faulkner worked on the novel during much of the time from 1934 on that he was producing and sending out to magazines the *Unvanquished* cycle (except for "Odor of Verbena," written after *Absalom, Absalom!*). Perhaps the difference in sensibility can be explained by the way the *Unvanquished* pieces were conceived for magazines in a Depression market that wanted a certain amount of romance and affirmation in its stories of the Old South (like *Gone with the Wind*), while *Absalom, Absalom!* was a private obsession. But it seems to me that the *Unvanquished* stories and *Absalom, Absalom!* are really part of a continuum of Faulkner's struggle with limits—racial, gender, and class—and with loss, figured mythically for a white southerner by the Civil War, and with sexuality: purity and pollution. The Depression drove the South (as it did other regions) into a reimagining of its past, looking either for former grandeur and virtue or for origins. Faulkner, writing out of a Mississippi full of failing farms, shifting power structures, the beginning of a black migration north to escape the misery of sharecropping and the indignity of Jim Crow, creates in *Absalom, Absalom!* a kind of Yoknapatawpha Genesis, a myth both of first things and the Fall. Judith and Rosa and Quentin and all the Sutpens are ghosts haunting the twentieth-century South. They are not only its history, they are its perpetual crises.

The crisis is acute when it comes to women. Mr. Compson tells his son, "Years ago we in the South made our women into ladies. Then the War came and made the ladies into ghosts. So what else can we do, being gentlemen, but listen to them being ghosts?" (12). Though the overweening, dynamic, phallic Thomas Sutpen, who "*tore violently a plantation*" out of the Mississippi wasteland, appears to dominate the past(s) being reconstructed and impersonated in *Absalom, Absalom!*, the feminine actually shapes these attempts at recovery of the South's "old ghost-times" (9). Like the first-edition dust jacket of *The Unvanquished* with the belle (presumably Drusilla) standing behind the cavalier, we might be tempted to place Rosa, Ellen, Judith, and Clytie behind the figure of Sutpen. But this would be a mistake. Rosa Coldfield, Clytemnestra Sutpen, Eulalia Bon, Ellen Coldfield, the Octoroon, Judith, Milly: these are the specters, living or dead; inhabiting, frustrating, held hostage to, Sutpen's "design." They are the ghosts worth listening to as they conjure the past "out of the biding and dreamy and victorious dust," a past that intrudes on Quentin Compson's present, a past that intrudes on Faulkner's present, and a past that intrudes on ours.

The stories they tell, these female ghosts, sabotage the stories put forth by the masculine narrators who seem to dominate by sheer force of numbers: four to one. Mr. Compson, Quentin, Shreve, and Faulkner (the most elusive of the narrators) try to make of the Sutpen saga an intelligible, logical tale; like detectives, they try to discover what "really" happened, focusing on difference and definitions, each making a "history" of Sutpen's rise and fall. However, the feminine imperils the hierarchies set up in the southern social order: male over female, white over black, virgin over whore, angel over demon. Though Miss Rosa invokes class decorum in castigating Sutpen, sniffing, "He wasn't a gentleman. He wasn't even a gentleman," she herself becomes multiple in sexuality, gender, and place, "all polymath love's androgynous advocate," giving play to the slippages of the past (14, 146). Though Quentin corrects him incessantly, Shreve keeps calling her "Aunt Rosa" (the title is more appropriate in the South for an old black woman) rather than Miss Rosa, the honorific of a white lady, collapsing two perceived opposites. Though Mr. Compson sardonically imagines Judith as the flower of the plantation garden, the symbol of Sutpen's wealth, she exhibits "masculine" qualities. While Judith's heroism, bravery, silent stoicism, and apparent distance from desire might seem to place her within the Confederate Woman narrative, the different places she occupies in the various stories that make up the novel complicate her. She is not exclusively represented by the unitary classical body, the statue on the pedestal at which men look up. She is also master, mother, lover, sister, daughter, and outlaw. She interrupts the stories and, like Drusilla, subverts the expectations her father, mother, and brother have for her. She is another instance of Faulkner struggling with his cultural inheritance, remaking the Confederate Woman in a modernist, uncertain moment.

I call this ghost in the "machine" of the narrative(s) "feminine" because it is fluid, multiple, and playful, "the concentric and bisexual spaces between the 'manifest text' of Faulkner's male creative consciousness and the 'unconscious discourse' of its own feminine subjectivity" (Gwin, Feminine 35). Quentin himself becomes a "feminine" speaker at times, in love with Judith and Charles Bon, lying in bed with Shreve, who, in The Sound and the Fury, is called his "husband," just as Charles Bon oscillates be-

tween the masculine and the feminine in his relationships with Judith
and Henry. This bisexual space from which the Sutpen stories emanate
disrupts the false absolutes of history, class, race, and gender. Plantation
culture (as reported by Mr. Compson) subdues and trisects the feminine
into "three sharp divisions, separated (two of them) by a chasm which
could be crossed but one time and in but one direction—ladies, women,
females—the virgins whom gentlemen someday married, the courtesans
to whom they went while on sabbaticals to the cities, the slave girls and
women upon whom that first caste rested and to whom in certain cases it
doubtless owed the very fact of its virginity" (109). This configuration of
sexual possibilities with the upper-class virgins depending on the availability of lower-class white women and slaves is presented as the simple
gender politics of the Sutpens' world. Chastity is a fiction of the upper
classes—without a class system, Mr. Compson implies, all women could
be subject to rape. But the South, with its love of artifice and definition,
builds its social system on the "purity" of the white women who create legitimate heirs to the property and the "impurity" of slave women
who produce more property for their owners. The classical body is left
intact on the pedestal only because of the accessibility of its opposite, the
grotesque body of the lower-class or black woman.

   Yet southern culture is devious. Private truth does not match publicly proclaimed ideology; the feminine ghosts of the narratives are like
poltergeists disguising, shifting things around, creating diversions. The
tripartite division of women is no more true than the southern story
that declares black and white racial absolutes. Henry Sutpen learns (according to Mr. Compson) from Charles Bon, the feminized man—apparently
white, secretly black—that gender relations are much more complex than
he thought, particularly down in New Orleans with its mulatto culture,
where every racial mixture is given a separate name. There the virginity
of mixed-race girls is closely guarded until such time as they are taken
to be a white man's mistress, and the institution of marriage blurs in the
plaçage arrangement whereby a white man can have a legal (white) wife
and a kept mulatta, each with her own establishment (see chapter 3). For
all that Mr. Compson expounds his erotic theory of the black (or mulatta)
woman's sexuality as "a female principle which existed, queenly and complete, in the hot equatorial groin of the world long before that white one
of ours came down from trees" in his "man to man" talk with his son,
attempting to cast Charles Bon as the "hell of a fellow" with drink, horses,

and women that Cash identified as the appropriate masculine in southern culture, evocations of Bon's "femininely flamboyant" New Orleans, "its atmosphere at once fatal and languorous, at once feminine and steel-hard," as well as Bon's wearing a "feminized gown," saturate this section (116, 109, 95). Men also partake of the feminine.

Moreover, there are constant references to Bon's "seduction" not only of Judith but also of Henry, and Henry's seduction of Judith. Despite Mr. Compson's "patriarchal authority," gender and sexuality (and race) slip and remix like loose mercury. If gender is thus unanchored, where does that leave the character we expect to find in a southern Civil War novel, the Confederate Woman, a figure defined by her fixity of class, race, and "morality"?

Miss Rosa's story, too, is not what it seems. She is one of the "also dead" who writes Lost Cause poetry yet despises and subverts the verities of plantation culture (65). One imagines her verse sounding like the Daughters of the Confederacy doggerel carved on the memorial in Montgomery, Alabama:

> When this historic shaft shall crumbling lie
> In ages hence, in woman's heart will be
> A folded flag, a thrilling page unrolled
> A deathless song of Southern chivalry.

While officially celebrating "Southern chivalry," the verse sets up the masculine as transitory and the feminine as eternal: the masculine "shaft" is destroyed while the "folded flag" of the feminine memory remains. Rosa Coldfield wears a convincing disguise as a Daughter of the Confederacy with her evocations of honor and her political support of the South, as much a rebellion against her pacifist father as patriotism. She is the local "poetess laureate," whose job it is to memorialize the Confederate dead, yet the real tale she has to tell is not about gallant exploits and chivalry but about the evils of men toward women (11). She creates not in an "heroic" mode but a gothic mode, her diction dark with "demon," and "curse," and "expiate." The historical gothic novel was a "feminine" genre, produced largely by and mostly for women: Miss Rosa talks like a devoted reader of Ann Radcliffe.[14] While in her poetry—suppressed in the novel—Miss Rosa reinscribes the southern social order, in her fiction she subverts it; where she might praise the soldiers in gray in verse, in prose she tells of the horrific lives of women: specifically herself, Ellen, Clytie, and Judith.

Between Mr. Compson's and Miss Rosa's narratives, Ellen appears as the gothic heroine who has made a dangerous marriage to a man who "*came out of nowhere*" and "(*Tore violently a plantation, Miss Rosa Coldfield says*)— *tore violently . . . and begot a son and a daughter which*—(*Without gentleness begot, Miss Rosa Coldfield says*)—*without gentleness*" (9). Not only is Sutpen a demon, he is a rapist: the gothic male monster par excellence. But whereas Ellen is the fleeing maiden in Miss Rosa's discourse, she becomes a parody of the plantation mistress, a Confederate Woman gone absurdly wrong, in Mr. Compson's. He consistently theorizes women as either helplessly sexual or in need of class definition, status. The very institution through which Ellen tries to define herself collapses on her. Her attempts to be the queen of the district, as ironically described by Mr. Compson, to live up to the image of the Lady of the Big House, are desperate: "When she shopped (there were twenty stores in Jefferson now) she unbent without even getting out of the carriage, gracious and assured and talking the most complete nonsense, speaking her bright set meaningless phrases out of the part which she had written for herself, of the duchess peripatetic with property soups and medicines among a soilless and uncompelled peasantry" (69).

Ellen as written here tries to become a Thomas Nelson Page plantation mistress, but her story is mediated by narrators who don't believe in the essential virtue of the image. *Gone with the Wind*, published the same year as *Absalom, Absalom!* and, in some ways, a revision of old representations, does take the madonna of the Big House seriously in Ellen Robillard O'Hara, Scarlett's mother, who was "the best-loved neighbor in the County. She was a thrifty and kind mistress, a good mother and a devoted wife. The heartbreak and selflessness that she would have dedicated to the Church were devoted instead to the service of her child, her household and the man who had taken her out of Savannah" (58). This could almost be a paraphrase of Page's passage on the "devotion" of the plantation mistress to everyone and everything but herself, earning a quasi-religious reverence. Ellen Sutpen does her damnedest but can't pull it off. Miss Rosa has no mercy on her, calling her a "blind romantic fool," while Mr. Compson is downright nasty about her pretensions: for him she is "a woman who, if she had had the fortitude to bear sorrow and trouble, might have risen to actual stardom in the role of matriarch, arbitrating from the fireside corner of a crone the pride and destiny of her family, instead of turning at the last to the youngest member of it and asking her to protect the others" (69).

In Mr. Compson's version, Ellen reads the role of plantation mistress badly. She manages neither heroic nor maternal self-sacrifice. She doesn't even seem to have a womb; she is the "swamp-hatched butterfly," the "foolish unreal voluble preserved woman" who lives "unimpeded by weight of stomach and all the heavy organs of suffering and experience" (69–70). She becomes a victim of her inability to translate her dream constructs into hard reality (like her husband), victim as well of his "design," finally dismissed in the narrative as a mere ornament of air, a chatelaine to furnish Thomas Sutpen's cloud castle. Ellen Sutpen is not Ellen Robillard O'Hara, the perfect mother and plantation mistress. It is interesting that in the mid-thirties a character once so standardized in southern fiction as to be practically invisible would be raised, then ultimately dismissed in the fictional world she inhabits. Scarlett's mother, like Melanie Wilkes, is an exemplary Confederate Woman, yet both Ellen O'Hara and Melanie Wilkes (like Ellen Sutpen) are finally seen as inadequate to deal with the realities of the South's downfall.

Ellen Sutpen, like Ellen O'Hara, is practically bodiless, signifying the acceptable feminine of the Old South, supposedly a "time when ladies did not walk but floated," the representation of the classical body (31). Like Granny Millard, she has nothing under her bell-shaped skirt. She denies the body, which, to Mr. Compson, is a denial of the fundamental truth of biology: anatomy is destiny. In the end, Ellen does not so much die as disappear: "the butterfly of a forgotten summer two years defunctive now— the substanceless shell, the shade impervious to any alteration of dissolution because of its very weightlessness: no body to be buried: just the shape, the recollection" (126). The Confederate Woman—a counterfeit woman—just vanishes.

But what of Judith? Her body is less present in the various narratives than her mother's (though most present in Miss Rosa's narrative). She is a series of negatives, swift sightings, a childish face in the loft, a gaunt adult face "impenetrable and serene" as she gives Charles Bon's letter to Mrs. Compson (125). Mr. Compson records her getting thinner and thinner as if she were going to be erased altogether, "the Sutpen skull showing indeed now through the worn, the Coldfield flesh" (126). The one moment when Judith's body is most powerfully imagined is in the scene, evoked by Miss Rosa, Mr. Compson, and Quentin, of her in her patched wedding dress, standing there while Henry "practically flings" the "bloody corpse" of Charles Bon at her feet (18). In Quentin's much more sexually loaded visualization of the scene, Judith stands in her "underthings" in the bedroom, "looking at the door, the yellowed creamy mass of old intricate satin and lace spread carefully on the bed and then caught swiftly up by the white girl and held before her as the door crashed in and the brother stood there" (172). Dressed (or about to be dressed) as a bride, awaiting the bridegroom, Judith is the emblem simultaneously of the virgin and of the sexual woman. She is on the threshold of trans-formation, from the *absence* and *emptiness* that characterize the virgin body in Mr. Compson's and Quentin/Shreve's construction of it, to *presence:* the "seeded" field or the "girlname" where the essences of Henry and Charles could meet (326, 120). Quentin "gazes" on more of Judith's interdict body, imagining her undressed, covering herself before her brother's eyes with her wedding dress: she is most real for him. The "crashing" door suggests violation, the sexual menace of the brother-lover.[15]

In white, the "blank" color of purity, Judith might well seem an exem-plar of the classical body, the daughter of the great house who is the focus of the romance, the focus of Ellen Sutpen's "design" the way a son is the focus of Thomas Sutpen's "design." Yet, like Drusilla Hawk in her wedding dress, the image is deceptive. Judith is represented by neither the clas-sical body of the lady nor the grotesque body of the sexual woman (or the black woman). Where is she on the spectrum of responses Faulkner makes to the Confederate Woman? I would argue that while *The Unvan-quished* is a lesser achievement than *Absalom, Absalom!* and Drusilla a less complex being (she is the production of only one narrative sensibility), Judith and Drusilla are related in the ferocity of their rebellion from the fixed and static gender that ladyhood demands. Both press at the bound-aries; both speak when their culture demands silence and acquiescence.

Judith is first described (by Miss Rosa) in the novel *screaming* like a ban-shee because the wild horses and the "wild negro," whom she could stir into a frenzy, making the carriage the family went to church in run away, have been replaced by her mother's sedate phaeton and "old gentle mare." She screams so much that she has to be taken away "ill" (25). The dull, safe carriage and horse are identified with the ladylike behavior that Judith wishes to flout: "It had been Judith, a girl of six, who had instigated and authorized that negro to make the team run away. Not Henry, mind; not the boy, which would have been outrageous enough; but Judith, the girl" (25). The next time Henry and Judith appear, it is Henry who is "screaming and vomiting" as he runs away in terror from his father's bloody wrestling matches with slaves, crying and hanging onto his mother's skirts while Judith illicitly watches the fight with her sister Clytemnestra (29–30). In both these childhood instances, Henry betrays "feminine" fears while Judith enjoys the violence, shocking her mother, perhaps, but not shocking her aunt, who is well equipped to document the slippage of genders and races among the "half-ogre" Sutpen children (13).

Miss Rosa, self-described as "androgynous," creates the "bisexual space" in which Judith and Henry (and Bon) move; there is no such direction in Mr. Compson's stories. In Quentin's and Shreve's re-creations and impersonations, Judith is sometimes the object of desire, sometimes the conduit for desire between the loverlike brothers, Henry and Charles. She moves in and out of positions: the masculinized "wild" Sutpen; the silent, patient fiancée; the shadow of Henry's body; the ghost. Because no one voice dominates, Judith must be multiple. She can never be simply the Confederate Woman some critics (imposing an external ruling voice on the novel's cacophony) have tried to make her, ignoring the narrative's contradictions and crises that represent her. Brooks praises her as "one of Faulkner's finest characters of endurance" (Yoknapatawpha Country 319) while Gwin (Black and White Women 115, 189–90) points to Judith's selfless actions in receiving the Octoroon, nursing the sick, even sewing maternity clothes for the young girl her father has got pregnant.

Judith is a portrait by various hands: her creators often have such different intentions and fixations that instead of a picture with more or less a sense of "classical" unity, what we get resembles a cubist composition. She is, perhaps, more a discursive strategy than anything else, dressed occasionally in the romance of the past. There is some attempt to represent Judith as a vessel; Mr. Compson makes her the bounded empty space to be filled by the masculine voice or the masculine seed, perhaps the spermatikos logos: "She was just the blank shape, the empty vessel in which each of them [Henry and Charles Bon] strove to preserve, not the illusion of himself nor his illusion of the other but what each conceived the other to believe him to be" (119–20).

Judith as a multiple being can be illustrated as part of the triangle formed by her brothers, Charles and Henry. Eve Kosofsky Sedgwick has defined this kind of relationship as homosocial: the woman is the conduit that enables men to communicate, to be together; the heterosexual bond is an acceptable substitute for a homosexual bond. It is "the use of women as exchangeable, perhaps symbolic, property for the primary purpose of cementing bonds of men with men" (25–26). Critics have made much of Charles Bon's name, "good," degenerating with his grandson into "Bond" as an evocation of slavery: it could, as well, slip into the other sense of bond, an evocation of desire or linkage. In the case of Henry and Charles, it may be that their bond is more than homosocial, moving over into the homoerotic. Yet Judith herself is not simply a "feminine" mirror reflecting her brothers. Her own gender position is fluid from childhood, as we have seen. As an object of desire, she is equally unfixed in "womanhood": Do Charles and Henry want her as a woman or each other as men? They themselves play alternately "masculine" and "feminine" roles; Mr. Compson speaks of how Charles "seduced" Henry "as surely as he seduced Judith" (96). At first the object of Charles's advances, Henry later becomes the masculine subject whose role it is to destroy Charles, who is simultaneously "feminine" and self-sacrificial, and masculine, threatening to deflower Judith.

Rather than a triangle, perhaps a more telling shape here would be Charles and Henry as parentheses with Judith as the space between: ( ). The question arises as to whether there is a Judith to desire. Is she just the construction by the narrators of a (shifting) object, a circumscribed space, nearly enclosed by her twinned brothers, as parentheses can enclose a phrase, or nothing at all? The scenario is complicated not only by being a homosocial (or homoerotic) relationship in which the woman is a conduit or "empty vessel," but also by being incestuous and miscegenous. Charles is not just Judith's brother, he is her black brother (at least in Quentin and Shreve's reconstruction of the story): their threatened marriage is transgressive in every way. Judith would be committing incest, though Henry, in Quentin Compson's version, finds a way to rationalize this, on the basis of historical fragments about "dukes" and "kings" who married their sisters. The incest is not the worst, however: in a sense, it is fitting for the two brothers to come together in their sister, to share her body. Indeed, Henry will be sexually "possessed" by Bon as much as Judith in their union, as well as sexually jealous of Bon's possession of his sister. Shreve has him think, "We belong to you; do as you will with us," then say: "I used to think that I would hate the man that I would have to look at every day and whose every move and action and speech would say to me, I have seen and touched parts of your sister's body that you will never see and touch: and now I know that I shall hate him and that's why I want that man to be you" (328).

Henry is willing to share his sister's body the way he would be willing to share his inheritance with the brother he desires so profoundly. For Charles, in Shreve's imagination, she is not merely Henry's female twin, unsophisticated and "innocent," she is an aspect of his denied birthright (if we accept that Bon knows who he is), his father and his father's property: "*I am not hearing about a young girl, a virgin; I am hearing about a narrow delicate fenced virgin field already furrowed and bedded so that all I shall need to do is drop the seeds in, caress it smooth again*" (326). The erotic implications of the "narrow fenced" space of Judith's body, awaiting the "seeds" to fill its emptiness, to impregnate it, underscore Shreve and Quentin's (re)construction of Henry and Charles's Judith. Here she shifts back to the feminine as the *hortus conclusus*, a supreme emblem of the plantation lady and the classical, closed body, and a type of *property*, representing the cultivated land of the plantation that Charles *also* desires.

The most serious transgression in the Charles/Judith/Henry relationship is racial—it is unbearable for Henry (again, according to Shreve and Quentin) that Judith commit miscegenation, although incest is not only tolerated but also encouraged. Irwin says that Charles is represented as the "dark self" because he is the unconscious self threatening to overrule the conscious will (92). Matthews reads the multiple references to Charles as a "shadow" or "shade" as evocations of his fictionality, his status as an "invention." For him the racial designation is symbolic: "Bon becomes a Negro only when he threatens to take Judith" (*Play* 148). I think both these readings can be incorporated into a literal (if such a word can be used in such a tangle of competing fictions) account of Charles Bon's blackness. The threat of miscegenation needn't be any more figurative or symbolic than the threat of incest. Charles "revealed" as Henry's and Judith's brother has the same status as Charles "revealed" as black—both are situated in southern culture as threats to the integrity of property and its emblem: the female, the lady's, body. I take Charles's projected blackness seriously not only because it is part of Shreve and Quentin's discourse of a "cursed" South full of secret darkness, but because in the context of both the plantation South and Faulkner's own South, the "pollution" of the white female body by the black male body was an explosive issue. Charles Bon's blackness may be no more "true" than anything else in the novel, but it is faithful to the racial and sexual anxiety that marked the South—Old and New. When Faulkner was writing *Absalom!*, Mississippi had a law (passed in 1930) forbidding miscegenation. "Blackness" was a highly ambivalent term, proved by the "drop of ink" idea which amounted to a social designation. Charles Bon's declaration of "blackness" is an utterance that marks him and his descendants as not only polluted but potential polluters of "pure" whites like Judith.[16]

Somehow the Confederate Woman, another fiction, another "shadow," comes back into play here. The arena returns to the historical and the social as Shreve and Quentin impersonate (or are possessed by, in this gothic novel) Henry/Charles and Charles/Henry. They confront each other over the body of the white woman. For a brief moment, Judith is constructed by her brothers (and their twentieth-century mediums) as the body on which the ideology of the South rests. She does not participate in this construction, but at this point in the reconstruction of the story, she is particularly powerless: mere property. The threat Charles Bon posed to Judith's body was not of mere archeological interest in the thirties. During the time Faulkner was working on *Absalom, Absalom!*, lynchings to uphold the "purity" of white womanhood were still happening with distressing regularity. The possibility that white women could ever be placed on an equal footing with black men was a terror that the South tried to stave off with legislation. At the time, Mississippi even had a law prohibiting the "printing, publication or circulation of material favoring social equality" (McMillen 174).[17] Charles is imagined saying to Henry the most inflammatory sentence anyone could say to a white man in the South: "I'm the nigger that's going to sleep with your sister" (358). Suddenly it is not only maleness Charles will inscribe on Judith's blank self, not just seed he will ejaculate into her "narrow fenced" body, but *blackness*. This echoes the kind of racial and sexual anxiety in *Othello*: as Judith is spoken of as an "empty vessel," Othello constructs Desdemona as "this fair paper, this most goodly book" on which the word *whore* can be written (in black ink, presumably). The double terror here is not only that black men will sleep with white women but that white women will desire this: female sexuality could destroy white supremacy and white property. The very blankness of the woman as she is constructed by these two sets of men becomes threatening—*anything* could occupy that white page. It is necessary not only that the black brother, the "nigger rapist," be destroyed but also that Judith be contained by a stereotype that "explains" her life and celebrates her asexuality.

But Judith is not contained—she is not a seamless vessel or a fenced piece of land or a framed mirror or any of the other bounded spaces her brothers (through Mr. Compson, Shreve, and Quentin) place her in. She and Henry are not discrete beings; they are "curiously alike as if the difference in sex had merely sharpened the common blood to a terrific, an almost unbearable, similarity" (172). They have "a relationship closer than the traditional loyalty of brother and sister even; a curious relationship: something of that fierce impersonal rivalry between two cadets in a crack regiment" (79–80). Snead points out that "the siblings' relationship throughout mocks strict sexual definition. . . . Male and female roles interweave without warning" (110–11). Judith and Charles become confused as Henry's object of desire while she and Clytie breach the distance that governs the issue of slave siblings by their relationship, which seems closer than the traditional loyalty of *sister and sister*. They share the Sutpen face, almost identical, looking down at the wrestling match as children; they even violate the convention that the slave sleeps on a pallet and the mistress on the bed: Miss Rosa says *"on more than one occasion Ellen has found them both on the pallet, and once in the bed together"* (140). Judith, Clytie, and Rosa become not distinct representatives of race and class specifics but *"three creatures who still possessed the need to eat but took no pleasure in it, the need to sleep but from no joy in weariness or regeneration, and in whom sex was some forgotten atrophy like the rudimentary gills we call the tonsils. . . . It was as though we were one being, interchangeable and indiscriminate"* (155).

Genderless, raceless, classless, this composite "creature" is another attack on the very uniqueness of the plantation lady. Judith constantly imperils her official position as the "heroine" by these dangerous incursions into masculinity and blackness. In doing so, she disorientates the narrative: as Quentin and Shreve "become" Henry and Charles (and, to some extent Judith), the separation of the past from the present is also disrupted. While there are many sites of merging and, as Snead puts it, "seeping" in *Absalom, Absalom!*, involving all the characters and narrators, Judith represents a central crisis in the officially "fenced" category of gender. She is a most unruly ghost in the text, one minute quiet and romanticized, with Bon one of "two shades pacing, serene and untroubled by flesh, in a summer garden," yet also genteelly troublesome: "The same two serene phantoms who seem to watch, hover, impartial attentive and quiet, above and behind the inexplicable thunderhead of interdictions and defiances and repudiations" (97). If she is a function of the narrative voices, she is also able to destabilize them; if she is the "blank space" for desire to be written on and in, she too writes. As Mr. Compson has her say to his mother when she hands over Charles Bon's letter: "All you have left is a block of stone with scratches on it provided there was someone to remember to have the marble scratched and set up or had time to, and it rains on it and the sun shines on it and after a while they dont even remember the name and what the scratches were trying to tell, and it doesn't matter" (127).

The marble is a tombstone, the scratches her forgotten name. This is Judith's longest "speech": after this she declines to near-silence in the narratives; calm and unrevealing before the door of the room where her dead lover/brother lies, she says to Rosa: "*Shall we go down stairs? I will have to speak to Mr Jones about some planks and nails*" (150). In an early draft of the novel, in a scene subsequently revised out, Judith has hysterics over Bon's death and has to be put to bed screaming, "Pity us" (Muhlenfeld xxvii). Since Judith began her incursion into the fiction by screaming, this apparent silencing by Faulkner and by the narrators is significant; indeed, it is one last brush with the icon of Confederate Womanhood. Silence is purity: "The young girl's muteness therefore figures her virginity, her ignorance of sexual commerce, or her fear before the act. Marriage—or union— reveals her sex (masculine perspective). According to the dominant masculine theory, her self-affirmation should stop there, and she should acquire speech only to abandon it at once" (Jean-Paul Debax, quoted in Brooke-Rose 310).

Yet the "masculine" idea that female self-expression comes only with the loss of virginity is challenged in Judith. She is freed to express herself, if not in language, in the very disruption she occasions. Where the narration—never her own—tries to circumscribe her, she haunts it:

> If woman has always functioned "'within" man's discourse, a signifier referring always to the opposing signifier that annihilates its particular energy, puts down or stifles its very different sounds, now it is time for her to displace this "within," explode it, overturn it. . . . And you will see how easily she will well up, from this "within" where she was hidden and dormant, to the lips where her foams will overflow. (Cixous, "Sorties" 39)

Judith survives as not just a ghost in the narrative but in the "real" ghost of Henry Sutpen, the "something" living in the remains of the gothic "mud-castle" of Sutpen's Hundred. She and her brother were one, "that single personality with two bodies"; now in Henry's wasted body, Quentin encounters the composite of Sutpen, male and female, black and white, present and past. When Clytie burns down the house, she makes ghosts of all of them. Quentin is haunted for the rest of his short life by the black and the feminine: the Others of the South that, though officially silenced, wail about the corners of ruined houses and distempered minds.

2 Mammy

Nobody cared whether Mammy Lu learned to read so long as she baked
the best spoon-bread in Alabama.—Sara Haardt, "Baby Chile"

The Politics of Aunt Jemima

Aunt Jemima in her kitchen, Hattie McDaniel lacing up Vivien Leigh in
whalebone and decorum, mammies in moonlight-and-magnolias novels
with biscuit dough up to the elbows helping "Old Mistis" ward off the
"damn Yankees" while burying the silver in the orchard, loyal to the white
family through decline, degradation, and death: hers is the shiny, acceptable face of black servitude.[1] In her uncomplicated fidelity and passive
Christianity, the Mammy validates a repressive social order that insists
she remain subordinate and that she enjoy it. Through her loving service
the Mammy absolves whites of guilt. She no less than the Confederate
Woman is a figment of white Old South nostalgia; indeed, she is necessary
to the Confederate Woman as a "female who was tougher, less sensitive,
and who could perform with efficiency and grace the duties of motherhood for her mistress and of course for herself" (Christian, "Shadows"
186). The Mammy as represented in southern ideology is not a woman
but a symbol of self-sacrificial motherhood, celebrated for denying not
only her gender but her race.

The Confederate Woman, the white lady, is defined by her difference
from the white man and her difference from the black woman, particularly that most central of southern stereotypes, the Mammy. The classical

body on the pedestal depends upon its "opposite," the grotesque body, characterized by "the gaping mouth, the protuberant belly and buttocks, the feet and the genitals" (Stallybrass and White 22). The dominant representation of the "ideal white woman tries to deny the gross physical aspects of being female, gross from the Southern point of view. In contrast, all the functions of mammy are magnificently physical" (Christian, *Black Feminist Criticism* 2). Where the classical body in the form of the white lady "keeps its distance," indeed, seems like no body at all (the absence under the hoopskirt), the Mammy's body is loudly immediate (Stallybrass and White 22). The exaggerated breasts of the Mammy provide milk; she prepares food, bathes, comforts, and instructs the white child—all activities the southern social order absolved its white ladies of just as it absolved them of sexuality. Indeed, the Mammy, taking over primary child care from the white mother on the plantation, treats the mother herself as a baby. As Gwin reports, white ladies liked "being infantilized"; Susan Bradford Eppes's "Mammy Lulu" still put her to bed when she was nineteen (*Black and White Women* 98, 92).

Faulkner negotiates representations of the mammy as he does the Confederate Woman, that is, incompletely, paradoxically, with no resolution or finality. Even the much-admired Dilsey in *The Sound and the Fury* (1929) is an ambivalent gesture toward revising or critiquing the old-time Mammy by trying to modify or erase her telltale body. The Mammy is trapped both in a sentimental vision of "noble" darkies and the extremely narrow expectations for women that southern whites endorsed. She is not a reality but an ideological tool, a creation of white culture to aggrandize and justify itself. As Hazel Carby remarks, "the objective of stereotypes is not to reflect or represent a reality but to function as a disguise, or mystification, of objective social relations" (22). Faulkner attempts to indict white southern society for its hypocrisy by showing the black mother as the "authentic" mother of the black and white southern family, but in doing so, he colludes in the stereotype even while he attempts to subvert it. As with the Confederate Woman, Faulkner's relationship with this black icon of the South is contingent on his conflicting romantic and critical understanding of the South's past. The society that created the Mammy was in flux, with new racial attitudes and new economic difficulties. Yet because the Jim Crow South was able to reinvent the racial hierarchy in a postslavery world, the Mammy was a more viable figure in the twentieth-century South than the Confederate Woman, fixed as she is in a specific historical period with reference to specific moments (the Civil War and Reconstruction). The Mammy was adapted to the New South: the plantation silver (if there was any left) didn't need to be buried in the orchard any more, but there were still white babies to be changed and biscuit dough to be beaten. Faulkner's own mammy, Caroline Barr, spanned the period between the Old South and the New; she was born a slave and she brought up both Faulkner and his daughter Jill until her death in 1940 at the age of one hundred. Frederick Karl calls her a member of the family, "a black Falkner" (58). Certainly she was very important to the Faulkners. When she died, Faulkner wrote to Robert Haas: "She was born in bondage and with a dark skin and most of her early maturity was passed in a dark and tragic time for the land of her birth. She went through vicissitudes which she had not caused; she assumed cares and griefs which were not her cares and griefs. . . . She was born and lived and served and died and now is mourned; if there is a heaven, she has gone there" (Karl 633–34). In his fiction, Faulkner is chiefly concerned with how the Mammy, the black mother, "lived and served"—the spaces between where she might voice a self unseen by whites are not explored. Faulkner could not explore them. He lived at a time when blacks were actors as well as servants. His representations of the Mammy are necessarily partial for all his authoritative tone.

Behind Faulkner's mammies are generations of a southern stock character praised and patronized by the white middle and upper classes. Mrs. M. F. Surghnor, in her Ku Klux Klan romance Uncle Tom of the Old South (1896), admonishes: "Children of the South, remember them with respect and affection,—but never more will you see the faithful old Mammy and the good Uncle Tom of the Old South" (391). In 1923 the United Daughters of the Confederacy suggested to the United States Congress that they be allowed to erect a monument in Washington to "Mammy" (Parkhurst 349). The Mammy operates as a focus both for nostalgic reimagining of the Old South and for its vindication in the New. Lillian Smith, in her autobiographical Killers of the Dream (1949), says that a white southern child's first intense feeling was toward its mammy. The bond between the black nurse and the white baby is one of the "ghost relationships" that haunt the South, and the figure of the Mammy is a reminder both of Arcadian antebellum days and the guilt of slavery, "the family-despot and the slave," the embodied oxymoron of the Southern attitude to blacks (Smith, Killers 109–13; Benet 160). The child associates love and nurture with the black woman instead of the white mother but sees that, powerless as the white mother is, the black mother is even more powerless. Power is white and, more particularly, male. Yet in celebrating the Mammy, southern culture "compensates" her for her lack of real status in giving her a bathetic role, lauded in novel after novel. She is "the positive emblem of familial relations between black and white," the only black figure allowed to have "power" over whites (Clinton 202).

The Mammy as romance character flowered early, well before the Civil War, though in southern writing she became most prominent in the post-Reconstruction era and on into the twentieth century. The Mammy's early importance is largely due to *Uncle Tom's Cabin* (1852) with its officially sympathetic black figures. The cornucopian Aunt Chloe is described in terms now as familiar as Aunt Jemima on the pancake-mix box. She is

> presiding with anxious interest over certain fizzling items in a stew-pan, and anon with grave consideration lifting the cover of a bake-kettle from whence steam forth indubitable intimations of "something good." A round, black, smiling face is hers, so glossy as to suggest the idea that she might have been washed over with the whites of eggs like one of her own tea rusks. Her whole plump countenance beams with satisfaction and a contentment from under her well-starched checked turban. (66–67)

Later in the novel we are presented with a mammy less associated with abundance of food than abundance of virtue: the St. Clare family nurse, "the best creature living" (261). Aunt Chloe and the St. Clare family nurse are Christian exemplars like Uncle Tom himself; he is, in a way, a male Mammy.

Outraged "answers" by southern writers to Stowe's reformist fiction present slavery as benign. But the Mammy remains the same, her perfection agreed upon by abolitionist and apologist alike. In Mary H. Eastman's *Aunt Phillis' Cabin* (1852), Aunt Phillis, a dignified and self-sacrificing slave on the Weston plantation, cures her dipsomaniac husband, encourages her children to act like white "ladies and gentlemen," and behaves in a consistently saintly manner. "How much can we all learn from good Phillis!" exclaims Mrs. Weston (209). Aunt Phillis dies a martyr to hard work and, like Uncle Tom, accepts her station and fate with Christ-like humility: "Oh! master, it's sweet for me to die, for Jesus is my friend" (258). In Mrs. Henry R. Schoolcraft's plantation novel *The Black Gauntlet*

(1852–60), another Aunt Phillis is a model of maternal piety, a mammy who raises both black and white children: "Phillis had nursed this child [the heroine] with her own infant, from her breast; and the acutest observer would have failed to ascertain which of the babies this affectionate slave loved the best" (205).

Actually, it is easy to tell which child the Mammy loves best: it is the white child. Faulkner celebrates the Mammy who mothers both a black child and a white child in The Unvanquished, where Bayard Sartoris and his servant Ringo nurse at the same breast, as well as in Go Down, Moses, where Zack Edmonds's white son and Lucas Beauchamp's black son are both raised by Molly Beauchamp. This questionable image of "brotherhood" and reconciliation is another strategy for romanticizing slavery: the white boys and the black boys are in no sense equals. It also underlines the collusion of the black Mammy in the white power structure. As Trudier Harris says: "These women's identities are so meshed with whites and white culture that they cannot change; nor do they have the level of consciousness which would even remotely suggest that change might be desirable" (25).

James Baldwin, in his essay "Many Thousands Gone," characterizes the Mammy as a full participant in the white system: "There was no-one more forbearing than Aunt Jemima, no-one stronger or more pious or more loyal or more wise; there was, at the same time, no one weaker or more faithless or more vicious and certainly no one more immoral" (28). Baldwin makes an important point about the Mammy's racial politics: her status, such as it is, is derived solely from the white world that values her as a good servant and shadow of her white mistress. The physicality of her being is simultaneously inscribed and contained. She must have no consciousness as a black person, no consciousness as a woman (no sexuality) in order to fulfill the role white society writes for her. She is a traitor to her race, as Baldwin says. Most perversely, it is precisely that treason against her race and her troubled relationship to her gender that makes white culture praise her.

This becomes clear in the way that the Mammy, in postbellum novels, is represented as an arch-conservative, a constant and verbose nostalgia merchant. Mark Twain sneers at this in Life on the Mississippi, recounting the story of the old mammy who, when someone remarks on the fineness of the southern moon, says, "Ah, bless yo' heart, honey, you ought to seen dat moon befo' de waw!" (365).

The Mammy is re-created and reinforced in an astonishing number of texts from Reconstruction on into the twentieth century. She is the choric voice of the Old South singing the heroic past over the pot of breakfast grits, the white South's supreme propagandist. And while she still represents the "gross" bodily attributes white women denied, she takes on many white values and amplifies them. In Thomas Nelson Page's story "Mam' Lyddy's Recognition," the old Virginia mammy moves north with the Frenches, her white folks, since they cannot get good "help" up there. She is a racist and a snob: "And when Freedom came, however much she may have appreciated being free, she had much too high an estimate of the standing of the Frenches to descend to the level of the class she had always condemned as 'free niggers.' She was a deep-dyed aristocrat" (Bred in the Bone 237–38). She is celebrated for her hostility to her own race: "When Negro rule was at its worst, Mam' Lyddy was its most bitter reviler" (243). Similarly, in the third volume of Thomas Dixon, Jr.'s Ku Klux Klan trilogy, Aunt Julie Ann works for northern interlopers while she awaits the messianic return of southern gentry rule. She overtly favors her old owner's family over the new employers who pay her wages, calling the scion "baby," even though he is thirty years old, allowing him clandestine access to his confiscated ancestral home with indifferent arrogance: "De very idee er me keepin' Mammy's baby outen dis house when I carry him across dis hall in my arms de day he wuz born" (The Traitor 14).

Even in fiction that critiques the South as a gothic realm rotten from within, the politics of the Mammy went unchanged, though not unexamined. In the black novelist Charles W. Chesnutt's 1901 novel, The Marrow of Tradition, dedicated to exposing the hypocrisy at the heart of southern racial "purity," there is an old-time plantation aunty: superstitious, status-conscious, utterly devoted to her white Miss 'Livy. Indeed, Mammy Jane is an active supporter of the Carteret family's oppression of her own people. Chesnutt shows how she is a product of and apologist for white racism; even dying she calls out not to her black family but to her white mistress, looking forward to being a slave in heaven as well as on earth.

Stephen Vincent Benét's John Brown's Body, published a year before The Sound and the Fury, places a mammy of mythic stature in the corrupt, if beautiful, plantation world:

> Fat Aunt Bess is older than Time
> But her eyes still shine like a bright, new dime,
> Though two generations have gone to rest
> On the sleepy mountain of her breast.

Wingate children in Wingate Hall,
From the first weak cry in the bearing bed
She has petted and punished them, one and all,
She has closed their eyes when they lay dead. (160)

Here the Mammy exhibits the usual maternal and racial signs: she is fat, her mountainous breast gives food, she provides nurture to the white Wingates from cradle to grave; she is a one-woman welfare state. She is seen as paradoxically essential to the existence of the Old South and a victim of slavery as well. There is something tremendously attractive about the Mammy, even to writers engaged in revising the plantation myth. And it could be that there were black house slaves who, in some instances, found that infantilizing the mistress and the master, and subtly usurping much of the household (though not the social or symbolic) role of the mistress, gave the Mammy a measure of at least emotive power that a field hand could never hope to have. Nonetheless, I hear in the celebrations of Mammy's perfection something similar to the subtexts of men's praise for women in general: all predicated on submission, on a power that is accorded only by convention or courtesy and might at any point be taken away.

It is interesting to see that more than a few writers, as late as the 1930s, go back, as Faulkner does, to an exploration of the Civil War and Reconstruction or else to traditional southern racial relationships as a response to the New South. Many of these are conservative counterblasts to scholarly and popular revisionism and northern calls for reform. "Baby Chile" by Sara Haardt (who was married to H. L. Mencken) celebrates Mammy Lu for loving her white "baby" Paulina more than her black daughters. When Paulina falls gravely ill, "Mammy Lu formally called on the Lord to take her own daughters, Georgia and Florida, instead" (175). Here again is the "treason" Baldwin indicts the Mammy for: black children as less valuable than white children. The privileged, and in white terms, "pretty," daughter of Mammy Lu's employer is more worthy than her own black— therefore less attractive—daughters. She is such a creation of internalized white discourses that her only identity is what whites write for her: comic, servile, maternal.

Gone with the Wind gives us the best-known mammy in twentieth century literature, later made even more famous by Hattie McDaniel in the film of the novel.[2] The alternately glaring, jolly, loving, snobbish keeper of the O'Hara household embodies the popular ideal: "Mammy was black but her code of conduct and her sense of pride were as high as or higher than those of her owners" (23). The potentially threatening, inferior black woman's body is defused: the Mammy is more upper-class, more ladylike than the whites who have the power of life and death over her. She is like a well-trained dog: a credit to her owners as well as a credit to her race.

White culture congratulates itself for the "civilizing" powers that turn a black slave into an "aristocrat" with standards beyond even those of her white folks. White culture also displaces guilt over slavery in the Mammy, who, just as she is more "refined" than her owners, is also more committed to the ideology of slavery. Mammy as a "member of the family" transcends her station as bonded wet nurse, cook, and maid, but her status is special, and any further mobility within the white hierarchy threatens her privileged position. As a woman, the Mammy is a contradictory image. Her place as a mother is central: she must be fecund, fat, and ample-breasted to objectify her generosity, her motherliness, and her place as a figure in childhood; yet her sexuality must be suppressed. She has become too "white" to sleep with her husband. Indeed, the Mammy's marriage is always troubled and therefore disguised as comic: until Faulkner's "Pantaloon in Black" and "The Fire and the Hearth," white writers rarely took black marriage seriously. Mammy wields the rolling pin while her husband—a gambler, drinker, or lecher—is systematically emasculated to the amusement of the whites. Constance Cary Harrison, in her memoir Recollections Grave and Gay (1911), writes comically of her cook, who, within a week of her husband's funeral, marries the deacon who had accompanied her home from the burial (Gwin, Black and White Women 98). Not only is the Mammy's sexuality suppressed, her religiosity—a potentially dangerous, subversive, freedom-preaching force—is undermined by making it "superstitious." The Mammy is tamed on all fronts: tamed into passive Christianity, tamed into sexless maternity.

The Yoknapatawpha Mammy

William Faulkner was brought up by a black woman. Her name was Caroline Barr. She was nurse, cook, and maid to the Falkner family, by all accounts a warm maternal presence in contrast to Maud Falkner's cool distance. While she had a most unmammylike habit of running off with various men, from which entanglements Murry Falkner often had to rescue her, it is not surprising that this sexual side to her personality is suppressed in the affectionate, somewhat patronizing manner her former charges, the Falkner boys, describe her; she could have been rolling out biscuit dough in a Thomas Nelson Page novel (Blotner 100). When she died in 1940, William Faulkner held the funeral in his white-columned house, presiding over her funeral like a plantation master, replicating the pattern of mingled love and condescension toward black house servants. He erected a headstone reading: "MAMMY: Her white children bless her" (Blotner 1035). No mention is made of her black children.

Faulkner's dedication of Go Down, Moses (1942) underlines this sentiment:

> To Mammy
> CAROLINE BARR
> MISSISSIPPI
> (1840–1940)
> Who was born in slavery and who
> gave to my family a fidelity without
> stint or calculation of recompense
> and to my childhood
> an immeasurable devotion and love.

This is the unexamined, uninterrogated Mammy. Yet Faulkner truly loved her. She represents, for him, a link with the southern past and a network of social relationships—many of which he would not defend— under siege in a changing nation where cries for equality grew ever louder. The black Mammy/white child relationship is central to the white South's myth of racial harmony, just as the Confederate Woman is necessary to the romanticization of defeat. The bond between the Mammy and the children she looked after is something Faulkner tries to honor and examine in fiction throughout his career. His approach ranges from embarrassing burlesques in early work and short fiction to the dignified, elevated portrayals of Dilsey Gibson and Molly Beauchamp. Faulkner wrote out of particular moments in history; he was, for a white, elite Mississippian who died before the Freedom Summer, a racial "moderate." He lived and died under Jim Crow, even though he knew that southern apartheid was doomed. He had to accommodate contradictory meanings for blackness and could, of course, achieve only incompleteness, pulled between a progressive sympathy for blacks and a nostalgia for the days of stable categories of black and white. Thadious Davis reminds us that

Faulkner "never knew or wrote about 'black' people as we today know and understand the term. He wrote about 'the Negro,' the white man's own creation" (2).

It is the white man Faulkner's "creation" of the Mammy, like Negro an historically and culturally specific term, that I am interested in here, not only his creation of her but how his fictive employments of her relate to the web of tensions and possibilities in southern culture. As in the last chapter, I begin out of chronological order, starting with how Faulkner represents the black mother in his more historically concerned fictions, especially Go Down, Moses. I save Dilsey for last because it seems to me that she presents the most problematic and most interesting reimagining of the Mammy in the "contemporary" (Faulkner's own) South. His less successful negotiations take place around The Sound and the Fury: in other words, there is not necessarily a chronological development in the character from the old nurse in Soldier's Pay to the same character (with the same name) in The Reivers. This reflects the tentativeness as well as the perpetual difficulty Faulkner had with the Mammy. He could revere her, as he did Caroline Barr, but where did she fit in the vexed New South?

Faulkner's fiction begins and ends with two Mammy Callies. The first appears in his first published novel, Soldiers' Pay (1926), and the last in his last novel, The Reivers (1962). Both given the name of his real mammy, Caroline; they are conventional types, no more profound or challenging than the super-Mammy in Gone with the Wind. It is as if by giving them the same name, Faulkner evokes a generic black feminine. They have exaggerated bodies made for enfolding children; they preside over food. They infantilize their white folks of whatever age. To Aunt Callie in Soldiers' Pay, the wounded war veteran Donald is still "my baby," and she is still "yo' mammy" to him. Aunt Callie in The Reivers is burlesqued rather than made poignant. In the reactionary Mammy tradition, she is the force restraining young Lucius Priest: she is supposed to curb his wild behavior and so maintain family honor—such is her investment in white values.

Similarly, the Mammy in Faulkner's Civil War fiction is no less a part of the war against the North than the captains and generals: the running joke is that Mammy is more terrifying than whole Rebel regiments as she fiercely wards off invaders and looters. Mrs. Compson's mammy faces a whole slew of Yankees: "Old Aunt Roxanne was standing in front of the outhouse behind the closed door of which Mrs. Compson was sitting, fully dressed even to her hat and parasol, on the wicker hamper contain-

ing her plate and silver. 'Miss in dar,' Roxanne said. 'Stop where you is' "
(*Collected Stories* 675). Here Mammy presides over the symbol of the earthi-
ness of the body—the outhouse which even "Miss" must occasionally
visit. But not officially. Officially "Miss" has no such dirty bodily functions. She is like a doll, wearing her hat and carrying her parasol while
Aunt Roxanne dares the soldiers to publicly implicate a southern lady in
bodily elimination. For herself to be so implicated is of no importance.
The Union hordes may win battles and devastate the land, but, in the
myth, domestic spaces such as kitchens and outhouses are still in the firm
control of mammies. And as the Mammy does exercise some command
over these private spaces, so she does have a kind of power in the family,
despite her status as a slave. Nonetheless, it is easy to see why James
Baldwin called her a traitor: her power is circumscribed by the limits—
physical and ideological—of the Big House. She is no subversive.

The obsession with saving the family silver, the badge of southern aristocracy, features in an astonishing number of Civil War anecdotes and is
used, unexamined if unadorned, by Faulkner in *The Unvanquished*. John Sartoris charges Mammy Louvinia to be wary of the potential silver thief in
their midst and knows he can trust her, even though the putative thief is
her own son. Louvinia identifies completely with her white family: there
is no overt irony in her determination to protect the silver, bought from
the profits of slave labor; no sense that her own people sweated and died
to purchase these objects of white status. Harriet Jacobs recounts a bitter story about how the white family that owned her refused to repay a
loan of three hundred dollars to her grandmother and bought instead silver candelabra: "I presume they will be handed down in the family from
generation" (20). This is how an "aristocracy" furnishes itself.

The Mammy is twinned with the Confederate Woman: Louvinia is the
black counterpart to Granny Rosa Millard, the guerrilla fighter, totally
committed to preserving the class structure from which she draws her
identity. And she is James Baldwin's "traitor." The moral discomfort of
having to spy on her son, indeed, to take sides against him, is never ques-
tioned: "Mammy's first loyalty is to her white folks" (Harris 54). Fidelity
to the Sartorises, to the preservation of their property, and to the prac-
tice and ideology of slavery, demonstrates, to the ruling-class whites,
Mammy's innate virtue. Louvinia proves her commitment to white values
by ignoring her own family and mothering the white Drusilla (whose
own mother rejects her as "fallen"), petting her, Bayard says, "in her arms

like she used to hold me." Hers is the nurturing body that makes children even of adults, returning them to infantilized "innocence" the way evocation of the old-time Mammy returns the white South to historical "innocence" (*The Unvanquished* 227).

Throughout his career Faulkner never stopped creating these *plus royaliste que le roi* mammies, whose role is to reflect, direct, and protect the class mystique of their owners or employers. Alice in *The Wishing Tree* is a disembodied voice of superparental discipline, issuing extravagant threats to unruly children. Elnora in *Flags in the Dust* and "There Was a Queen" represents the ancient dignity of the antebellum aristocracy; she is a stickler for decorum no less than Miss Jenny Du Pre, her Confederate Woman "twin." Elnora has no sympathy for Caspey, who has returned from the war in France with a lot of "New Negro" ideas about how he will no longer be put down by whites, indeed, how he will sleep with white women. Elnora isn't interested in social revolution or even social equality. Elnora is an arbiter of taste and "quality" amongst white and black: "I knows trash. I knows the way trash goes about working in with quality. Quality can't see that, because it's quality. But I can" (*Collected Stories* 734).

Having the black Mammy mouth the racist and classist statements through which whites justify their control of southern society defuses the ugliness of bald racism and snobbery while lending those tenets a perverse authority; if the underclass endorses the prevailing order, then the order must be sound. Faulkner sometimes seems blind to the Mammy's collusion in the white order which oppresses her. Louvinia's loyalty to the white aristocracy founded on the labor of slaves, and Elnora's loyalty to white class assumptions, indicate their willing participation in the Jim Crow South. This can be read as Christian stoicism, accepting their "place" and selflessly making the best of it. Or it can be read as an example of Faulkner's inability to reimagine fully the central stereotype of the Mammy.

However, there are places in Faulkner's fiction where he struggles with the received image of the Mammy and reproduces a black mother at times operating counter to convention. The narratives of most of his contemporaries replicated Mammy as a stock "darky" with few "serious" possibilities. The mammy in John Faulkner's (Faulkner's younger brother's) novel *Dollar Cotton*, published in 1942, the same year as *Go Down, Moses*, is two stock characters in one: in youth the accommodating sex object, in old age the faithful mother who sacrifices not only her own money but her only son for her white former lover's wife and children. The mammy (actually named Mammy) in *Dollar Cotton* occupies the two most dogged stereotypes of black women: the promiscuous Jezebel seen as "natural" (and sexually accessible) by white men and the mother—Jezebel past menopause. John Faulkner's dual representation of the black woman as sexual receptacle and maternal martyr reinscribes the crudest version of the South's understanding of blacks.

Go Down, Moses complicates this over-simple two-stage representation of black women. It is more than historically appropriate that the novel is dedicated to Caroline Barr, with her unstinting "fidelity, devotion and love" without adequate "recompense," because *Go Down, Moses* is about self-sacrifice and self-denial as well as the coherence of the family. It insists that family identity can transcend the categories of black and white; this is doomed to fail because southern society—most whites—insist on rigid definitions. Black motherhood in the form of Molly (sometimes spelled "Mollie") Beauchamp is seen as a possible point of departure from the hierarchy of white over black. *Go Down, Moses* contains places where the Mammy is refigured, only to slip back, in other places, into the inexorable racial and historical context that circumscribes her. In the end, black motherhood, Mammyhood, is reenshrined. Nonetheless, Faulkner's struggles with and modifications of the Mammy are worth exploring.

I agree with Thadious Davis that although *Go Down, Moses* "seems to refute myths about the Negro, it actually substitutes more personal and palatable myths (similar to those in *The Sound and the Fury*) for the more disturbing cultural ones in *Light in August* or *Absalom*" (242). Molly Beauchamp in *Go Down, Moses*, is still the nurse, the cook, and she is relatively uncomplex compared to her mulatto, excessively self-aware husband Lucas; but Faulkner views her place in the McCaslin plantation world seriously and thoughtfully. The mechanics of Mammyhood, the scolding, the feeding, the pronouncements of class and custom, are still in place, but Molly is rendered with dignity, perhaps as a memorialized, fictionalized Caroline Barr. The words of Faulkner's dedication are similar to those in the text used to describe Molly: "who had given him [Roth Edmonds], the motherless, without stint or expectation of reward that constant and abiding devotion and love which existed nowhere else in this world for him" (117). As Thadious Davis points out, the "key words are *fidelity, devotion* and *love*, which reverberate throughout the book" (242). Like Caroline Barr,

Molly is celebrated for her qualities as a good servant/mother. The dignity Faulkner brings to her is located not in some new vision of the Mammy's role, or some deepening understanding of her femaleness or her blackness, but simply in insisting that the black mother is the *authentic* mother: "He knew that his own mother was dead and did not grieve. There was still the black woman, constant, steadfast, and the black man of whom he saw as much and even more than of his own father, and the negro's house, the strong warm negro smell, the night-time hearth and the fire even in summer on it, which he still preferred to his own" (110–11).

To assert that the black woman is the genuine mother of the black *and* white family undermines the insisted-upon separation of races in the South, displacing the officially deified white mother. Does the black woman gain in power from this substitution? The answer is yes and no; the structure that keeps the races officially separate and unequal is not overturned. Despite the growing calls for integration in the South, despite increasing northern criticism of the vestiges of the plantation system, despite the black diaspora to urban centers and the accelerating destruction of the southern wilderness (so central to Faulkner in *Go Down, Moses*), Faulkner does not invent a prescription for a new South that would allow the girl in "Delta Autumn" a legitimate place in the white McCaslin family or absolve Molly of her tragic motherhood. Where the Mammy gains something is in the way she deviates from type, stepping out of martyrdom at times, represented by a more complex body than the usual over-present, fat, protuberant body.

Molly almost walks out of her own story when her husband "betrays" her by his destructive behavior. *Go Down, Moses* is about the betrayal of blood and the betrayal of the land: the potent underground cousin-ship of the Chickasaw, the Beauchamps (the black McCaslins), and the Edmondses (the white McCaslins). Their indivisibility, even in the face of self- and social definitions as slave and master, black tenant and white planter, is underlined time and time again. In "The Fire and the Hearth," the first section of *Go Down, Moses*, Molly demands a divorce. "I got to go clean away. Because he's crazy," she says (101). Lucas has become obsessed with finding buried money and no longer fulfills his obligations. "He's sick in the mind now," Molly tells Edmonds. This could have been comic, the old aunty with the shiftless husband, Aunt Phillis refusing to put up with any more nonsense from Uncle Bacchus. But there is a strange dignity to Molly, despite her near invisibility—at least to the white sensibility of Edmonds, who at first does not recognize her away from her own yard. Her body is nearly insignificant, a conscious reversal of the copious body of the conventional Mammy. She is "a small woman, almost tiny" with arms so thin they feel like reeds and layers and layers of petticoats concealing the rest of her (100). Over and over she is called "tiny," as if she were a child. But she has been the mother at whose breast Carothers Edmonds was nourished. Her body in the text is described as either shrunken or else as a breast at which both white and black children (Roth and Henry) suck. Yet in the knotted Edmonds/McCaslin/Beauchamp sexual history, she is a body in the middle of a dispute. In her youth she was not only wet nurse to Roth but possibly mistress to his father, Zack, reinforcing her status as the actual mother. The text flirts with the traditional Mammy image: nurturing both black and white children, representing the literal and symbolic truth that the white upper-class southerner takes in his nourishment from the black breast. There is a high degree of identification between the black mother and the white child, and confusion between the black servant and the white wife that Molly's husband, Lucas, sees and resents: "and he standing over her, looking down not at his own child but at the face of the white one nuzzling into the dark swell of her breast—not Edmonds' wife but his own who had been lost" (50). Molly's body is present in contrast to the absent—perhaps *erased* would be a better word—white mother. The white woman is only talked of in terms of her insignificance and invisibility: she is not even given a name but is called "a thing of no moment unsanctified, nothing" (46). Like Ellen Coldfield Sutpen, even in death she has no physical being: "It was as though the white woman had not only never quitted the house, she had never existed" (46). Snead points out "how few of the key [white] women in the novel have any other title than 'wife'" (188–89). The nameless, bodiless white lady is just another ghost, as if her mandated delicacy, gentility, and *whiteness* render her incorporeal—another instance of the bodiless classical body. Molly, on the other hand, has borne numerous children. She does not disappear like smoke. She is the authentic giver of life, taking into her hands the infant Roth as the white woman dies in childbed. Her *blackness* seems to signify her motherliness, here the signifying breast. Molly's body with its smells and its warmth and darkness, her house associated with food and sleep, provides the formative child care that becomes the paradigmatic relationship of upper-class white to black in the South.

    This relationship is the "original erotic connection with another race, beginning at the black mammy's breast—an 'infant' experience, both as *infans* (an infant is one who is 'speechless') and *infandum* (socially 'unspeakable'); what the white infant could not speak of, the white adult does not wish to admit" (Snead 193). It is "unspeakable" because it collapses the hierarchy of white over black and disrupts the pieties of sacred white womanhood. It is also unspeakable because the access a white child has to the body of the black woman is only an "innocent" version of the access a white man has to the body of the black woman. As a young woman, Molly is both mother and *object of desire*. In chapter 1 of "The Fire and the Hearth" Molly is "borrowed" by Zack Edmonds; her husband suspects she may be taking the white woman's sexual place as well. This sets up the major confrontation between the black McCaslin Lucas and the white McCaslin Zack, fighting over the symbolic bed. Years later, Roth remembers the rift between his father and Lucas, but the story is suppressed: "*It was a woman, he thought. My father and a nigger over a woman. My father and a nigger man over a nigger woman* because he simply declined even to realize that he had even refused to think *a white woman*. He didn't even think Molly's name" (115). Roth makes the story almost impersonal, detached from the personal, *named* histories of his black and white family. Molly disappears again here, hidden in "*nigger woman*" and a refusal to speak her name as a body in dispute. What Faulkner stresses is the kinship, the similarity between the two men: they are spoken of as "almost twins." Molly is an historical bone of contention between white master and black dependent, the central sexual conflict of the old plantation, where first rights to black women belong to white masters even if the women are "married" to black men. Molly in this context is a sexual commodity; possessing her implies power. Her body is an object to be controlled, in every sense— as object of desire to be penetrated, as well as breast to be nurtured at, yet that body is alternately present and absent (where the white mother's body is almost entirely absent).

To go back to Molly's position as black mother to the white Roth Edmonds, "the only mother he ever knew," her movement from disputed sexual body to disappearing mother is highlighted at the end of "The Fire and the Hearth" (131). This once-powerful dispenser of food is literally dried up, likened to a "rotted stick." She is so frail, Roth almost carries her in and out of the courthouse for the divorce that never happens. Finally, Lucas hands her a peace offering, a sack of candy for her to suck—she becomes the one in need of nourishment: Mammy infantilized. Though his father may have failed in his responsibility to Lucas and

Molly, Roth (here, at least, though not in "Go Down, Moses") fulfills it as Molly's son (though not Lucas's). And Molly remains a figure of immense dignity, chiefly because she is so mystified—we never know the truth of her relationship with Zack. She is Mammy, yet she is more: or perhaps she is the representation of the Mammy that raises the stereotype from racist emblem to embodiment of the erotic and familial involvement of black and white in Faulkner's South.

Molly appears again (now spelled Mollie) in the final and title section, "Go Down, Moses." She almost has the last word as the grieving mother of a family that now includes not only black and white McCaslins, but black and white Worshams as well. Gavin Stevens sees Molly as infantil-ized again: "She's not as big as a ten-year-old child" (379). As she demanded a divorce from Lucas, she now demands a local funeral for her grand-son, executed for murder in the North. Samuel Worsham Beauchamp is obviously a casualty of the black diaspora, a black McCaslin done out of his inheritance by Roth Edmonds, who "sold my Benjamin, sold him in Egypt" (381). The language of slavery (and of deliverance) focuses atten-tion on the interdependence of black and white in this complex family. Molly is finally Mammy transcended into mother, matriarch. While she is not a subversion of the symbolic order that places white over black in Faulkner's South, neither does his fiction force her into unexamined collusion with it.

The Romance of Endurance: Dilsey

Go Down, Moses is Faulkner's most comprehensive attempt to "solve" the historical, religious, and social problems of race in his fictive South. It presents not a unitary answer but several responses to the damaging in-volvement of white with black (and red), allowing Faulkner to reinvent a range of black characters from Old South myth: the Tragic Mulatta (see chapter 3), the Trickster, and the Mammy. However, Faulkner's full-est, and arguably most fruitful, engagement with and reinvention of the Mammy comes earlier in The Sound and the Fury (1929). I would argue that the Mammy is the central representation of white nostalgia. She is the figure on whom the longing for maternal care and racial reconciliation rests, overlaid with an historicizing of this fantasy in the southern past. The achievement of Dilsey in The Sound and the Fury is to ruthlessly decon-struct, then reassemble the Mammy in the degenerate New South.

Conventional wisdom (from white critics, at least) on Dilsey Gibson has been to call her the "moral center" of *The Sound and the Fury*, "a special embodiment of humanity," "a unifying and sustaining force" (Peters 138, Brooks, *Yoknapatawpha Country* 342). In an early review Evelyn Scott said, "Dilsey isn't searching for a soul. She is the soul" (9). Dilsey is immune to history: "neither the past nor the future nor the present is oppressive to her because they are all aspects of eternity, and her ultimate commitment is to eternity" (Brooks, *Yoknapatawpha Country* 330). If Uncle Tom is Christ, Dilsey is a madonna; she suffers yet transcends mortal pain.

Recently, however, there has been a movement, especially among some black critics, toward reading Dilsey historically in her position as black, as a woman, as a servant. Thadious Davis, for example, says that "in the Gibson family Faulkner succeeds in capturing the symbolic and spiritual significance of a whole generation of Southern blacks as they are understood by the white South" (71). Dilsey is the Mammy reactivated in the moral darkness of the New South: a critique both of the New South and of the old Mammy. She is celebrated for her "humanity," yet she reenacts a structure in which blacks and women—especially black women—are denied humanity, denied any possibility of stepping out of a self-abnegating role. Thadious Davis tries to have it both ways, insisting that Dilsey "transcends symbol or stylized type" while admitting she is connected "to a long line of actual and fictional portraits of 'mammy,' the loving black servant praised for her service to a white family" (105, 104). What makes Dilsey Faulkner's most interesting mammy is that the discourses surrounding her are not comic or merely nostalgic but religious. She suffers and looks forward to some resurrection, just as Uncle Tom, body broken by white viciousness, turns toward heaven. Her power as a redemptive figure is fragmentary and limited. Yet it stands as a significant countervoice to the unmitigated despair and destruction of the Compsons. It is undoubtedly true, as Myra Jehlen acidly puts it, that "Faulkner realized that no degree of endurance by a nigger mammy could reverse the disintegration of the aristocratic South" (37). The stereotyped religiosity of the old-time mammy becomes something tragic (because of its inability to redeem the family, especially Caddy and Quentin) in Faulkner's coinage of the figure for 1928. Dilsey is the product of unassimilable historical moments: the Old South of black-fed, black-served, plantation order and the New South of poverty, racial retrenchment, and racial unrest; Janus-faced, looking to past and future in equal confusion. Like everything else about *The Sound and the Fury*, searching for absolute order among the ruins is pointless.

Dilsey as a product of religious discourses could be a rehearsal of entrapping binaries; women are either virgins or whores, blacks are either saints or rapists. Blacks in sentimental white novels have often been depicted as more truly Christian than their white masters and mistresses; Aunt Phillis and Uncle Tom die in a grace somehow above that of whites. Dilsey does not die but struggles on, demonstrating the stoicism Faulkner expected from, and admired in, black women.

Yet Dilsey's activities in the Compson household do not include anything outside the province of the conventional mammy. How could they? In 1928, as in the sixty years of "freedom" before that, black women served whites. The kitchen is her special domain; she is associated with the inevitable biscuit dough. She puts the children to bed, she is the judge of proper behavior, constantly uttering the rhetorical question of all mammies: "Aint you ashamed of yourself?" She heals, she protects the weak, shielding Quentin II from her angry uncle: "He aint gwine so much as lay his hand on you while Ise here." She is the way to religion: "You's de Lawd's chile, anyway. En I be Hisn too, fo long, praise Jesus." She is mother of the motherless: "Who else gwine raise her 'cep me? Aint I raised eve'y one of y'all?" (35, 37, 112, 189, 120). In keeping with the conservative Mammy tradition, Dilsey could, at this level, be read as an unadulterated white fantasy of black martyrdom. It is true that she treats her own family curtly. Dilsey is especially harsh to her sons and grandsons over care of Benjy: Versh, T.P., and Luster do, to some extent, fulfill the racist notion of "trifling niggers." Luster in particular derives from the cliché of the shiftless black boy, lazy and dishonest. Dilsey's constant admonition to him is, "Dont you sass me, nigger boy" (34). He, too, suffers from Jason's malice, as when Jason teases him with the quarter for "the show" and benefits from Dilsey's kindness: " 'A big growed man like you,' she says. 'Git outen my kitchen. Hush,' she says to Luster. . . . 'I'll git you a quarter fum Frony tonight and you kin go tomorrow night' " (153). The Compson children can hardly be said to merit Dilsey's care. Though she tries to protect weak (white) members of the household from Jason Compson's vicious spite, she does not sentimentalize them; they are not put in place of her real children. Indeed, Dilsey has a realistic view of the Compsons, particularly Caddy, astutely calling her a "devil" at one point and saying prophetically of her soiled drawers that the dirt had soaked clean through. Dilsey reads both Compsons and Gibsons with detached, compassionate accuracy. She handles Jason's sadism with grim grace, copes with Mrs. Compson's hypochondria to keep the house running, and shows active love to Benjy without being destroyed in the culture of decay and violence the Compsons inhabit.

Yet for all her self-contained integrity, what the reader—and "Faulkner" the narrator—sees is not a *black* woman (to go back to Thadious Davis's delineation of terms) but a Negro cook. Perhaps this accounts for the ways in which she crosses at times into Mammy territory. We see this in her relations with her husband. She speaks to Roskus with ironic contempt, sending him on menial errands, echoing the old-time mammy who had little respect for her no-count man. The black marriage where the wife is censorious and long-suffering while the husband is impossible and child-ish is another facet of southern racial myth. Faulkner quotes it in "The Fire and the Hearth" with Molly and Lucas: here the Gibsons' marriage is drawn quite crudely. Sexual feelings within black marriage seemed un-imaginable (though Faulkner treats the idea with dignity in "Pantaloon in Black"); black male sexuality is threatening. Molly and Lucas are accorded some sense of their own sexuality though expressed in the context of white exploitation. Faulkner's concern with Dilsey is sufficiently iconic that there is no question of her having a sexuality, much less expressing it.

In some ways, Dilsey is in danger of becoming a mammy-saint, yet she is resistant to some of the central conventions of Mammyhood. Per-haps the most interesting challenge to the old-time Mammy comes in the careful physical description given her. Thadious Davis notes that Dilsey's "maroon velvet cape" and "dress of purple silk" are "the colors and ma-terials of royalty" (103). The fabrics are traditional; Jessie Parkhurst points out that the Mammy often wore her mistress's cast-off finery for Sun-day (353). While the "voluminous skirts and headgear may rely generally upon conventional types and specifically upon his own mammy, Caro-line Barr," Dilsey is far from the fat, animated breast and belly of the stereotype (Thadious M. Davis 105). Dilsey is queenly; she is compared to an impressive ruin. This aggrandizing strategy undermines the comic Mammy convention. However, underneath the regal trappings, her body is not fecund and nurturing:

> She had been a big woman once but now her skeleton rose, draped loosely in unpadded skin that tightened again upon a paunch almost dropsical, as though muscle and tissue had been courage or fortitude which the days or the years had consumed until only the indomitable skeleton was left rising like a ruin or a landmark above the somnolent

and impervious guts and above that the collapsed face that gave the impression of the bones themselves being outside the flesh. (158–59)

Women's bodies in The Sound and the Fury appear and disappear in curious ways, presented usually in the fragments of someone's obsession. Caddy, for Benjy, is a smell of trees (or later, of perfume), a shoe, and arms that hold him; for Quentin she is pieces, constructed around evading sexuality: a veil, the scent of honeysuckle, a throat, a shifting, unlimited entity. For all the narrative voices, Mrs. Compson is a diseased body, often reduced to a complaining voice whose physicality is almost deleted in the text. She is certainly not a welcoming maternal presence: Quentin thinks, "If I just had a mother so I could say Mother Mother" (105). Quentin II's body is the object of Jason's rage; he insists she should keep it covered while describing its display: "Her kimono came unfastened, flapping about her, damn near naked" (111). The white woman's body is the focus of so much Compson anger and pain, yet it is elusive. As we have seen, there is a cultural underpinning to this: the lady is so circumscribed as to be invisible. Her invisibility makes the black woman perversely visible: Dilsey is the most present body in The Sound and the Fury, represented by her work of cooking and nursing. Dilsey's body is whole, neither apotheosized nor effaced, neither constructed as the object of ultimate desire nor reduced to one defining element. She is represented neither by the unreachable classical body nor the multifarious, open, grotesque body. Dilsey is associated with food, but not with the all-nurturing breast. While Faulkner goes on in Go Down, Moses to insist more coherently on the black mother as the authentic mother, at this stage of his reactivation of the Mammy, the black woman's body is more an antitype. Molly once had the sustaining breast, before she became reinfantilized as tiny and toothless. There is no suggestion that Dilsey ever wet-nursed for the Compsons (though it would make sense if she had). Neither Dilsey nor Molly is like the Aunt Jemima of myth, as if abundance disappeared with the Old South. Dilsey is, if anything the "ruins" of the Mammy for New South, a kind of memento mori for the Compsons: she looks as though her skeleton is on the outside of her flesh. The fat, milky mammy signified the plenty of the plantation—plenty for the whites who received the wealth, anyway. Dilsey's bony outside, her appearance as an impressive architectural ruin, signifies the Compson house (and the House of Compson): reduced, once grand, undernourished, and dying.

Insisting that the Mammy is not merely the breast of the white family but its soul does not alter Dilsey's situation as a black woman in a white household, celebrated as a servant/mother who, unlike Benjy, Quentin, and Jason, is not allowed to speak her own life. Critics disagree about why this is while trying to spare Faulkner any charges of racism or condescension. Thadious Davis insists that the third-person Dilsey "lends decorum and distance" (106); Reed argues that it assures "absolute objectivity" for the final part of the novel (82); Waggoner calls the section "effectively" Dilsey's (55); Faulkner himself said it was "Faulkner's" and that it "still was wrong" (Gwynn and Blotner 32). Matthews cautions that it "explores the resources of conventional narrative discourse to learn that they can compose no more authoritative telling of the story than the inside accounts that have gone before" (*Play* 111). Where Gwin asserts that she can "hear" Caddy Compson's voice amidst her brothers' obfuscations, I would say it is much harder to really "hear" Dilsey, even though the novel is full of reports of her speech. Where Caddy's fluid selves surround and inform her brothers' narratives, Dilsey is much more their construction: each Compson, needing different forms of care from Dilsey, contributes to her assemblage. Snead suggests that whereas the "first three sections of the novel have shown the failures of white society and its discourses," the last section "tests whether non-whites can negate such a white language with a non-denotative language of otherness" in the black Easter service creating "an integrated narrative voice" (37). Certainly the Reverend Shegog "answers" the Compsons' problems, as Matthews has shown (*Play* 108). Yet this does not explain why Dilsey cannot speak her own experience but must have it mediated through the white voices—however limited or disturbed—of Benjy, Quentin, Jason, and finally Faulkner himself. Why must the Mammy be spoken for? Perhaps it is because for her to appear the all-loving, strong, giving devoted mother, she must be defined only as she affects others, not through an inner life that might prove to be disruptive. A society run by the Law of the Father, as the southern social order is, requires, as Irigaray points out, "that woman maintain in her own body the material substratum of the object of desire, but that she herself never have access to desire" (*This Sex* 188). Dilsey is valued not for what she might reveal of herself but what she suppresses of herself in giving to the Compsons. And perhaps the most compelling reason is that the voices constructing her, including "Faulkner" in section 4, and Faulkner the author, cannot know her. She is, at the risk of belaboring Davis's point, a "Negro," a white construction. The first section, "April Seventh, 1928," is filtered through Benjy's atemporal consciousness. Here Dilsey is warmth, love, and authority. She represents continuity as years flow forward and backward in Benjy's mind. Dilsey, like Caddy, is a nurturing force, calling Benjy her "baby" even when he is in his thirties: standard Mammy speech, yet also quite appropriate. It is Dilsey who sees to Benjy's daily needs, never complaining, treating him as a human being, not a mere "idiot," even buying him a cake for his birthday with her own money.

She hardly appears at all in Quentin's section, "June Second, 1910"; she is part of the scenery of his life in Mississippi, one of those "Negroes" who were to his childhood constant background noises and indispensable furnishings but whom he barely notices until he leaves for the North. He finds that Dilsey is part of the Other necessary to his self-definition, "a sort of obverse reflection" of him (53). Quentin's mind abstracts everything except Caddy, his obsession.

In Jason's section, "April Sixth, 1928," we see Dilsey through the eyes of her opposite, the adversary who calls her "an old half dead nigger" (112). Jason is Dilsey's true spiritual foe, his values completely opposed to hers. Jason and Dilsey, materialist and moralist, engage in the real power struggle in the Compson menage, grimly battling over Quentin II, over Benjy, over, indeed, the smallest domestic details: trips to the cemetery, morning coffee, meals. Their relationship is a bitter parody of a conventional marriage: Jason is the breadwinner and masculine disciplinarian while Dilsey is the child minder and cook. The war they wage against each other reflects the power structure of the traditional family, where the male is in charge of money and discipline while the female is in charge of food and values. Here it is rendered grotesque: Dilsey isn't literally the mother, Jason is nobody's father. Mrs. Compson has abdicated her role, Mr. Compson drank himself to death, and the "children," Benjy and Quentin II, are beyond nurture. The old-time Mammy may have held together the plantation and the white folks in War and Reconstruction, but in Faulkner's version of the Fall of the South, she is powerless, her sacrifice useless in the face of history.

The Mammy has often been given a sort of mythic dimension: Benet's "Fat Aunt Bess is older than Time"; Faulkner's Old Het in "Mule in the Yard" seems to be "around a hundred and at least triplets" (Collected Stories 249). This exaggerated freedom from ordinary time is an attempt to detach her from history. But Dilsey belongs quite firmly in a specific time;

she is central to Faulkner's investigation of what it might have been to be a white southern aristocrat in the early twentieth-century South. If Faulkner does not succeed in entirely accounting for the black experience in the early twentieth century, it is because of his own situation as a white man from an upper-middle-class family. Yet, without privileging the last section, there is at least some sense that, as Thadious Davis points out, Faulkner seeks to shift from the white world to a "Negro-centred world" (118). This consciousness is reflected in the way, for example, the Reverend Shegog changes from "white" speech to black in the course of his sermon. Yet it is a black-centered world nonetheless circumscribed by white romanticizing. Setting the last section on Easter Sunday, filling Dilsey's speech with apocalyptic import: "I seed de beginnin, en now I sees de endin," tempts us to read Dilsey as herself redemptive (371). Dilsey's understanding of time allows her to "endure" it, though not to beat it, even with the Christian resurrection. This transcendent discourse may have been particularly associated in the southern mind with blacks, who have had to perceive time as apocalyptic with "freedom" always coming in the future. The fourth section of *The Sound and the Fury* does not represent Dilsey's "transcendence" of time but her involvement in an alternative time as well as an alternative language. Snead reads this section as a "crossing the fence," transversing the barrier between white and black to the Easter service in Nigger Hollow, where blacks can speak freely outside the confining white context: "Black words are hardly language at all" (Snead 37). While the Reverend Shegog's liberation sermon affirms the black community, the Dilseys and Lusters and Fronys have to return to the white power structure just as the narrative returns to white discourse. Dilsey's differentness has been rendered authoritative, but she is not freed from her role.

Dilsey endures, but she does not triumph. It is true that she alone in the decomposing world of the Compsons manages to be both engaged and stoic. She represents "the blood of the remembered Lamb," a sacrifice, a literal interpreter of Christian *caritas* even Jason's rage cannot erase:

> She came hobbling between us, trying to hold me again. "Hit me, den," she says, "ef nothin else but hittin somebody wont do you. Hit me," she says.
> "You think I wont?" I says. (112)

Quentin II does not even appreciate Dilsey's abasement on her behalf, responding to her touch by striking away the old woman's hand and call-

ing her "You damn old nigger" (112). Dilsey is so saintly (or Uncle Tom–
like) she can even put up with this wretched treatment. She takes on the
sins of the Compsons, answering their coldness with warmth, looking
heavenward with vast understatement, "I done de bes I kin" (189). Of
course, much has been made of the "theological" structure of the novel,
especially the third and fourth sections, set on Good Friday and Easter.
The fourth section is concerned with the possibility of redemption and
resurrection, first and last, beginning and ending, alpha and omega. The
sermon, Dilsey's expressed faith, even the parody of the empty tomb beg
a reading of the novel in a religious context. But there is also an historical
and social context. Matthews points out that while 8 April 1928 was indeed Easter, 9 April was the date of Lee's surrender at Appomattox, and
2 June, the date of Quentin's section, is Jefferson Davis's birthday and the
date widely celebrated as Confederate Memorial Day (Lost Cause 84–86).[3]
Although it would not do to make too much of this, the framing of the
novel with two dates central to the fall of the Old South and the invention
of the Confederate myth suggests an historical situating of the novel that
better grounds Dilsey's experience as a black servant in a white household that, like the Old South from which it derived its original status, has
collapsed. Jefferson Davis, a Mississippian himself, became the focus of
the southern sense of failure and the failure of the whole Confederacy: it
is somehow fitting that Quentin's last day on earth should be his birthday
(and the day to honor the Confederate dead). The surrender at Appomattox (hardly commemorated in the South) should not be crudely linked
to a "surrender" of the Compsons to chaos, but the juxtaposition of the
fourth section's date to the sixty-third anniversary of the last hope of the
planterocracy Quentin's grandfather General Compson fought to defend
surely should not be ignored.

It isn't just the suggestion of significant Confederate dates that invites an
historicist reading of The Sound and the Fury. Faulkner's own "afterthought"
on the novel, the Compson Appendix (written in 1945 for The Portable
Faulkner), places the Compsons firmly in the rise and fall of the South.
He wanted it called "Compson 1699–1945," saying it was "an obituary."
It is also a history, telling the story of the white planters of Mississippi
as they flee the failure of Jacobitism, are "given" land by the Chickasaw,
make a plantation, lose a war, lose the land, and sell the plantation house,
and finally, as Jason says, "in 1865 . . . Abe Lincoln freed the niggers from
the Compsons. In 1933, Jason Compson freed the Compsons from the
niggers" (234). The Appendix, with its projection of Jason's final "domes-

ticity" with the prostitute Lorraine, Dilsey's old age in Memphis, even the fanciful placing of Caddy as a companion of a Nazi general, insist on the specificity of the Compson experience. Dilsey's own entry is, however, the most mythic, saying "They endured." This grand, plural pronouncement, coming sixteen years after *The Sound and the Fury* was published and five years after the death of Caroline Barr, might seem to work against contextualizing Dilsey. But perhaps an examination of what *endurance* means will resituate Dilsey as an emanation of the Mammy, after all.

Enduring unceasing oppression by whites is, in Christian terms, admirable; politically, it can seem an endorsement of that oppression. Enduring implies no rebellion, no real resistance, only acceptance. Once again, a white text congratulates a black woman for colluding in a structure that imprisons her in a narrow definition of possibilities. What Dilsey receives in return for her commitment to servitude (she evidently receives practically nothing in wages) is perhaps inclusion in the white family, insofar as "mother" has any meaning for the Compsons. In a reading that searches out "universal human values" this can be seen as affirmative: in a recalcitrant, historicized reading, Dilsey is another reinscription of Mammy.

Amongst the Compsons, authenticity of family is a ceaseless debate. There is much discussion of status and naming: what defines Compson-ness as opposed to Bascomb-ness, particularly by Caroline Bascomb Compson. Because Benjy is retarded, his name is changed from a Bascomb one (he was called Maury for Caroline's brother) to one with fewer dynastic associations (Compson men are called Jason or Quentin).[4] Indeed, in giving him the name of Benjamin, an exile, the Compsons indicate he is an outcast. He is likened to a "bluegum," a wild Negro with a poisonous bite, or a cannibal: "*Versh said, Your name Benjamin now. You know how come your name Benjamin now. They making a bluegum out of you*" (43). In contrast, Dilsey's identity must be "solid" when all else is fluid: this is part of the romance of her endurance. She insists on the inviolability of her name:

> Folks dont have no luck, changing names. My name been Dilsey since fore I could remember and it be Dilsey when they's long forgot me.
> How will they know its Dilsey when it's long forgot, Dilsey, Caddy said.
> It'll be in the Book, honey, Dilsey said. Writ out. (53)[5]

Quentin says, "a nigger is not a person so much as a form of behavior; a sort of obverse reflection of the white people he lives among," implying, in the case of the Compsons, that blacks act out "family" where they cannot. Black servants must, paradoxically, be "white" (as John Sartoris insists to Louvinia in The Unvanquished), yet must be unalterably Other. Blacks must internalize white values, such as truth, honor, fidelity, compassion, modesty, bravery, and faith, on behalf of morally malnourished whites. It is a flattering picture of the black capacity for virtue, yet it relies on a definition of blackness as a receptacle for an ethical system whites have discarded as they might give away old clothes to the servants. Whites entrust (or burden) blacks—and men entrust women—with the values they identify as essential to culture yet must, as the empowered race and gender, lay aside in order to maintain power: the dominant group defines the subordinate group as morally "better" as a means of control.

Lee Jenkins in Faulkner and Black-White Relations notes that Dilsey is "a suitable benediction" on Caroline Barr's life, as much as Molly Beauchamp is (165). What Faulkner said of Caroline Barr at her funeral could be equally true of Dilsey: "She asked no odds and accepted the handicaps of her lot, making the best of her few advantages. She surrendered her destiny to a family" (Blotner 1035). In some ways Dilsey surrenders her destiny and, to some extent, her voice. She also surrenders her race and her gender to become a sexless image of all-giving motherhood. Occupying the moral pinnacle previously inhabited by the white lady of the plantation, she takes on the burdens of that position, to be divorced from desire (yet a symbol of motherhood), to be self-abnegating, giving everything to men and children: "The true Southern maid is the mammy whose ineffective compromise in the home of the white mistress causes her to identify completely with the status quo; she believes within her heart in the rightness of the established order of which she is a part" (Harris 24).

Yet Dilsey does offer some resistance, imposing her own (religious) order on chaos by her attendance at the Reverend Shegog's sermon. Even though only temporarily, she escapes the white context that reduces her while pretending to elevate her. It is only a partial counteraction, yet it offers a glimpse of Faulkner trying to understand the black beyond the "Negro."

Cleanth Brooks says of Dilsey that she can "make sense of past, present, and future. All are aspects of eternity, and Dilsey, in her simple religious faith, believes in an order that is grounded in eternity" (Yoknapatawpha Country 328). This points to the romance of race at the heart of Dilsey's portrayal. Faulkner, speaking at the University of Virginia, reiterated the sacrificial model: "she held the family together for not the hope of reward but just because it was the decent and proper thing to do" (Gwynn and Blotner 85). Dilsey is part of the social reality (for whites such as Faulkner) of 1928. Though Brooks says, "Faulkner does not make the mistake of accounting for Dilsey's virtues through some mystique of race in which good primitive black folk stand over against corrupt wicked white folk," nevertheless there is a "mystique of race" (and gender) operating here; Dilsey's spiritual stature is a function of her being a black woman (343). Is the Mammy safe and sentimentalized because she is not a challenge to the status quo? Is Faulkner being subversive here yet pulling against the complex reality that might have freed him from the convention altogether, or simply responding to a deep-seated white need for forgiveness? The Mammy refuses to blame the system.

Dilsey is an attempt to acknowledge the centrality of the black mother without challenging the system that defines her. Barbara Christian suggests the black woman's maternal talents probably stemmed from the sacredness of the mother-and-child relationship in Africa: white southerners tended to interpret this not as something deriving from culture but as animal instinct. Christian goes on to show how this demonstrates the contradiction in southern ideas of motherhood: on the one hand, it is a revered estate; on the other, it is turned over to "a being less than human," indicating that, for all the gyneolatrous rhetoric, women's work was devalued, whether performed by black or white women (*Black Feminist Criticism* 188). And in middle- to upper-class southern households, women's work, especially mothering, was carried out by the Mammy.

Dilsey is, perhaps, a new kind of mammy. Her body is present as the black woman *must* be present: to nurture, comfort, feed, clean, mediate, and suffer. Yet it is not trivialized. Nonetheless, in celebrating the self-sacrificial all-mother, the exemplary Mammy of the old southern model partially, but significantly, reasserts herself. No one laughs at Dilsey the way they might at the mammy in *Gone with the Wind*, serving as the saintly plantation mistress's viceroy of virtue, reminding Scarlett O'Hara when she strays from the moral precepts endorsed by her mother. But Dilsey performs essentially the same function. She nurtures not just the bodies but the souls of the unsalvageable Compsons. *The Sound and the Fury's* shifting narratives subvert the reductive stereotyping of the black mother as laughing, fleshy feeder, while at the same time reinforcing the discourses that deny her liberty. Dilsey endures, but she does not escape.

3 The Tragic Mulatta

The curse of my ancestors has fallen heavily on their child.

—Cora Munro in THE LAST OF THE MOHICANS

Secret Blackness and the Terror of the Self-Same

Confined to the kitchen, contained in asexual maternity, the Mammy is no threat to the symbolic order: as a creation of the white mind, she endorses it. Yet the Mammy has an opposite, also a creation of the white mind but not a comforting maternal presence. What Bakhtin described as the grotesque body expresses many features of the black female body as understood by the white South. The Mammy's roundness, the focus on her breasts, literal and symbolic source of nourishment, typify the kind of "protuberance" that characterizes the low Other. Another feature of the low Other is the genitals: the grotesque body is open. Black women are not only breasts and bellies but also available sexual receptacles. Under slavery the black woman was legally and practically accessible to white men. An industry of sorts, the "black" (though she often could pass for white) kept woman, became part of the secret sexual economy of the South. Thus the Tragic Mulatta was invented.

In the white South's tangle of racial myths, a black woman can be constructed an erotic object, repository of fantasies about "Negro" sexuality. White women are locked into the chaste Confederate Lady ideal, represented by that orificeless classical body, but the young black woman is physically as "present" as the Mammy, though not for nurture: created to be seduced or raped. She is doubly Other, both an endorsement of and a threat to the prevailing ideology, "impure" vessel of negative images that prop up the white lady's purity and delicacy. The black woman is a wish fulfillment figure. As W. J. Cash says: "Torn from her tribal restraints and taught an easy complaisance for commercial reasons, she was to be had for the taking. Boys on and around the plantation inevitably learned to use her, and having acquired the habit, often continued it into manhood and even after marriage. She was natural, and could give herself up to passion in a way impossible to wives inhibited by Puritanical training" (84).

Cash's broad-brush portrait is more important as an attempt to understand the "blackness" of sexuality as it was constructed in the mythic South than as serious investigation. The Mind of the South is a species of fiction, a creative description of a region through its mythic characters recast in the revisionist, troubled climate of the 1930s, writing through mystifications of race and gender. It is what Thomas Nelson Page tried to do in The Old South (1892). Writing the Lost Cause, justifying the ways—particularly the racial ways—of the Old South to the New became a growing enterprise in the twenties and thirties. Faulkner's fictions cover some of the same territory; he too was present in the South of the twenties and thirties as it reinvented race relations through Jim Crow, lynchings, and anxieties over "mongrelization." Black women were, like white women, a central part of this protean collection of responses to the past.

The reduction of black women in slavery to "commercial" property to be "used" by white men is not something Faulkner's fictions condone, yet the southern social order allows them no other role. Faulkner protests the inhumanity of their treatment and, as with his revisions of the Mammy, both reinvents the stereotype of "Jezebel," the sexual black woman, and insists on her inclusion in the white southern family. The young black woman disrupts and confuses the defining binaries of the South: white over black, virgin over whore.

While Faulkner's narratives try to reject the cultural discourses surrounding black women's sexuality that allow, even encourage, rape, they situate the sexual exploitation of young black women not as a crime against women but as a crime against the family: incest. Most young black women in Faulkner's fiction are of mixed race. The cultural stories Faulkner draws upon are rich in American fiction and the popular imagination. The heroine of these stories, the Tragic Mulatta or Tragic Octoroon, has been the subject of novels, stories, and plays since the 1830s. Faulkner's representation of the mulatta is contradictory and troubled: sometimes she is a conventional (though incomplete) player in a narrative that challenges southern society, as in *Go Down, Moses*. At other moments, the mulatta story is displaced to question the official oppositions of southern racial myth, as in *Absalom, Absalom!* The white world creates the "Negro"; it creates the role of prostitute that the officially black woman was expected to play. By insisting on the mulatta's place in the white family, Faulkner questions the hierarchy of white over black, but in a way that reveals not only anxiety in southern culture over the *difference* of blackness but a radical fear of the *sameness*—an undefined and unregulated, fluid blackness "hidden" in women who look white. Perhaps race is a smokescreen, perhaps this is really a story about sexuality "hidden" in women who are told to behave asexually.[1]

At any rate, Faulkner produced these fictions in a South almost hysterically concerned with defining the limits of race. Legal (and cultural) parameters of whiteness and blackness actually became more conservative during the twenties and thirties. In the New South, "many Southern whites became extremely anxious—perhaps paranoid is not too strong a term—about the specter of 'invisible blackness'" (F. James Davis 56). "One drop" legislation, basically labeling as black anyone who had a "known" black ancestor, was adopted in many southern states in the late twenties and early thirties: until then the laws varied from one-thirty-second part black to one-eighth part black constituting "blackness." There were various strategies to separate black from white as well, stemming from a fear of creeping "social equality" (underneath which lurked the terror of miscegenation). Jim Crow laws often took bizarre and seemingly overdetermined forms. In 1926 in Atlanta, black barbers were forbidden to serve women or children under fourteen; a 1930 Birmingham city ordinance banned "a Negro and white person together or in company with each other" from playing dominoes or checkers (Woodward 116–18). Mississippi passed an antimiscegenation law in 1930. It could be that this growing rigidity resulted from worry over the growing (though often suppressed or discounted) achievements of blacks in education, journalism, and other areas.[2] One should also bear in mind that it had been illegal in Mississippi only since 1920 to publish material advocating "social equality" (McMillen 174). Most appallingly, these anxieties over the scandalous "touching" of black and white manifested themselves in lynchings: there were two violent lynchings in Oxford, Mississippi, in

1935 and 1936, right under Faulkner's nose, as it were. Such social forces could not but affect the production of literary texts.

"Oh, who am I?" cries Amantha Starr, daughter of a slaveowner and a slave in Robert Penn Warren's *Band of Angels* (1955), articulating the agony of racial uncertainty that is the mulatta's existential inheritance. However white she looks, the Tragic Mulatta is previolated by her race, a commodity in a white world that traffics in black women's bodies.

The South's dominant story insists on a hostile binary of supposed "opposites": white and black. These states of being, white on top and black on bottom, are constructed as absolutes that can in no way touch, though it is their touching that creates the need for the South to erect a system in which white and black *cannot come together*. So southern culture assembles stories about how whites have a "natural" physical aversion to blacks (though if this was so, why did they need laws prohibiting white/black marriages?), and that if blacks and whites were to "mate," the result would be a "mongrel," sterile as a mule. Indeed, the word *mulatto/a* comes from the Spanish *mulato*—"mule."

However, *white* requires *black* in order to have meaning, so the insisted-upon opposites aren't really opposite at all but exist in a state of "antagonistic interdependence"; the normative needs the alien in order to exist. Yet black and white slip into one another constantly: they "touch" (in all possible senses), and we can call on historical evidence to show this. In the old lower South before 1840 or so, when social rank was still fluid, some mulattoes and mulattas could define themselves as white and be treated as such (Williamson, *New People* 13–30). However, as the caste system ossified, shades of color were not tolerated. Williamson in *New People* remarks: "External pressures demanded internal order and there could be no anomalies; everything at all black must be unfree and white must be privileged. Mulattoes must be made black, and the unfreedom of blacks must be defined and made universal" (14).

Defining even blond and blue-eyed mulattas as black was not only a reassurance of the "purity" of the white race, it was good economics; in a slave-based system a mulatta, even the daughter of the plantation master, was only another piece of property. The whiter the slave, the higher the price. It was also a way of absolving the South of the guilt of miscegenation: "By classifying the mulatto as a Negro he [the southerner] was in effect denying that intermixture had occurred at all" (Jordan 86). Of course, like everything a culture shrilly insists is either forbidden or does not exist, it *did* occur and was acceptable if kept quiet; in some circles (not polite society), it was even applauded, a badge of southern male virility: "Miscegenation between a white male and black female posed almost no ethical problems for the antebellum Southern community, so long as the rules, which were fairly easy to follow, were discreetly observed" (Wyatt-Brown 307). The rules included official silence: this story was not to be told outside the privileged group, that is, white men. The rules were entirely different for white women: as early as 1681, a law was passed in Maryland prohibiting white women from marrying black men, since the only possible reason for this breach of racial decorum would be the "Satisfaccion of theire Lascivious and Lustfull desires," (Jordan 44). For a white woman to so "demean" herself was an "indecent outrage on her own womanhood, and sin against God," (Van Evrie 154). Most states defined a person's status through the status of his or her mother, *ad ventrem*: black children of white mothers were not slaves, not profitable, and thus the situation that could create them was suppressed.

James Baldwin drily remarks, "Negroes are associated in the public mind with sex" (53). Blackness has long been equated with lust: the Spirit of Fornication in Francis Bacon's *New Atlantis* (1624) is "a little foul ugly Ethiop." Images of women in the Victorian South ranged from the Angel in the House, apparently conceiving children by parthenogenesis, to harems full of supine dark women. The culture accommodated both, participating in its own erotic legend by producing mulattas solely for the enjoyment of white men. It is surely no coincidence that one of the most popular works in the antebellum South was Thomas Moore's orientalist fantasy *Lalla Rookh* with its eternally faithful, compliant Arabian women.

In the South, these stories, based more on sensational metaphor than sociological truth, were thought to be factual: "All negresses are wantons and strumpets. All white men in the South firmly believe that" (Stribling, *Birthright* 199). Van Evrie explains black female "looseness" by saying that black women do not blush and therefore cannot compare with the pink-cheeked "moral perceptions and elevated nature of the white woman" (89). Mary Boykin Chesnut blames mulattas for usurping the place of white wives: "An abandoned woman is sent out of any decent house elsewhere. Who thinks any worse of a negro or mulatto woman for being a thing we can't name? God forgive us but ours is a *monstrous* system" (29). Her sympathies lie with "my countrywomen" who "are, I believe, the purest women God ever made"; she reviles "those beastly negress beauties. Animals—*tout et simple*—cordifiamma—no—*corpifiamma*." Chestnut, mindful that her own father-in-law was thought to have a brood of mulatto children, locates the mulatta's identity in her sexuality (243).[3]

The story of black sexual insatiability was created to underscore the convenience of regarding black women as less than human. One cannot commit adultery with an animal; one cannot rape property. The sexual accessibility white men ascribed to black women reflected their legal relationship: master to chattel. It scarcely matters in this context that slaves believed in marriage and fidelity to the same extent as whites; the myth that chastity is foreign to black women remained unshakable.[4]

While later novelists, both black and white, appropriate the mulatta for abolitionist fiction (the first real mulatto novel is Richard Hildreth's 1836 *The Slave*), James Fenimore Cooper, in *The Last of the Mohicans* (1826), creates the first Tragic Mulatta in American literature in order to destroy her, making America safe for "pure" white colonization. The novel operates in a political space defined by the threatened intermixture of races. Cora Munro is racially ambiguous owing to her mother's West Indian "Creole" background; she looks white but has "rich blood," as Cooper delicately puts it. She and her fair, pure, and "pure-blooded" sister Alice are thrown into a brutal North American wilderness where "evils worse than death"—rape by racially inferior Indian men—await them (88).

Characters are defined racially; with whites, Indians, and mulattas inhabiting the same claustrophobic, hostile landscape, Cooper sees a frightening potential for miscegenation. Definition—the reassertion of the violent hierarchy—becomes imperative. The Indians distinguish tribes amongst themselves; the whites distinguish themselves from the Indians; Natty Bumppo is proud to call himself "a man without a cross," that is, all white; and Cora stands alone, saying she is "cursed" by her black heritage. Alice's virginity must be preserved at all costs. Alice must become mother of children "without a cross"; her "superior" whiteness demands she must not be a victim of rape and miscegenation. When both the dark and fair sister are captured by the would-be ravisher Magua, Cora pleads for Alice, crying, "Her soul is as pure and spotless as her skin" (378). But Cora, like Hawthorne's black-haired heroines, is assumed to have a strong streak of latent passion in her, an inherent sexuality. This is what Magua sees (he is not interested in Alice) as he offers her the choice between concubinage and death. Cora, descendant of slaves but brought up a white lady, dies a sacrifice on the linked altars of racial integrity and sexual purity.

Cora's dual burden is misinterpreted by critics insisting on the apolitical nature of the romance. Erskine Peters compares her to some of Faulkner's Tragic Mulattas and says: "Even though Cora Munro dies tragically, her death is not tainted by racial circumstance, for unlike her literary successors, she is accorded her birthright by her father who loves, protects, and acknowledges her" (115). It is true that Cora's father is (in some ways like Faulkner) a racial liberal. He probably even married Cora's mother. But Cora cannot produce "pure" heirs. Her "dark" blood must not be allowed to mix with a white man's and carry the "curse of my ancestors" down to the next generation of Americans engaged in conquering the continent for Anglo-Saxon Christianity. Yet unhallowed cohabitation with an Indian is unthinkable for a refined woman brought up, at least, to be white. Her double funeral rite, Indian and Christian, represents the ambivalence. The mulatta is born to be martyred for her "better" self, her white self, the white sister, quieting the turbulence of race and passion in the grave.

The mulatta rarely appears in apologist romances of the Old South; her existence undermines the official story. She does, however, feature in works by writers interested in propagandizing the place of the part-white in a slave society. Race is destiny as the victims of plantation droit du seigneur are made dramatic emblems of the persecuted and dispossessed. More important, the problem of desire is articulated by the mulatta and in her: her own body testifies to the sexuality that goes beyond "Christian" containment in producing heirs within legal marriage. Mulattas were rarely protected by legal marriage; they often understood desire as death. In J. H. Ingraham's The Quadroone (1840), Azélie, in love with the white aristocrat Don Henrique, declares: "I am outcast and degraded, and can look on this noble brow only with dishonour. There remains no bridegroom for the doomed Quadroone but death—no bridal robe but the winding mantle of the grave!" (115). Azélie's mulatta mother tries to force her to become a courtesan, the role prescribed for quadroon girls in New Orleans. The root of Azélie's problem, like Cora Munro's, is her presumed sexual availability: she, unlike Estelle, the white heroine of the novel, cannot demand marriage. She will always be "the intended victim of white men's lust." The "taint" of race and the "taint" of gender become nearly indistinguishable.

The mulatta narrative of rape or seduction, children, reenslavement, and death, is found in a good deal of nineteenth- century fiction. Rosalie, in Lydia Maria Child's "The Quadroons" (1847), dies of a broken heart when her white lover leaves her. Their daughter is sold, raped, and dies insane. In William Wells Brown's novel *Clotel; or, The President's Daughter* (1853) the mulatta Clotel thinks she has a "marriage" with a white man "sanctioned by heaven although unrecognized on earth" until he abandons her and her child to marry into a politically influential white family (80).

William Wells Brown was himself a mulatto and an escaped slave whose sister was, as he says in his memoir, "sold to sensual slave holders" (13). *Clotel* is based partly on his experiences and partly on the story that Thomas Jefferson had children by his wife's slave Sally Hemings, one of whom would have been Clotel. Historically valid or not, the idea of a president's child sold for fifteen hundred dollars, enslaved, and degraded, was a strong vehicle for Brown's antislavery argument.[5] He subscribes to the prevalent sentimental racist idea that mulatta heroines had to be "beautiful" according to the convention of the day, that is, near-white. This heightens, for Brown, the sexual insidiousness of the double standard that *requires* mulatta women be overwhelmingly sexual while white women must be asexual breeders of heirs: "Society does not frown upon the man who sits with his mulatto child upon his knee, whilst its mother stands a slave behind his chair" (55). Brown is quite clear, as Faulkner will be after him, on the exploitation of sexuality and race; however "noble" the liaisons between mulattas and white men, these women are products of, and subject to, a system that does not hold white men responsible for what is often rape: "What must be the moral degradation of that people to whom marriage is denied?" asks Brown (58).

The sense of "taint" that the mulatta articulates on behalf of women in general, indicating the guilt and fear that white culture has taught them to attach to their sexuality, defines the mulatta heroine. Cassy in *Uncle Tom's Cabin*, like Cora Munro and Azélie, feels unclean: "We live in filth and grow loathsome, till we loathe ourselves! And we long to die, and we don't dare kill ourselves! No hope! no hope! no hope?—" (515).

According to the Tragic Mulatta myth, the mulatta responds to rape as a white woman would (a black field worker, like any peasant, would, according to the southern myth, take small notice of her bodily violation, or would not be able to articulate it if she did). Her fine sensibilities are shattered. Yet there is no possibility of redress. Joel Williamson recounts an incident in 1859 of a Mississippi overseer who raped a slave and was murdered by her husband. The courts ruled that "adultery" was no excuse: the overseer was not seen to have committed any sexual misdemeanor (*New People* 54). On the body of the mulatta is inscribed over and over not only the politics of slavery but of gender oppression; white female sexuality could be controlled through an ideology that disallowed its expression and black female sexuality could be contained in rape.

In Dion Boucicault's popular play *The Octoroon* (1859), Zoe of Terrebonne Plantation, daughter of Judge Peyton and a quadroon slave, is given the chance to save her father's land if only she will become the mistress of the Legree-like overseer M'Loskey: land is equated with the female body, agricultural property with sexual property. Zoe subscribes to the conventional divorce between white body and black body that informs the mulatta, declaring to her white suitor George that she is branded with a "dark fatal mark," and "of the blood that feeds my heart, one drop in eight is black—bright red as the rest may be, that one poisons all the flood; those even bright drops give me love like yours, ambition like yours—life hung with passions like dew drops on the morning flowers; but the one black drop gives me despair, for I am an unclean thing."[6] Like Cora Munro, Azélie, Cassy, and Clotel, she feels torn and corrupt, robbed of identity, at the mercy of a society that represents her as a culpable sexual commodity.

The mulatta is without a sanctioned role in society: the conventional protections accorded white women are unavailable to her. Not only is her body divided from herself in its "taint," but she is divided from the offspring of her body—her children. The quadroon mother in George Washington Cable's "Madame Delphine" (1881) refuses to acknowledge her daughter; she wants Olive to "pass" as white and (illegally) marry a white man, gaining the respectability she could never have. As the priest says: "She is a quadroon; all the rights of her womanhood trampled in the mire, sin made easy to her—almost compulsory—" (30).

The mulatta heroine was useful for fiction writers in the nineteenth century; unlike white women, she could be simultaneously sexual and virtuous. What happened to her body did not necessarily taint her soul as it would her white sister. She is a creature of parts, "black" blood and "white" blood, acting independently. She is formed of so many contradictory discourses—black and white, sexuality and innocence, "naturalness" and refinement—that she can barely exist. In the end, these contradictory discourses that construct her also destroy her.

Mulatta novels display a dual sensibility: their overt political purpose is to attack slavery as well as refute (certainly in Stowe's case) the idea that miscegenation necessarily produces inferior beings, but their covert purpose is more troubling. There is something almost hysterical, almost pornographic about the loving description of the whiteness of mulatta beauties. These women are cultivated, intelligent, often apparently as white as their mistresses, yet are predestined to be raped. The white boy in Lillian Smith's Strange Fruit (1944) excitedly compares his mulatta lover to his sister: "In the dusk she's as white as Laura" (6). The epiphany of powerlessness that comes when the young girl finds she is not the adored heiress of the house but a slave is titillating to a white audience not encouraged to think of real white women being raped. Counterfeit white women are another matter. The mulatta's sexuality—the core of her identity—is disguised in whiteness, making it all the more thrilling. There is a fear not only of the hidden Other, the alien "blackness" lurking inside the mulatta's fair form, but a terror of sameness that implicates white culture, producing its overinsistent stories. To borrow a phrase from Jonathan Dollimore, "the Other is inscribed in the self-same." The mulatta is doubly threatening for being both unbearable things at once: black and female, yet "like" whites as well. The tension produced by this collapsing of absolutes creates the suppression of the black and the feminine in texts that simultaneously attempt to demystify race and deny female sexuality.

In later nineteenth-century and early twentieth-century fiction by whites and blacks, the mulatta becomes less the sentimental heroine and more an avowedly political character. Howells's An Imperative Duty (1893) and Twain's Pudd'nhead Wilson (1894) ridicule the arbitrariness of "black" and "white" in American culture. Howells's Rhoda confronts the sexual connotations of blackness when she discovers she is a mulatta, but she is redeemed by liberal northerners who essentially laugh off her sense of "taint." Twain is less interested in the sexual role of the mulatta Roxana and more concerned with a sociological exploration of the influence of environment on character. In contrast, the popular novels of Thomas 'Dixon, Jr., whose Ku Klux Klan trilogy formed the basis of Birth of a Nation, warn of the consequences of "hybridization" and depict mulattas as dominating bitch-goddesses.

Black writers such as Frances E. W. Harper in Iola Leroy (1892) and Charles Chesnutt in The House Behind the Cedars (1900) appropriate the mulatta not as a white lady feeling "unclean" but as a woman attempting to accept and embrace her blackness: this is the vision followed by the writers of the Harlem Renaissance, whose fiction often deals with the mulatta.[7] Most white writers, on the other hand, continued to focus on the mulatta as the identityless soul or as a white woman whose secret soul is black and therefore sexual.[8] Sherwood Anderson's *Dark Laughter* (1925), with "brown women tending up to the job—getting the race lighter and lighter," is a celebration of the white legend of black female fecundity and "naturalness" (69). Thadious Davis suggests that William Faulkner's friendship with Anderson in New Orleans in 1924–25 may be cause to see the influence of *Dark Laughter* and other Anderson works on Faulkner's "natural" black women (45–56). This is possible but need not be so: the constant association of black women with animal sexuality was part of the creed of Faulkner's culture as he himself articulates it in *The Sound and the Fury*, where Caddy's promiscuity is described as "negro": "*Why wont you bring him to the house, Caddy? Why must you do like nigger women do in the pasture the ditches the dark woods hot hidden furious in the dark woods*" (56–57).

Faulkner's fiction struggles to untangle gender from race. Ultimately he fails because the cultural imperative in figuring female sexuality as something *dark*, something *negro*, is too strong. To create a mulatta that is not at the mercy of her own or a white man's desire—as he does with Clytie in *Absalom, Absalom!*—he has to practically ungender her. In his other mulatta fiction, he associates the mulatta with the land, violated woman with violated wilderness. Faulkner, too, is concerned with slipping definitions: Garber's "category crisis" in a definition-obsessed society. Yet the mystifications of race and gender—I don't know whether a veil or a web is the better metaphor—so implicated in "pollution" and hidden "truths," cannot be contained. In the mulatta blackness is nowhere—and everywhere.

"Amalgamation Is Incest": The Tragic Mulatta in Go Down, Moses

The woman of mixed race embodies the sub rosa state of relations between black and white in the South. Faulkner was interested in the ways mulattoism is invisible and silenced in a South desperate for definition, yet was, perversely, such a visible symbol of slavery. Where does desire intersect with subjugation? When does "black" become "white," or, using the preferred image of the purity-obsessed South, when does the "drop of ink" pollute the clean white page? Faulkner's fictions aim to negotiate the category crises that mulattas, by simply existing at all, create. In effect, he tries to find ways to "solve" the sexuality, the presumed sexual availability, that marks the mulatta as her blackness marks her. Really, the sexuality and the blackness are inextricable, even dependent on one another. I begin my discussion of Faulkner's mulattas with *Go Down, Moses* because, as with the Mammy, his reactivation and manipulation of the stereotype is closer to the convention here than in his earlier *Absalom, Absalom!*, which I come to in the third section of this chapter.

Sterling Brown dismisses the Tragic Mulatta as "an artificial sentimental white creation" (Zanger 64). She is literally a "white creation": white father and black mother, as well as a vessel for exploring the injustices of race in the South. Mixed-race women in *Go Down, Moses*, however, do not closely follow the elaborate romantic pattern seen in earlier fiction. The mulatta's delicacy, her anguish of unbelonging, the narrative of her thwarted love for a white man, and final escape or miserable death appear only in fragments. The radical elements of the myth do, nonetheless, make incomplete, enigmatic appearances in *Go Down, Moses*, complicated by the incest that haunts Faulkner's southern family.

Incest in Tragic Mulatta fiction was used to shock and could be deployed in both abolitionist and radical racist works. Hildreth in *The Slave* underscores the wickedness of slavery when the debauched Colonel nearly succeeds in raping his own mulatta daughter. In Thomas Dixon's *Sins of the Father*, incest is introduced to emphasize not white vice but black, to show mulatta depravity and ruthlessness. On the plantation miscegenation was often literally incest as well: fathers seduced or raped mulatta slave daughters; brothers seduced or raped mulatta half-sisters. Henry Hughes in his *Treatise on Sociology* (1854) equates miscegenation and incest: "The same law which forbids consanguineous amalgamation forbids ethnical amalgamation. Both are incestuous. Amalgamation is incest" (31). Still, despite such injunctions, interracial sexual encounters were a source of great anxiety. Sarah Haynsworth Gayle, wife of an early governor of Alabama, writes of a profligate planter and his son: "I think I heard, that his child and his grandchild have one mother?" Prefiguring the well-known comments of Mary Boykin Chesnut, she says: "And those fathers whose beastly passions hurry to the bed of the slave do they feel no compunction when they see their blood sold, basely bartered like their horses? This sin is the leprosy of the earth nothing save the blood of the cross cleanses from it" (Fox-Genovese 9).

In *Go Down, Moses*, Ike McCaslin is shocked by evidence of "amalgamation" and incest in his own family. The white McCaslins are historically guilty of ignoring the kinship between them and the black McCaslins. While the male black McCaslins ("disguised" as Beauchamps) articulate their betrayal, it is the women who suffer the original, *sexual* exploitation. Incest is a crime against daughters and sisters. White Ike McCaslin romantically connects the seduction (rape?) of his aunt Tomasina and the abandonment of his cousins by white members of his family with the destruction of the wilderness: land reflects the integrity of the culture the way virginity implies "virtue" in women.

Dispossessed mulatto and mulatta children haunt "Was," the opening section of Go Down, Moses, and "The Fire and the Hearth," which follows it. Turl, or Terrel, in "Was" is the half-brother (and nephew) of Uncle Buck and Uncle Buddy McCaslin, who chase him as if he were a fox and bet on him as if he were a racehorse. He presides, a sort of slave Hymen, over the imputed engagement of the wily Miss Sophosiba Beauchamp and Uncle Buck. Terrel himself marries the Beauchamps' Tennie, a girl who could be Miss Sophonsiba's half-sister or her niece. These two marriages, divided on racial lines, might be, in fact, the union of two Beauchamp sisters and two McCaslin brothers: one pair officially "white," one pair officially "black." The description of Terrel as he stands over his brother, dealing the cards that will decide their fates, places both families—and the entire text—in a mulatto space, between light and dark, in the dusk with his "arms that were supposed to be black but were not quite white" (29).[9] In earlier drafts Terrel was substantially "blacker," looking like "a very dark Arab" (Snead 204). Lightening him focuses attention on "the repressed and unspoken crimes whose visual traces are still evident" (Snead 204). Terrel's skin illustrates the slippage between black and white imperiling the sustaining fiction of separation on which southern racism based itself. This is similar to Faulkner's making the girl in "Delta Autumn"—originally just an unnamed black woman who looks white—a member of the Beauchamp/McCaslin family to underscore the exploitation and incest brought on black women by white men of Ike's family. To quote Snead once more, "Go Down, Moses commits a sort of narrative miscegenation, a negative reversal of original division" (205). The result of this "mixing" is, as stated before, a mulatto world where the hierarchy of white over black is imperiled and, in some places, destroyed. Though Terrel is the walking, breathing "evidence" of the crime, the suppressed story of his mother's and grandmother's lives haunts the narrative like a couple of sad ghosts.

Black women's bodies are objects of contention in *Go Down, Moses*. Lucas Beauchamp in "The Fire and the Hearth" is "the oldest living McCaslin descendant," but his seniority counts for nothing as he must demand his own wife back from Zack Edmonds, the white cousin he fears has slept with her: " 'How to God,' he said, 'can a black man ask a white man to please not lay down with his black wife? And even if he could ask it, how to God can the white man promise he wont?' " (59). Black men must defer to white men over black women's bodies, yet Lucas's "lightness" (more an idea of dignity and family pride than actual color) undercuts the racial binary. Still, the possibility that a white man has "lain down" with his wife is seen as his sorrow and his loss, not Molly's.

Ike's discovery of the truth about his ancestors, the truth of the patriarchs (there are hardly any white women in this family) he was taught to revere, seems to him like the activation of a curse. In the faded, near-illiterate, spare words of the ledger, he finds that in 1807 his grandfather, Carothers McCaslin, went to New Orleans, the center of trade in "fancy girls," and bought a slave called Eunice; she was almost certainly a mulatta, bred to be a white man's concubine. Carothers and Eunice had a daughter, Tomasina. When Eunice realized one day that Carothers had impregnated their child, she killed herself. The ledger is incredulous and terse: "*Drownd in Crick Cristmas Day 1832*," then "*June 21th 1833 Drownd herself*," then "*23 Jun 1833 Who in hell ever heard of a niger drownding him self*" (267). The ledger does not employ a consistent pronoun: articulation of Eunice's gender, like the articulation of her anguish, is momentarily suppressed. This is not, however, what centrally interests Ike. When he discovers that Tomasina's son is left a thousand-dollar legacy in Carothers's will, he suddenly realizes the truth: "*So I reckon that was cheaper than saying My son to a nigger* he thought. *Even if My son wasn't but just two words*" (269–70).

To Ike, Carothers's failure to say "my son" is more significant than his failure to say "my daughter." In T. S. Stribling's "Forge" trilogy, published about ten years before *Go Down, Moses*, the slave Gracie is also the master's daughter. Her father dies in her arms, refusing to acknowledge her as his child, seeing her only as "nigger." Her brother, likewise refusing to acknowledge the truth, rapes her. The great-grandson of Gracie and her white brother Miltiades Vaiden, ends up a candidate for lynching as one of six "nigger rapists" accused in a South where (ironically enough, considering the treatment of black women by white men) "black man" and "rapist" were virtually interchangeable. Miltiades Vaiden does not understand why she would ask him and not the boy's "colored family" for help. She says: "Colored relations! What colored relations? . . . Toussaint, the son I had by you was nothing but a Vaiden on both sides. . . . Who would my grandchild come back to see except white people, Miltiades?" (*Unfinished Cathedral* 224). Despite the blatancy of kinship, the white Vaidens and McCaslins try very hard to deny that sexual exploitation—in both these cases, incest—ever happened. Ike McCaslin calls the knowledge of McCaslin guilt what the mulatta calls the knowledge of her black "blood": that is, a "curse." He tells Carothers's black granddaughter:

> "Dont you see?" he cried. "Dont you see? This whole land, the whole South, is cursed, and all of us who derive from it, whom it ever suckled, white and black both, lie under the curse? Granted that my people brought the curse onto the land: maybe for that reason their descendants alone can—not resist it, not combat it—maybe just endure and outlast it until the curse is lifted. Then your peoples' turn will come because we have forfeited ours. But not now. Not yet. Dont you see?" (278)

The talk of "my people" and "your people" is ridiculous: they are one, and Ike knows it. He is aware that Fonsiba stands in exactly the same relationship to the founder of the family as he does himself. Though Ike seeks her out to give her a share of the legacy, Fonsiba gets nothing of value from the white McCaslins. Her husband is rebuffed by Ike's cousin McCaslin Edmonds as a "nigger" and a "Yankee" when he comes to announce to the man he considers "chief" of his fiancée's family his intention to marry her. He gets no blessing. Yet Fonsiba is the one black McCaslin woman of the novel who does not behave as a white-controlled sexual commodity. She responds to Ike's weak paternalism with "I'm free" (280).

In his identification with the exploited and dispossessed black members of his family, particularly the women, Ike becomes more and more a feminized character himself, though he cannot, finally, overcome the racial categorizing he was brought up with. He is economically powerless, refusing the inheritance that could establish him as patriarch of the McCaslins and Edmondses; he is sexually powerless, shrinking from his wife's desire (her sexuality is directly related to his forfeited land), impotent in old age to stop the rape of the land he now identifies with, finally denied a place in that masculine ritual, the hunt. Ike's "chivalric" family heroes have played him false; he realizes what bondage really means, that women were sexually enslaved by his own "gallant" grandfather, all because of a web of fictions that assures white culture that blackness is an absolute and that black women are creatures whose sexuality exists to be exploited.

We never hear the voices of the first two wronged women in the McCaslin family, but their stories contain traces of the literary Tragic Mulatta. Eunice and Tomasina enact fragments of the traditional narrative as part of the deep structure of the McCaslin "curse." Their lives illustrate the false binary of black and white; their deaths, in suicide and childbed, are appropriate, even conventional, reponses to their exploitation at the hands of their white owners, reflecting the sexual roles they have been forced to play. Eunice, in bearing her master's child, partially rehearses the pattern of the Tragic Mulatta: the submissive body, the victim, the product of a fashion that white gentlemen should have, as Hubert Beauchamp in "The Bear" does, a "high yellow" concubine with her "nameless illicit hybrid female flesh" (303). Yet in her suicide Eunice registers a protest beyond being merely a sentimental object. She refuses to collude any longer in a system that reduces her to "nigger"; she exercises power in choosing to die.

Amantha Starr, the much-violated heroine of *Band of Angels*, says to the man who would transform her from beloved to casual whore: "Oh, I know—I know—it's just you want to make a nigger of me—that's what you want—a nigger—a nigger—" (215). Intercourse between master and slave is a microcosm of the plantation power structure, not a romance. Harriet Jacobs says the slave woman can expect no law to protect her against the sexual demands of white men: "She will become prematurely knowing in evil things. Soon she will learn to tremble when she hears her master's footfall. She will be compelled to realize she is no longer a child. If God has bestowed beauty upon her, it will prove her greatest curse. That which commands admiration in the white woman only hastens the degradation of the female slave" (45–46). Ike realizes that these women had no choice; he contemplates Eunice, apparently as fascinated with her fidelity as her suffering, as she dies the death of Clotel and so many other mulatta heroines, seeming "to see her actually walking into the icy creek on that Christmas day six months before her daughter's and her lover's (*Her first lover's* he thought. *Her first*) child was born, solitary, inflexible, griefless, ceremonial, in formal and succinct repudiation of grief and despair who had already had to repudiate belief and hope" (271).

Tomasina, her daughter by Carothers McCaslin, has no status as a family member or even a human being, though Ike tries to soften his grandfather's actions: "*But there must have been love* he thought. *Some sort of love. Even what he would have called love: not just an afternoon's or a night's spittoon*" (270). He tries to excuse the old man "lonely in the house" needing "a young voice"; yet he cannot hide his disgust: "*His own daughter His own daughter No No Not even him*" (270). But there was *not* love, any sort of love, there was only power and desire; Ike eventually faces the truth and ceases to believe in McCaslin chivalry, rewriting his grandfather as an "evil and unregenerate old man who could summon, because she was his property, a human being because she was old enough and female, to his widower's house and get a child on her and then dismiss her because she was of an inferior race" (294). Tomasina, too, dies a traditional death, expiring as she produces a mostly white son, killed, as the mulatta is always killed, by her own sexuality.

Both Tomasina and Eunice, silent in Go Down, Moses, largely reinscribe the passivity, helplessness, and pathos of the Tragic Mulatta. The nameless girl in "Delta Autumn" also reenacts the pattern of white-over-black sexual exploitation. Like them, she disrupts the pretended absolutes of race. Indeed, "she confuses all expected figures of social division" in her "colorlessness" and her clothes, which are countrified and masculine, yet she is clearly feminine, maternal, and sophisticated (Snead 206). She is a "descendant of Tomey as well as her most recent avatar," speaking with the composite voice of Eunice and Tomasina and the violated wilderness (Vickery 130). The invisible Tragic Mulatta inhabits the narrative of McCaslin history; now she haunts Ike's beloved woods in the form of a girl so white he only realizes "You're a nigger!" when he is told her aunt takes in washing, one of the "signs" of blackness in the culture.

This character is "passing" in several ways: she is legally black but looks white, she is a woman but wears men's clothes. She has, in a sense, cross-dressed to allow herself freedom of movement in the Jim Crow South, and in doing so, she imperils both the essential binaries of race and gender: "These transvestite representations often appear, significantly, within a context that includes 'crossing' (or 'passing') simultaneously as an element of gender and of race . . . [this] suggests some useful ways to interrogate notions of 'stereotype' and 'cliché'" (Garber 268). Certainly, the "Delta Autumn" woman's multiplicity (white and black, male and female) interrogates the insisted-upon absolute racial and gender positions in the South. Yet her various "crossings" do not really imperil the stereotype or cliché of the Tragic Mulatta; in her is contained already this element of destabilizing transvestitism. The "Delta Autumn" woman has the power to shake Ike's world, but does she have the power to pass out of the subjugated position she still holds with regard to the white McCaslins?

In some ways, she appears to accept the passive, unsanctioned position of the mulatta, an exemplar of the black woman's "endurance" Faulkner so admires. Her namelessness reiterates the way southern culture attempts to erase her. In a novel where names—McCaslin, Edmonds, Beauchamp—are badges of race, class, self, she has nothing—nothing but a literary tradition of exploitation and suffering. As her blackness is all but invisible in her, she is rendered invisible to the white McCaslins: "No one sense test is capable of validating the existence of the Negro; even sight has traditionally been insufficient, not only because blacks who are visibly white in color exist, but also because the white southerner has persistently refused to see the Negro, despite living and dying with the effects of his presence" (Thadious M. Davis 181–82). She admits she does not expect marriage of Roth Edmonds, reading his white, male ethics astutely: "I knew that to begin with, long before honor I imagine he called it told him the time had come to tell me in so many words what his code I suppose he would call it would forbid him forever to do" (358). She seems to have accepted, up to a point, her invisibility.

Despite her competence with language (Ike says she sounds as if she has been to college), despite her obvious intelligence, there are ways in which she colludes in the Tragic Mulatta narrative, living with Roth in New Mexico, where "I could at least sleep in the same apartment where I cooked for him and looked after his clothes" (358). Not only does she fulfill the sexual role of the mulatta; she takes on the traditional tasks of the black woman in southern society: cooking and cleaning.[10] She accepts her fate (though she shows up for one last try) not accepting that she is merely "an afternoon's or a night's spittoon." When Ike suggests that she take Roth's money and go north to marry a black man who will cherish her for her whiteness, disappearing back into the race, she rebukes him in the name, we feel, of her tongueless ancestresses: " 'Old man,' she said, 'have you lived so long and forgotten so much that you dont remember anything you ever knew or felt or even heard about love?' " (363).

The "Delta Autumn" woman struggles to be heard; she resists erasure by Ike's world of white men who would reduce her to an anonymous "nigger girl." Yet she isn't anonymous after all; she has a name, two names.

She is a Beauchamp and a McCaslin, even though this is suppressed. To underline the narrative of sexual exploitation, it is imperative that the girl be a Beauchamp (that is, a McCaslin). In the 1940 version of this story, written for magazine sale, the girl is simply an unconnected mulatta, light enough to "pass" but not a McCaslin. Faulkner rewrote the story for *Go Down, Moses* to make "Don" into Roth Edmonds, and the girl a granddaughter of Tennie's Jim and a great-great-granddaughter of Carothers McCaslin. She is the living body, the objectification, of the past sins of the McCaslins; she inhabits "two juridically defined, racially polarized bodies," crossing into hostile territory looking for justice for her child, at least (Berlant 111)—or if not justice, a McCaslin who will take responsibility. This woman and child are the embodied evidence of the crimes of southern history.

Ike, for all his sympathy, his own feminization, his powerlessness, and his guilt, has not escaped his place in McCaslin racial politics. He fails to take responsibility. He gives her his hunting horn for the baby as a sort of acknowledgment, however pale, of their cousinship, yet he labels the woman "nigger." It was because she was a "nigger" that Carothers McCaslin could impregnate his daughter; it was because she was a "nigger" that Eunice's suicide made no sense to the McCaslins; and it is because she is a "nigger" that James Beauchamp's granddaughter cannot claim recognition and marriage as her right. A "nigger" is not a human being, as Amantha Starr finds when her lover calls her "nigger" to rape her, and as Nonnie in Lillian Smith's *Strange Fruit* is forced to face when the white father of her child reduces her to "nigger girl" in order to assault her with impunity.

The ravished land that Ike so loves takes on the personality of the "Delta Autumn" woman even as Roth, avoiding his responsibility to his lover and his son by hiding out in the forest, is killing deer, leaving the woman and child denial and "just money." While I agree with Snead that the woman who enters Ike's tent "embodies and therefore violates several zones," her transgression is both an act against masculine hegemony and a reclamation of the feminine, reinscribing her body and her integrity. The land, the Delta, is a female shape and symbol. We are aware of entering a female space from the opening sentence: "Soon now they would enter the Delta" (335). In case we miss the point, Faulkner includes the elemental, feminine letter *delta* inverted, "this ∇-shaped section of earth between hills and River" (343). The deer that Roth shoots—"just a deer"—becomes a doe, a wounded mother. The hunting horn that signifies Roth's child as a sort of McCaslin heir, linking him to the masculine (and cross-racial) world of the hunt, is not acknowledgment enough, even as Ike protests against amalgamation and incest like an old-time romantic racist, crying out that the fruit of the curse can never be made legitimate as once before he declared to Fonsiba, vainly denying the kinship his heart, his soul, is moved toward: "*Maybe in a thousand years or two thousand years. . . . But not now! Not now!*" (361).

Not now. Not yet. Maybe someday. Several generations of southerners (and others) said things like this. The "Radical Racists" said *never*: the conservatives and later the moderates (and Faulkner himself) advocated a "go slow" policy toward integration and "social equality."[11] "Delta Autumn" neatly places *Go Down, Moses* in its context, historical and social. The anxiety over miscegenation had not abated in the thirties and forties: if anything, it was more intense than ever. Secret blackness was a worry: "Your very neighbor might be a Negro, they whispered in their minds, your son or daughter might marry one" (Williamson, *Crucible* 467). The "Delta Autumn" woman is the embodiment of the "drop of ink" hysteria—Ike can tell she's legally black only when *she* (quite on purpose) gives him the requisite cultural information about the laundry. She makes the choice to identify herself as black so she can claim kinship with the McCaslins and Beauchamps. Surely it could not have been an easy choice to come down from the North to Mississippi and announce to your white lover's family that you are black—no matter how white you may look. In "Delta Autumn" Faulkner articulates the fears of his own time over miscegenation and secret blackness. There seems no absolving the South of its family curse.

The unnamed woman in "Delta Autumn" is one of the most articulate female characters in all of Faulkner's fiction, yet despite her intelligence and dignity, the truth is that she, like Eunice and Tomasina before her, cannot be equal in a liaison with a white man. She speaks of love, but the heart of this society is better revealed by the men who tease Roth about her: "He's got a doe in here. Of course an old man like Uncle Ike cant be interested in no doe, not one that walks on two legs—when she's standing up, that is. Pretty light-colored, too. The one he was after them nights last fall when he said he was coon-hunting, Uncle Ike" (337).

The crudity of the "doe hunting" and "coon hunting" jokes belies the lyrical talk about how a man and a woman coming together are God (348).

Reality for the mulatta is sexual exploitation, even if she is a sister, daughter, or cousin of whites. Female sexuality is a mask for blackness and female blackness a representation of sexuality: mulattas are branded by both being different, by embodying the Other, and by being the same. Perhaps they, like all the Coras, Cassys, and Azélies, would echo Gracie Vaiden (if only they were allowed to talk) when she "wished she could fling away her whole generative organ. It was like a daub on her" (Stribling, *The Forge* 164).

"But Let Flesh Touch with Flesh": The Terror of the Self-Same in Absalom, Absalom!

I have said that Faulkner's Confederate Woman ends up a disembodied spirit, a banshee wailing around the ruined gothic edifice of the Old South. In *Absalom, Absalom!* Judith Sutpen acts as a ghost in the narratives of her family's decline and fall. But she is not alone. Her sister—in some ways her twin—Clytemnestra Sutpen also haunts the fiction; the mulatta is a specter, a skeleton in the closet of the plantation South. Like *Go Down, Moses, Absalom, Absalom!* (1936) creates what Sundquist calls a miscegenous space, a chiaroscuro world of part white and part black where race and gender, officially fixed and opposing in southern society, break free.

The Sutpen narratives do contain traces of the conventional Tragic Mulatta story (though in some unconventional guises); Clytemnestra, Clytie, slave daughter of the plantation owner Sutpen, interrogates and subverts the traditional mulatta story. Her recognition in the Sutpen family is not a matter for agonized debate, it is a fait accompli because it *apparently* does not challenge the symbolic order. This, in itself, is an important departure from the more familiar denial the mulatta usually meets with from her white family. As she appears (and disappears) in the Sutpen narratives, Clytie seems fluid, able to slip from black to white and from slave to master. Clytie's unfixed state disrupts the hierarchies with which the South defines itself. *Absalom, Absalom!*, in many ways a response to the idea of the lady (see chapter 1), is also a response to the Tragic Mulatta. If Judith is a quotation of, as well as a subversion of, the Confederate Woman, the seamless, elevated, desexualized white classical body constructed to suppress the feminine, and the Mammy represents the food-giving, fecund, grotesque body endowed with all the messy physical properties found distasteful in white women, then Clytie negotiates the troublesome space in between. Just as in childhood she sleeps sometimes in Judith's bed and sometimes with Judith on the floor pallet, Clytie oscillates from high to low, white to black. Her fluidity, her protean identity, negates the seductive, sexually exploitable black body of the Tragic Mulatta in *Absalom, Absalom!*. Though Clytie's story is rewritten by men (with an important countertext by a woman, Miss Rosa) into silence, asexuality, and "endurance," she is nonetheless an attempt to represent *blackness* and *femaleness* (the Other) as well as *femaleness* and *whiteness* (the Self-same) in one person.

If we accept Quentin and Shreve's reconstruction of history, Clytie and Charles Bon share a father in Thomas Sutpen: this is one of the "secrets" of the novel. She defines herself as black, performing the signs of blackness: sleeping on a slave's pallet, acting as a servant to her white sister. Perversely, she is accepted as a responsible member of the family, controlled by the fiction of her "alien" status, though officially a slave, considered no threat to the dominance of the white Sutpens. Charles Bon, on the other hand, defines himself as white, according to Quentin and Shreve's narratives (at least until the crucial moment before he dies) appropriating, for a time, the signs of upper-class male whiteness—fine clothes, university education, even (twist of twists) a mulatta *placée*. These signs of whiteness, maleness, class, and power, however, crash down on him. *Absalom, Absalom!*, among its myriad complexities, is a set of related (but not parallel) stories about the pitiless and deceitful black/white categorizing practiced by the South. Like the social status of both Clytie and Charles, the Sutpen plantation is founded on a set of unstable fictions: a labyrinth of unacknowledged miscegenation and blood money, the "truth" of which is scattered like the broken colors of prism light. *Absalom!* offers intuitive narratives: there are few "facts" but a great deal of impersonation and dream. As I suggested, these narratives negotiate a miscegenous space, a space where the violent hierarchy of "white" and "black" dissolves or mixes into something more troubling and, at the same time, more creative.

The narrators acknowledge this in the obsessive way they keep telling fragmentary but recognizable versions of the Tragic Mulatta story. Charles's mother, Eulalia Bon, is a construct of the white romantic mind, possibly (if we believe Quentin and Shreve) a mulatta embittered by her "drop" of black blood. The nameless Octoroon, formed as well largely by the white male narrators, represents the mulatta as suffering sexual vessel. Charles Bon as suffering hero (as opposed to Miss Rosa's version of him as the object of her multiple desires) is also created by the young white men of *Absalom, Absalom!*: the desiring Henry, or the desiring Quentin, or the wry Shreve. He does not act out the role of the Prodigal Son, but is a Tragic Mulatta himself, dispossessed, an incest threat, becoming more feminized just as Clytie, his half-sister, becomes more "masculine," shifting power from the male and white to the female and black, temporarily subverting the patriarchal control of the plantation. In the "end," Clytie's dominance is consumed in flames and subsumed in a male narrative that claims the last Word: nonetheless, in her very being she has shaken the foundations of the southern order. Like the unnamed woman in "Delta Autumn," she transgresses zones of control and confounds expectations.

Again, it is not at all surprising that Faulkner was preoccupied with racial limits and definitions: the white South had been obsessed with the issue since Emancipation and carried on debating it legally, morally, and culturally until after the high-water mark of the civil rights movement. Purity and pollution both racial and sexual (frequently they seemed indistinguishable) were central to the South's (and America's) post–Civil War, post–World War reinvention. As we have seen, Jim Crow laws and laws refining and narrowing the realm of whiteness were toughened in the twenties, thirties, and forties in the South. Blackness was to be isolated and segregated, not assimilated. Yet it so often was assimilated, invisible. Whites feared this above all. *Absalom, Absalom!* undoubtedly reflects the anxiety over racial slippage, as did a number of (white) novels of the period and on up into the sixties, including *Show Boat, The Fathers, The Forge* trilogy and *None Shall Look Back*. Oddly enough, *Gone with the Wind*, most famous of southern reinventions of the past, seems, at least, almost oblivious to the racial pathology of its day. However, Joel Williamson has suggested in an intriguing essay that racial anxieties are exhibited in rather an unlikely place in the novel. Margaret Mitchell "was born into a social universe that was obsessed with blackness and yet she wrote a novel that seemed so totally white" ("How Black" 87). Williamson explains this gap by pointing out the ways Rhett Butler's representation intersects with that of a black man, a "hipster-trickster," a criminal, a rapist. Mitchell, like Faulkner, grew up in an atmosphere of racial paranoia, lynchings, riots, rumored epidemics of black men attacking white women, and increasing nervousness over race mixing. The "black" Rhett Butler has some relevance to the "black" Charles Bon, as I shall explore a little later. But first, I shall look at *Absalom, Absalom!*'s representations of miscegenation.

The narrators present and re-present stories; the reader can try to gather them into some kind of explicable text or else to allow them to move around, unstable, mysterious, contradictory. Sutpen's "history," as it is given (and regiven), is fatally enmeshed with mulattoes and mulattas. He marries the heiress of a Haitian plantation, but when he discovers her "defect," her supposed mixed blood, he must "put her aside," since her son could not, according to the rule of absolutes in the South, legitimately inherit and pass on the plantation. With his first wife relegated to what he thinks is the confining past, Thomas Sutpen gets himself a second one, a woman "without a cross," able to breed "pure" white heirs. He becomes the father of Henry and Judith; he has already fathered Clytemnestra by one of his "wild" slave women. Clytie and Charles both mirror and over-shadow their white siblings, signifying the nexus of race, class, gender, and history that tangle to destroy his plan.

Sexuality is the principal site of racial contention in the South, presided over by the mulatto/a who, in his or her "mongrel" flesh, announces the scandalous absence, contrary to the official story, of barriers. Sexuality is the "language" through which black and white communicate (though it is rarely an equal intercourse). In his story Mr. Compson "writes" Charles explaining the nuances of male-female relations: the black brother teaching the white brother about sex just as the black girl traditionally gives the white boy his first experience of it. Henry contemplates the New Orleans system of the placée, the socially sanctioned mulatta mistress, one of which is kept by Charles himself: "the morganatic ceremony—a situation which was as much a part of a wealthy young New Orleansian's social and fashionable equipment as his dancing slippers" (100). The custom of keeping a quadroon or octoroon lover was well known, openly acknowledged in New Orleans while it was discreetly ignored in the rest of the South. The Victorian actress Fanny Kemble says, "In New Orleans, a class of unhappy females exists whose mingled blood does not prevent them from being remarkable for their beauty, and with whom no man, no gentleman, in that city shrinks from associating" (14). Frederick Law Olmsted in The Cotton Kingdom recounts in careful detail the quadroon balls with their convent-educated girls, and the contracts that take place between the girls and upper-class Louisiana men, lasting until the white man marries for legitimate heirs and sometimes beyond (236–39). Olmsted describes New Orleans as a hedonistic but highly ritualized culture with special names for each product of amalgamation, an attempt at making order from racial chaos: a *griffe* results from a black and a mulatto, a *sacatra* from a *griffe* and a black woman, a *marabon* from a *griffe* and a mulatto, and so on. The categories are an historical bagatelle; these people were still fundamentally and inexorably black in the eyes of the law and society. And these women were inevitably a sexual commodity.

In the mulatta the contradictions of the Other and the Self-same are apparent (but not resolved) in one body. She combines the European beauty white men found pleasing with the supposed "African" passion white women were "innocent" of. She is a scandalous being because in her the black/white opposition is telescoped into the object of desire: white in upbringing, appearance, "refinement," and "delicacy" (black women were held to be coarse and bestial), yet essentially black (that is, sexual) as well as unprotected by social laws governing the official chastity of ladies. She is a compendium of: "ancient curious pleasures of the flesh (which is all: there is nothing else) which her white sisters of a mushroom yesterday flee from in moral and outraged horror—a principle which, where her white sister must needs try to make an economic matter of . . . reigns, wise supine and all-powerful, from the sunless and silken bed which is her throne" (*Absalom* 116–17).

The Octoroon in *Absalom, Absalom!* is constructed to gratify white male desire. She has no name; she has no sanctioned place in everyday society, either. She is married, yet not married, to a white man who is really a black man. This tangle of stories about gender, sexuality, and race is gazed on in adolescent fascination by the naive Henry as he (according to Mr. Compson) regards "the apotheosis of two doomed races presided over by its own victim—a woman with a face like a tragic magnolia, the eternal female, the eternal Who-suffers" (114). As Mr. Compson's black *Ewige Weibliche*, the Octoroon in her Aubrey Beardsley dress, emblematically black and white, her sad, languid face all-knowing, represents the most traditional blossoming of the Tragic Mulatta in Faulkner. She is not a character but a feminine force "created of and by and for the darkness." The mulatta suffers voluptuously, undiluted by consciousness. She has undergone little change from her first appearance in "Evangeline," the story Faulkner wrote in 1931 containing the germ of *Absalom, Absalom!*, where she has a "doomed and passionate face with its thick surfeitive quality of magnolia petals," (*Uncollected Stories* 609). She is a victim; she is a fantasy. According to the mulatta myth, as recounted by Mr. Compson, though the white woman is her "sister," the white woman attempts to restrain the man in marriage: "an economic matter." With the mulatta a white man is truly free: she allows herself to be "covered" by him and makes no demands in return.

One wonders why Quentin and Shreve did not give Eulalia Bon a "face like a tragic magnolia." She is nearly invisible, a story that almost can't get told; Quentin constructs her as "the woman, the girl, just that shadow which could load a musket" in the Haitian uprising (248). Shreve calls her "the old Sabine," making her an hysterical avenger grooming Charles Bon for his fatal moment as she and the lawyer maniacally speculate on Sutpen's legitimate offspring: "Daughter? daughter? daughter?" (309). We hear her posited voice a little, triumphing in her revenge plot to have her part-black son seduce his white sister, saying to Henry: "So she has fallen in love with him," but this is no more "real" than any of the other mulatta stories in Absalom, Absalom! (335).

Eulalia reads more like the sinister mulattas of Thomas Dixon than the languishing heroines of mulatta romance. Perhaps Shreve is thinking of Lydia Brown in The Leopard's Spots; perhaps Faulkner was thinking of Cleo in The Sins of the Father, published in 1912. Cleo uses incest as retribution on the white man who betrayed her.[12] For all we know, Eulalia does not even exist; she might be completely a literary a/illusion. As the mulatta represents the dangerous forces of blackness and female sexuality, having Eulalia behind Sutpen's downfall "explains" the direction of the plot. Eulalia lives in Shreve's and Quentin's young male imaginations, contained. She moves their stories but she cannot take on reality beyond their construction of her; she is a reminder of just how unstable reality in this text can be.

Charles Bon's body itself is part of the wandering "reality" of the text. In one crucial representation he tries to define himself not only as black but as the black personification of rape: "I'm the nigger who's going to sleep with your sister." Such a sentence is the ultimate in fighting words, both in 1866 and in 1936. Threatening pollution of the sacrosanct white body of the sister, perhaps, looking at the situation as a homosocial triangle, threatening as well to pollute Henry, could elicit only one response: destruction of the black menace. In 1865 or 1866 it was a private murder; in 1910 or 1936 it might have been a lynching. Like Rhett Butler, who plays the "black rapist" to Scarlett's white lady (the scene somewhat parallels representations of "nigger rapists" such as Gus in Dixon's The Clansman), Charles is both a powerful body that must be neutralized and a powerless, feminized body. Rhett Butler is an outcast from aristocratic society: Charles Bon is a hopeful entrant.

Perhaps an even more relevant Mitchell "text" might be her early effort, now destroyed, called " 'Ropa Carmagin." [13] In it, a young white aristocrat called Europa, living in a crumbling plantation house, falls in love with a mulatto man who is probably her half-brother. It was as if Mitchell had started to write *Absalom, Absalom!* in 1927 and was stopped by her husband's dislike of the story. *Gone with the Wind* seems altogether tamer. Still, it was inevitable that someone tell that southern story about the black brother and white sister who wanted to become lovers: it was the unarticulated nightmare of the South.

Fay E. Beauchamp, in an unpublished dissertation, suggests that Charles Bon acts out the female Tragic Mulatta legend (159–70). As we have seen, there are a number of points in the narratives where Bon slips into a "feminine" position; more to the point, he acts out the sentimental mulatta drama. He is "refined," he has no position in the plantation aristocracy, and he suffers the pain of a forbidden relationship with a white lover and a lack of acknowledgment from his white father. His death might be read as a sort of suicide, the passive death of Cooper's Cora Munro and Faulkner's Eunice. Like the Tragic Mulatta, Charles Bon's identity is located in his desire—his being is stripped down to the "one you wouldn't want your sister to marry," or worse, the "nigger rapist." Mr. Compson's earlier descriptions of him in his "Frenchified cloak" or his "flowered, almost feminine garments of his sybaritic privacy," a "hothouse bloom" of a character out of the *Arabian Nights*, show how Charles Bon inhabits a number of cultural, racial, and gender positions (*Absalom* 95, 96, 97). He may be, to Henry, the potential bridegroom for his sister, but in Mr. Compson's fin-de-siècle rendering (which might have influenced Quentin's version as well) he is also the woman. And in invoking the *Arabian Nights* there is a suggestion of the harem, an image often used in description of the *plaçage* system of New Orleans. Both southerners and northerners frequently referred to the slave owner's "harem" of available, captive women. Mary Chesnut speaks of a planter's "hideous black harem" while Harriet Beecher Stowe depicts the slave South as orientalized: gorgeous, fecund, implying the sexual power white men exercise over black women. Marjorie Garber has written about the multiple meanings of "crossing" or "passing" genders or races, reading the black male body in feminized clothes as a strategy for emasculating the mythically potent black man. Certainly one crossing implies another. Yet the emasculation apparently signified by feminine clothes does not always displace white anxiety over blackness. Garber quotes Richard Wright's "Man of All Work," where a white man imagines shooting his black "maid," actually a man in women's clothes: "I was protecting white womanhood from a nigger rapist impersonating a woman! A rapist who wears a dress is the worst sort!" (Garber 294). Charles Bon is a sort of "nigger rapist" in a dress. He dies at the hand of the Beloved; he is a Tragic Mulatto as well as a masculine threat, penetrated by Henry's bullet in an unequal *Liebestod* all over the race and gender map.

As Charles is denied identity, name, birthright, racial definition, and finally life, erased even to the point where no one sees his body, Clytie in contrast grows more powerful, more defined, more "masculine," more embodied, more present. Her situation as the mulatta daughter of the plantation master, maid to her white sister, would appear to make her the ideal candidate to fulfill at least a portion of the traditional Tragic Mulatta plot. Yet in Faulkner's gothic tapestry of mulatta women exploited and drowned, raped and dead in childbed, banished and alone, Clytie is an anomaly. A product of plantation droit du seigneur, Clytie is not used and abused as an object in the expected manner of the Tragic Mulatta in a white world. In "Evangeline" the Sutpens' slave Raby, described as "pretty near whiter than she is black; a regular empress, maybe because she is white," has Clytie's dignity and dedication to preserving the household, and carries out the essential actions of nursing Henry and burning down the house (*Uncollected Stories* 585, 597–601). By the time Faulkner reworks the material for *Absalom, Absalom!*, the black Sutpen sister and her white counterpart become conservators standing in contrast to the self-destructive Henry and Charles. While their brothers go off to war, the sisters become not the belle and her darky maid waiting to become wives but heroic and unvanquishable illustrations of endurance, appropriating "masculine" power. Clytemnestra and Judith, named after ancient, fierce, man-killing queens (though Judith is accorded the full dignity of her name while her slave sister has to make do with a nickname), hold the estate together, with Miss Rosa, creating a little society in which men are superfluous.

In some ways Clytie has more in common with the figures of the Mammy and the Confederate Woman than the passive Tragic Mulatta. She achieves authenticity and her own kind of legitimacy in the Sutpen family to an extent unmatched by any other black woman in Faulkner, even

Dilsey.[14] A black slave playing Confederate Woman, brave, chaste (as far as anyone knows), points up the absurdity of her official status. It is true, as Brooks remarks, that Clytie is "accepted because acceptance on this level does not imperil Sutpen's 'design,' " while "acceptance of Charles Bon, in Sutpen's opinion, would" (*Yoknapatawpha Country* 299). However, Clytie's triumph of self comes not only out of the "acceptance" the Sutpens give her, but out of her own self-definition, paradoxically, that of blacks in a slave society. She is powerful at the expense of her desire. Judith the white sister is made the locus of Henry and Charles's struggle over and with the feminine; Clytie the black sister is relegated to a supporting role, especially by Quentin and Shreve. For a black woman to achieve the dignity and stature of not only the plantation mistress but, after all the white Sutpens are dead, plantation *master*, she must be distanced from the stereotype of the lurking animality in the black woman's body, however white she appears.

While Charles Bon aligns himself with the white world in everything from his university place to his New Orleans *placée*, Clytie covers herself with blackness like a cloak and is accepted as a member of the family through the fiction of her "blackness." Though she once slept with Judith as an equal, when Charles Bon's son comes to live in the rotting old house, she sticks to her servant's pallet on the floor as if her determination to be black will somehow make this boy white, or, at least, *whiter*. Clytie's self-definition, like her fidelity to Sutpen's Hundred, is perversely a function of her status as a member of the Sutpen family and her "black" quality of endurance. Yet there is something frightening about Clytie, something the men "telling" her story do not see but that the one female narrative voice identifies. Whereas the Octoroon represents a mostly satisfying containment of the Other in the Self-same, circumscribed by her conventional sexual subservience, Clytie embodies the terror of the Self-same. Rosa says: "*Clytie who in the very pigmentation of her flesh represented that debacle which had brought Judith and me to what we were and which had made of her (Clytie) that which she declined to be just as she had declined to be that from which its purpose had been to emancipate her, as though presiding aloof upon the new, she deliberately remained to represent to us the threatful portent of the old*" (156–57).

This is one of Rosa's more difficult passages, a syntactically fraught struggle of negatives and qualifications rehearsing her struggle with the contradictions and likenesses that Clytie embodies. Under slavery Clytie is not a slave; emancipated, she refuses to be free of her family. Her "pigmentation," which is neither black nor white, is the focus of what Rosa sees as the "debacle" of the Old South, the sin not just of slavery but of miscegenation that creates the powerful anomalous mulatta, the woman that is both mirror-image sister and shadowy alien. Clytie disrupts the sustaining myths of the South about blackness: "A white world is created in broad historical outline and sufficient psychological depth to subsume the myths of the Negro, but that world fails, and the vision creating it is reduced to an emotional paralysis" (Thadious M. Davis 180).

More even than Clytie's presence, her *touch* destroys the violent hierarchy of white over black on which the fragile order of the South rests. Her black/not black hand on Rosa's flesh demands acknowledgment. In a sense, Clytie takes the masculine role, ready to "penetrate" Rosa:

> *Because there is something in the touch of flesh with flesh which abrogates, cuts sharp and straight across the devious intricate channels of decorous ordering, which enemies as well as lovers know because it makes them both—touch and touch of that which is the citadel of the central I-Am's private own: not spirit, soul; the liquorish and ungirdled mind is anyone's to take in any darkened hallway of this earthly tenement. But let flesh touch with flesh, and watch the fall of all the eggshell shibboleth of caste and color too.* (139)

Minrose Gwin reads this moment as "a parable of the Old South. Clytie's touch is both female and black. It asks for human connection, for human community. Rosa's slap both recognizes that touch and rejects it" (*Black and White Women* 17). I would carry this a bit further: Clytie's touch does demand sisterhood, but it is also a *masculine* touch, a *violation* of Rosa's citadel of self. Rosa cries out in the agony of watching the absolutes of her world—white/black, male/female, collide in one being, in the pressure of one hand: "*And you too? And you too, sister, sister?*" (140). The central I-Am is reached in a parody of the rape that created the mulatta in the first place, the mind to be "taken" in a dark corridor, the whole world constructed as an erotic power game. But here it is the "black" woman who is the sexual aggressor: the parody even extends to that central postbellum southern paranoia, the rape of white women by free black men. Snead's reading of Rosa's relationship with Clytie shows that "whiteness" has been mixed from the beginning, citing Rosa's perpetually black clothes and the "merging" with Judith and Clytie that destroys both gender and color (112–13). They become "*not even as three women, but merely as three creatures . . . one being, interchangeable and indiscriminate*" (155). I see Clytie as able to be both male and female, penetrator and fluid surrounder of the Sutpen world. She stands not just for black men and mulattas, but for white women ("*sister, sister*") and white men (she is in charge of the plantation) as well. Impossibly, she has become the fusion of absolutes, "twin-sistered" yet opposite, beyond an argument for the black woman's inclusion in the white family; in perhaps the most subversive moment in a subversive text, we see Clytie is the family, the true heiress to Sutpen's "design," the child closest to his own mind, in a way, sprung from it like Athena from the head of Zeus.

Clytie partakes of both whiteness and blackness, both maleness and femaleness. Marjorie Garber says, "To change power is to change sex"; but to change power is also to change *race* (271). In Clytie, Faulkner rearranges the pattern of southern class, race, and gender. Clytie, dying in 1910, represents the final collapse of the Old South: Henry Sutpen, Rosa Coldfield, and Quentin Compson all die in 1910, in a kind of replay of the fall of the South in the Civil War. Clytie can be read as a literary character, a rewriting of a standard cast member of the plantation drama, the master's darky daughter, activated by Faulkner at a time when segregation laws and the culture of violent enforcement of black submission conspired with great efficiency to push blacks toward invisibility. Yet sexuality, if not black-man-to-white-woman, was hard to regulate; no white man was ever lynched for making "improper advances" to a black woman. Race mixing carried on. In 1921 a grand jury in Natchez reported that southern "gentlemen" had so many "Negro concubines" that "our commonwealth [was threatened] with a mongrel race" (McMillen 17). Mississippi's own Theodore Bilbo published his *Take Your Choice: Separation or Mongrelization* in 1947. Clytie is nothing so crude as an "argument" for tolerance or for repression: she does appear to be an anomalous figure at a time when much southern fiction was doing the cultural work of reifying traditional hierarchies and reinventing a mythical past. Rhett Butler may be, in some way, "black," but Mitchell in *Gone with the Wind* presents the prelapsarian Old South as a time of racial order and grace. Faulkner, on the other hand, presents the Old South as already gothic, decaying from within, with Clytie, even more than Sutpen himself, presiding over its last moments before complete chaos.

Rosa Coldfield's insight into Clytie's true subversiveness is finally drowned out by the other narrative voices, the male narrative voices of Mr. Compson, Shreve, Quentin, and Faulkner himself. The sexual and racial politics they espouse do not complicate the mulatta figure or reveal her revolutionary potential; instead, they romanticize her. Mr. Compson has Charles Bon draw her as "a female principle which existed, queenly and complete, in the hot equatorial groin of the world long before that white one of ours came down from trees and lost its hair and bleached out" (116). He follows with an erotic wish-fulfillment description of her sheltered cultivation: she was "trained to fulfill a woman's sole end and purpose: to love, to be beautiful, to divert" (117). He even has Bon say, "Sometimes I believe that they are the only true chaste women, not to say virgins, in America, and they remain true and faithful to that man not merely until he dies or frees them, but until they die" (117). This pornographic dream, the perfect mulatta lover, has the face of a (white) angel, the pliancy of a whore, the manners of a princess, and the fidelity of a dog. The Octoroon is a nonperson, one of those vessels to be "filled" by male desire, a representation that Faulkner questions in Go Down, Moses. Against this harmonious and untroubling (for white men) sex object, Clytie interjects a discord. She is both like the Octoroon and unlike, a mulatta but not a Tragic Mulatta. The brief moment when, in Rosa's story, Clytie becomes a dangerous entity, a focus for destabilization—masculine and feminine, white and black, sister and father—is lost in Quentin's final recollection of Henry on his bed reciting his name. Clytie has retreated into what seems another fiction, a gothic tale-with-a-twist, just the ghost haunting the old mansion, no longer the volatile element encompassing all the anxieties of a culture.

Clytie offers a glimpse into a world on the brink of racial and sexual collapse. It is interesting that the embodiment of this potential destruction is a woman and the voice that exposes this potential destruction belongs to a woman. Perhaps this precipitousness was simply unbearable, for the final words we hear belong not to Rosa (quieted in the grave) but to Quentin. His exclamation "*I dont hate it! I dont hate it!*" defers the catastrophe, changes it from the possible explosion of a whole social order to a personal crisis. The twin terrors of the Other and the Self-same are finally unresolved. Yet the final word on the racial future of the South, Shreve's last dig at Quentin, is to imagine a mulatto world: "I think that in time the Jim Bonds are going to conquer the western hemisphere. Of course, it wont be quite in our time and of course as they spread toward the poles they will bleach out again like the rabbits and the birds do, so they wont show up so sharp against the snow. But it will still be Jim Bond; and so in a few thousand years I who regard you will also have sprung from the loins of African kings" (378). Not just a mulatto future (for more than just the South) but a world of secret blackness—blacks who now look white yet are still "Jim Bond." Is this vulgar antiamalgamationism (Jim Bond is, after all, an idiot) or is it a subversion of the message the South sent itself and the world in the twenties, thirties, and forties? The end of *Absalom, Absalom!* looks on radical chaos and offers no prescriptive rebuilding of the barriers. Perhaps Clytie has the last word after all.

4 The New Belle

She wuz de light o' dis plantation!—Thomas Nelson Page, "Meh Lady"

Little Miss: Her Fall from Ideal to New Idea

The Confederate Woman became a sacred invocation of the South's "epic" (meaning white, aristocratic) past. She metamorphosed gracefully from the Yankee-shooting amazon to the unvanquishable grande dame who walks out of *Gone with the Wind* as soon as Sherman's name is mentioned. The Southern Belle, heiress of the Confederate Woman, survived the Civil War and Reconstruction and was carried on into the modern world like an icon held before a ragged army. She is the heroine of the white South's most cherished story about itself: its designated work of art, bearer of its ideals (Seidel xv, Westling 15). The body of the Belle was inscribed with the integrity and glamour of the South itself. Her sexual purity translated her into the emblem of racial purity. Despite its nationalistic attractions, this story eventually ceased to be believed. Its tellers became shrill and insistent, or contradictory stories about young women—promulgated by Freud and D. H. Lawrence or such homegrown fictionists as Frances Newman, James Branch Cabell, Erskine Caldwell, and William Faulkner—challenged the old stories, even while exhibiting nostalgia for them.[1]

In Faulkner the Belle becomes a precarious figure, inhabiting both the vestiges of the reverent space belonging to white upper-class southern virgins and a new, perilous sexual territory where the female body seems more powerful than ever. Women like Caddy Compson and Temple Drake negotiate masculine and feminine realms, just as they negotiate between purity and pollution. The oppositions between masculine and feminine, virgin and whore are disabled, and, just as the Mulatta collapses the imaginative distance between black and white, the Belle pioneers a bisexual space, challenging the hundred years of piety that went into her construction.

The southern landscape has always had, as Annette Kolodny asserts, a radically feminine essence, both receptive and attractive, "cultivated" as the fenced plantation domain (115–32, 135). In the sustaining stories of plantation sensibility, womanhood and nationalism are inextricable: the South is the Mother, the Bride, the Queen, a female entity, "she" as Ireland is "she." As Kolodny remarks, "Implicit in the metaphor of the land-as-woman was both the regressive pull of maternal containment *and* the seductive invitation to sexual assertion" (67). Constructed as a territory to be first penetrated and enclosed, then made "fruitful," women are imaginatively contained. Like the passive land, which is "taken," ploughed, planted, and harvested, the woman has no agency and thus no voice. She represents the "classical body," seamless, closed, denoting "the inherent form of the high official culture" (Stallybrass and White 21). It is no accident the southern lady is often likened to a statue; Lillian Smith, in 1949, decried the legacy of the Old South: "They listened to the round words of men's tribute to Sacred Womanhood and believed, thinking no doubt that if they were not sacred then what under God's heaven *was* the matter with them! Once hoisted up by the old colonels' oratory, they stayed on lonely pedestals and rigidly played 'statue' while their men went about more important affairs elsewhere" (*Killers* 137).

Sacred womanhood was a story that denied white women significant activity: they had to inhabit a pedestal—a notoriously small space in which to maneuver—yet many things were done in their name, on their "behalf"; Jim Crow laws, lynchings, and a rigid class system were maintained in the South partly out of a fear that the purity of white women would somehow be compromised by the right to vote, contact with blacks (other than servants), the theories of Darwin, and socialism.

The white lady is represented as a vessel or as a garden or as a statue on a high, narrow pedestal; disruption is a fall—expulsion from Eden or a tumble to the ground, breaking a marble limb or two. The Civil War and

Reconstruction were inscribed as a violent descent from grace: the land was "raped"; "Paradise," built by the slave economy, was lost. If the land lost its innocence, its walking symbol, the southern woman, was in danger of losing hers. Cash writes of the "rape complex," a knot of nationalist and racist passion in which the "ravishment" of the land during the war by "invaders" became the feared ravishment of white women by black men (114–17).

White men (and some white women) wrote and spoke of the Civil War and Reconstruction as if it drained their political and sexual potency: control over their land, control over their legislatures, control over blacks, and control over women was, to some degree, lost. So they adopted strategies to regain their power, including activities like the formation of the Ku Klux Klan, the Knights of the White Camellia, and other such groups. The Kappa Alpha Order, founded in 1866 at Washington College (later Washington and Lee) is still, as a popular college fraternity, in the business of selling Lost Cause nostalgia. The Confederate generals "Stonewall" Jackson and Robert E. Lee became the brothers' patron saints; they dedicated themselves to chivalry and the memory of the Old South. In the 1890s there was a controversy over having chapters in the North—KA, like Rebel Yell bourbon and Bryan's hot dogs, was, for a while, sold only below the Mason-Dixon line. Every year the fraternity still has a large party called Old South, at which the members wear Confederate uniforms and their dates wear hoopskirts. Organizations like this, along with the Sons and Daughters of the Confederacy, did the work of not only enforcing segregation but also of propagandizing the jewel of the Old South, the Belle.

The terror of losing jurisdiction over women's bodies created discourses of nostalgia and threat. The importance of white female purity went along with the fear of its pollution by free blacks. Williamson in *The Crucible of Race* says it was a "kind of psychic compensation" for white men to project their fears (and their fantasies) onto "the black beast rapist" and invest white women with all goodness (115). The more bestial the black man seemed, the more immaculate the white woman had to be in contrast. Perhaps white men saw the black "rapist" as the only creature who could have sex with a white woman without guilt: they had made her too much the objectification of the combined mother–virgin land to "defile" her with impunity. They both hated and envied black men and harassed and lynched them in a "conjunction of sex and race that seized the South in 1889, and has not yet let go," as if ritual murder would somehow avenge the northern humiliation of their land, the sacred space implicated in the sacred space of their women (Williamson, *Crucible* 115).

The economy of sexuality became a new battleground as the symbolic order struggled to keep its hierarchies intact: women's bodies had to be "protected" from external menace. But what of attacks from within? Parallel to the fear of lower-class rapists assaulting white ladies was the fear that ladyhood wasn't what it used to be. Given that the Civil War was such a radical marker in the way southerners understood their history, it is inevitable that "ravishment" and sexual corruption be seen in historical terms, a romantic decline of "purity" and integrity from the mythologically intact past. History and class are bound up in Faulkner's fictive interrogation of ladyhood, as we have seen in his Confederate Women. In his representations of southern society, Faulkner seems to look to the present for weakness, to the past for virtue. Perhaps this relates to a larger (white, Protestant) American sense of pioneer fortitude versus modern middle-class ease, most graphically represented in women. The South is hyperaware of its history (or histories), often making women emblems of both the seamless past and the decayed present: ancient "moral" strength as a code for sexual chastity is nostalgically compared to the sexual permissiveness of today, no matter how "past" and "present" are defined. In Faulkner's South, ladyhood is often a function of the forever-lost past; something more fluid, unfixed, and threatening happens to the lady's descendant, the Belle, in the cacophonic present. The "ruin" of the Belle makes the forfeit of Eden ever more momentous.

There were, of course, good social and economic reasons why such a cherished representation of white southern values might be shaken off her pedestal. After 1920 women could vote, despite the opposition of southern senators, which delayed the Nineteenth Amendment for nearly a year. Women went to work in the textile mills in some southern states; women were beginning to get more education and began to involve themselves in political and cultural clubs. As a result, women began to question their "elevation" and the restrictions it placed on them. The Association of Southern Women for the Prevention of Lynching was founded in 1930; led by Jessie Daniel Ames, white women began to protest the system white men had devised for their "protection" from supposedly rapacious blacks. This was no doubt confusing to many white southerners. Though white women were beginning to challenge the old roles available to them, at the same time southern culture erected new limits. In memorializing the past and reinscribing feminine virtues in such organizations as the United Daughters of the Confederacy and campus sororities, the South sent confusing signals to middle-class women.

As a character in the popular imagination, the Southern Belle is tiresomely familiar and strangely contradictory. She is pure, or provocative; innocent, or sultry; guileless, or knowing; submissive, or rebellious; decorous, or hoydenish. As a cultural emblem, simultaneously representing the image of ladyhood so dear to the white South's sense of its own past while covertly embodying the oppression, racism, and classism on which such an historical account is based, the Belle inhabits much twentieth-century southern fiction. Debating the place of the lady is central to New South discourse: ladyhood is in a volatile state. The Belle is no longer the light of the plantation but a vehicle for exploring a shift in the understanding of female sexuality.

One of the first writers to shove the Belle off her pedestal in a most unchivalric manner was a Virginian who had certainly been indoctrinated with the official version of the South's Palladium found in pious fictions like Thomas Nelson Page's "Meh Lady." But whereas Page, also a son of the Old Dominion, celebrates the ethereal chastity of the southern white girl, James Branch Cabell means to reveal the body under the marble shell, insisting that belles feel desire. Jurgen, Cabell's 1919 best-seller and succès de scandale (it was the object of an obscenity trial), parodies the connection between virginity and ladyhood: the hero has a series of erotic adventures with Helen, Guinevere, and other great queens of legend. Throwing off the official shackles of chastity, women are aggressively sexual: Jurgen is constantly molested by overeager damsels as he makes his way through a dream landscape in pursuit of a false female ideal, Dorothy la Desirée. Dorothy turns out to be not a goddess but a dumpy middle-aged woman. Jurgen's succession of mistresses, initially lustful, become postcoitally shrewish, confining, and domesticated. Cabell denies a transcendant quality in women, just as he savages the idea of purity.[2]

Cabell's fellow Virginian Ellen Glasgow also critiqued the southern code of "woman worship" (as Cabell's 1927 novel Domnei is subtitled), though in a realist rather than a romance mode. Her novels also insist on women's radical sexuality. Virginia (1913) and Life and Gabriella: The Story of a Woman's Courage (1916) demonstrate how the restricting rules of chaste bellehood imposed on women by the southern code can destroy their lives. Virginia, the perfect, self-abnegating lady, loses her husband to a woman who recognizes the importance of sexual love. Though Glasgow's heroines do not, unlike Edna Pontellier in *The Awakening*, view sexuality as a higher personal imperative, they do show that the old rule of inaccessibility is a trap: rigid chastity does not protect women but destroys them.

Glasgow's reservations about gyneolatry and her acknowledgment that women, too, feel physical desire were intended to be liberating. A great many attacks on the chivalric system, however, turned into attacks on the women themselves, as Cabell's misogynistic fictions show. The violent hierarchy of madonna/whore collapsed: moral superiority and sexual innocence were no longer accorded women, but neither was full humanity. Many American writers felt that if women could not be very very good, then they must be very very bad. F. Scott Fitzgerald, for example, pulls the young American heroine off her pedestal into a pit of depravity. Though he was not a southerner, Fitzgerald could be said to have an intense engagement with southern models of belleship (to use a word coined by Virginia Clay). In *This Side of Paradise* (1920) Isabelle and Rosalind are products of the transformation of the lady from perfection to monster: "The 'belle' had become the 'flirt,' and the 'flirt' had become the 'baby vamp'" (62). Rosalind is "a sort of vampire" (178). Vamps not only flout Victorian middle-class morality, they violate the class imperative of sexual unavailability that kept them "morally" superior.

Fitzgerald did a great deal to codify and popularize the new literary type of "fast girl" or "speed." His wife, Zelda Sayre, brought up from birth to be a belle, blurred the line between fiction and reality, appearing in glossy magazines as the Flapper Muse. Her background is similar to some of Faulkner's upper-middle-class white heroines, particularly Temple Drake. Zelda Sayre was the debutante daughter of a judge, brought up in Montgomery, Alabama (called "the Cradle of the Confederacy"), where she was subject to the severest conditions governing ladyhood: beautiful posture, beautiful manners, white gloves. Zelda Sayre was, in a term that still had resonance, a "great belle"; at the University of Alabama Key-Ice ceremony, she and other girls were congratulated for being as pure as water and as cold as ice, and she was the toast of Zeta Sigma (for Zelda Sayre) fraternity at Auburn University. Still, she resisted, and her relation to her husband's fiction (some of which she not only inspired but may have written), is complex: did Zelda inspire the Fast Girl or did she write herself into the part? The fiction becomes inseparable from the reality it is supposed to represent. For his part, Fitzgerald, like Faulkner, records the flight from sexual repression of these women while remaining somewhat invested in the image on the pedestal. Frustrated over Zelda, he wrote in his ledger: "I used to wonder why they locked princesses in towers" (Milford 45; my italics).

Fiction in the South of the early twentieth century contended with issues of sexuality shaped by influences from within and without the region. D. H. Lawrence insisted on the power of female sexuality as a disrupter of class divisions and old models of decorum. Francis P. Gaines remarks that in the modern southern novel "the Magdalen has eclipsed the Madonna" (176). Novels such as Edith Everett Taylor Pope's Not Magnolia (1928) and Zelda Sayre Fitzgerald's Save Me the Waltz (1932) challenge the relevance of the Belle in sexual terms: repression drives the heroines in both novels to illness and misery. Sexuality saves. If women do not surrender, they risk coercion. In Ruth Cross's The Unknown Goddess (1926), Noel, the "innocent" heroine whose dormant but evident sexuality "inflames" men, is raped by a man her parents idolize, only to find herself condemned for her "promiscuity" as critics have condemned Temple Drake for her "nymphomania."

The sexuality the Belle now finds herself indulging in, or being forced to confront, is not necessarily liberating. There are few Lawrentian celebrants of the mythic grandeur of unfettered intercourse hanging about the small towns of Mississippi and Georgia where these fictions are set. The "tainted" Belle now finds herself the target of her society's (and sometimes the author's) rage, emblematically bearing on her body the marks of the South's social, economic, and "spiritual" pollution. Isa Glenn's biting novel Southern Charm (1928) contrasts two sisters: Alice May, who is pretty and "ladylike," and Laura, who is rebellious and was raped (by a northern man, one of countless reenactments of the Civil War on the body of a southern woman).[3] In the graduation ceremony of the Seminary for Young Ladies, where Belles learn to be Belles, Miss Cassandra Toombs (a woman prophesying, in a sense, from beyond the grave of the dead Old South) exhorts: "Always remember, girls, that a lady must be pure. Among common people, women sometimes do awful things. But, when a lady does an awful thing, God punishes her. She is no longer a LADY: she becomes the Scarlet Woman of Babylon!" (128).

The state of ladyhood is a site of contention in southern novels, documenting the struggle between the free play of sexuality and the social discourse demanding containment of the female body. The debate is played out in *Flags in the Dust* and *The Sound and the Fury*, where Narcissa Benbow and Caroline Compson speak for tradition: either you are a lady or you are not. Those who have fallen from purity have it written on them, a scarlet mark, or an odor: Narcissa says Belle Mitchell smells "dirty," and when Caddy is no longer a virgin, she ceases to "smell like trees" to her brother Benjy.

Frances Newman's *The Hard-Boiled Virgin* (1926) satirizes the class-bound nature of chastity: the novel dismantles the absolute division between ladies and "common people" in their fascination with doing "awful things." As with Zelda Sayre's *Save Me the Waltz*, the novel is somewhat autobiographical. Frances Newman was herself an Atlanta debutante, like Zelda Sayre and Temple Drake the daughter of a judge. *The Hard-Boiled Virgin*, banned in Boston in 1927 and everywhere reviled for its sexual candor, specifically attacks myopic southern society for its useless gentility: "In Georgia no lady was supposed to know she was a virgin until she had ceased to be one" (174–75). Katharine Faraday eventually ceases to be one, becoming aware of the simmering sexuality all around her. As a child in chapter 1, she witnesses her blue-blooded parents copulating. Yet again, sexuality does not free her for anything except alienation. Awareness of her body costs Katharine her place in the symbolic order; it is a troubled liberation.

Some early southern feminists hailed the death of the Belle. Nell Battle Lewis proclaims:

> The idol, thank God, is broken beyond repair. For, graceful though it may have been, romantic though it certainly was, it was only an image after all. And whatever its artificial beauty, it lacked the beauty of life. In its place is a woman of flesh and blood, not a queen nor a saint nor a symbol but a human being with human faults and human virtues, a woman still only slowly rising to full stature but with the sun of freedom on her face. (Mims 241)

This proved to be overoptimistic. The idol may have been broken but its fragments still haunted the South. And though southern women might be no longer queens and saints, they were not allowed to be "flesh and blood" humans either. The discarded myth of the "shield-bearing Athena" left a vacuum that only a demonic myth could fill. Two stories about the young upper-class white woman are presented simultaneously in Faulkner and other writers: one that she should be the untainted vessel of all goodness, the other that she is a cauldron of boiling vice. They depend upon one another, as if the angel cannot exist without the succubus. As we have seen, these apparent oppositions (male/female, white/black) are unstable, constantly slipping into one another. Behind them lurks the idea that a woman's purity "protects" community integrity, that controlling a woman's sexuality implies order in the community: "Let a woman throw off her feminine character and her power to benefit society is lost; her loveliness, her dignity, her own chief protection is lost" (Rogers 190).

In other words, women are threatened with punishment, sometimes with rape, if they step down out of the clouds. Faulkner's New South Belles cannot inhabit the sphere of heavenly purity, yet they do not necessarily transgress against purity by themselves. In Flags in the Dust and Sanctuary, society rests on a discourse of rape in which young upper-class women are confronted by sexuality, while in The Sound and the Fury rape is decentered and the fluidity of gender takes precedence. Leslie Fiedler refers to Faulkner's treatment of Belles as an "almost hysterical campaign against the myth of the pure young girl" (No! in Thunder 117). Fiedler meant this comment as a criticism of what he saw as Faulkner's misogyny, but it can be looked at another (more playful) way. In The Newly Born Woman, Hélène Cixous says of the hysterical woman: "if she succeeds in bringing down the men who surround her, it is by questioning them, by ceaselessly reflecting to them the image that truly castrates them, to the extent that the power they have wished to impose is an illegitimate power of rape and violence" (154). Women in Faulkner's fiction must negotiate a realm of violence—"illegitimate power" directed at their bodies. In "voicing" the feminine, Faulkner's fiction both represents and becomes the "hysteric," causing the virgin/whore binary to fall in on itself, subverting the narrative of rape to suggest a bisexual space where the female/male binary is itself imperiled.

Caddy and Quentin: The Bisexual Voice

"To me she was the beautiful one, she was my heart's darling," says Faulkner of Caddy, "too beautiful and too moving to reduce her to telling what was going on" (Gwynn and Blotner 6). Like Dilsey, Caddy is constructed on the authority of other voices: Faulkner says he felt it would be "more passionate" to write her that way. Where Benjy, Jason, and Quentin have their own sections of The Sound and the Fury, Caddy, their chief obsession, seems to live only through them, a fiction "belonging" to them. Like Judith Sutpen, Caddy has been read (or not read) as the blank page on which her brothers inscribe their fear and desire or as an immobile center (Sundquist 10). She is a creature of paralyzed desire: "There is no room for female desire, and so there is no space for Caddy's subjectivity, her version of her story" (Matthews, Lost Cause 91). Yet Caddy exists as a southern white upper-class woman at a particular moment in history when the South struggled to solve the problem of the modern feminine: was she to be the South's Palladium or the Scarlet Woman of Babylon, the Angel in the House or the Devil on the Dance Floor? This debate is tied up with the sense that speaking is pollution for women. If Caddy tells her own story, she will incriminate herself (as Drusilla Hawk, Temple Drake, Rosa Coldfield, and Joanna Burden do). So, although she is, in so many ways, the opposite of all that the southern lady should be, Caddy's alleged silence is part of a net of responses to ladyhood.

In an intriguing reading, however, Minrose Gwin insists that Caddy is not a passive tabula rasa awaiting inscription by the agency of her brothers but a speaking woman. Working through the theories of Julia Kristeva in particular, Gwin sees Caddy as a means by which women's "libidinal energies" can be expressed (Feminine 35). The feminine enfolds and saturates The Sound and the Fury: it cannot be fixed, yet it marks a locus of creative energy from which Caddy's voice, "muted but articulate," can emanate, disabling the control and "balance" of the masculine narratives.

This reading is particularly attractive because it validates Caddy on her own terms, not those of her brothers, and honors the feminine energies in Faulkner's fiction. I am nevertheless not wholly convinced by it: the "voice" that Gwin hears as Caddy's is not unadulterated, not "pure": unpacking the novel to get at this hidden treasure comes close to valorizing the feminine as somehow more worthy than any other voice. Gwin's thesis is most helpful in "hearing" Caddy when her brother Quentin is factored into the equation; while Benjy, Jason, and Faulkner/Dilsey are also points from which to "enter" the feminine space inhabited by Caddy (as Gwin points out), Quentin constructs a bisexual space where the play of presence and absence, of seduction and maternity, is energized. I would argue that to hear Caddy is, at least in part, to hear Quentin, and to hear Quentin is to hear Caddy, so imperiled is his status as masculine, as separate.

I should like to examine Caddy for a moment not as a voice in a bodiless space (like Dante's Francesca, whom Faulkner evokes), trying to be heard, but as a woman situated in a specific society. As the daughter of the House of Compson, Caddy embodies the unstable binary of virgin/whore: intrinsically sexual underneath the petticoat layers of upper-class social conditioning. If we listen for a while to the external voices determined to construct Caddy for us, she appears as nurturing, a mother to her retarded brother Benjy and her pain-paralyzed brother Quentin. In contrast, her brother Jason lays at her feet the destruction of the Compson family; he blames her for not sustaining the marriage that will restore the family fortunes.

Female "honor," that is, chastity, as a verifier of family status, is a Compson fixation. Like *Absalom, Absalom!*, *The Sound and the Fury* is concerned with the possibilities of ladyhood and the relationship of the woman to the family, to the land, and to society. The daughter of the aristocratic family is an emblem of their status and an economic asset. As Gayle Rubin has pointed out, women are "gifts," goods to be transacted in marriage, "a conduit of a relationship rather than a partner to it" (176). In the eyes of her family, Caddy removes herself from the marketplace. Caddy dares to give herself, to act not as an object of transaction but as a transactor. It is inevitable that she be punished. She is "damaged goods," a woman "fallen" out of the southern economy that invested young women with so much symbolic import and so much obfuscating rhetoric. Her own mother, also a product (or victim) of what Rubin (and Emma Goldman before her) called "the traffic in women," ironically responds to her now-valueless state most viciously. Quentin hears Mrs. Compson defining Caddy as biologically polluted, saying to Mr. Compson, "Who can fight against bad blood . . . she not only drags your name in the dirt but corrupts the very air your children breathe" (64).[4]

In the classist views of Mrs. Compson and Jason, Caddy becomes a curse, not a positive presence but an absence, a nonbeing whose name cannot be spoken within the sacrosanct precincts of the Compson mansion. As reported to us—for her voice is also transmitted through male agency—Mrs. Compson has the most highly developed sense of the "good name" of all the Compsons: her definitions of Compson-ness and Bascomb-ness are ironclad, as are her parameters of "ladyhood": "I was taught that there is no halfway ground that a woman is either a lady or not" (63). She sees herself as upholder of a position, not an individual, embattled in the family's slipping gentility: "What reason did Quentin have? Under God's heaven what reason did he have? It cant be simply to flout and hurt me. Whoever God is, He would not permit that. I'm a lady. You might not believe it from my offspring, but I am" (179). When Caddy is no longer a "lady" with all the talismanic power that absolute state (like grace) implies, she is as good as dead. For them, she has no being. Jason reports "that time when she [Mrs. Compson] happened to see one of them kissing Caddy and all next day she went around the house in a black dress and a veil and even Father couldn't get her to say a word except crying and saying her little daughter was dead" (138). To her mother, Caddy has descended to an unreachable location, a "fate worse than death." When Caddy later tries to send money for her daughter, to buy her an Easter dress (the badge of southern young-girl innocence) Mrs. Compson responds coldly: "We Bascombs need nobody's charity. Certainly not that of a fallen woman" (132).

Caddy's father commodifies her in a different manner altogether, at least in Quentin's version of him. Instead of constructing her as the precious virgin vessel of Compson honor and status, he acknowledges that society imposes "ladyhood" on women who are fundamentally sexual beings. Rather than mourning or constructing elaborate fantasies to evade the fact of his daughter's sexuality—the old discourse of southern masculinity—he adheres to an alternative masculine story: "It means less to women, Father said. He said it was men invented virginity not women. Father said it's like death: only a state in which others are left" (48).

In Quentin's representation of his father, Mr. Compson denies the possibility of virginity in trying to correct Quentin's hyperromanticizing of it. He says virginity is *negative*, it is "contrary to nature" and therefore untenable. He equates women with nature and nature with chaos. Ladies are women with a list of rules used to control themselves and others; women are animals, fundamentally dirty, "periodical filth between two moons balanced" (78). *The Sound and the Fury* marks an early evocation of the Faulknerian hero's long obsession with menstruation, the badge of women's Otherness. It could be argued that though it is Mr. Compson who is supposed to be speaking, the fixation with female "uncleanliness" is really Quentin's—his experience of women is of Caddy's muddy drawers, Natalie the "dirty girl," and the grimy-faced little Italian child. Quentin takes his sense of this dirtiness and translates it to a moral state, here expressed in his father's "theories" about women: "*they have an af-*

finity for evil for supplying whatever the evil lacks in itself for drawing it about them as
instinctively as you do bed-clothing in slumber" (59). Menstrual "periodic filth" assigns women to a preconscious, involuntary world of organic functions.
They cannot be understood, and they cannot be overcome. Denial of this
"natural" force is equal to death. But sexuality is also death, at least to
Quentin. The body will not be silenced.

Jason's viciously funny monologue declares its sexual politics from the
opening sentence, "Once a bitch always a bitch, what I say." He is speaking not only of his sister Caddy but also of the product of her "bitchery,"
her daughter Quentin. Quentin II is a reminder of the two people Jason
blames most for the failure of his life's ambitions, Caddy and his elder
brother. Caddy's "honor" not only represented the status of the Compson family; for Jason it was the guarantor of future success: her husband,
Herbert, was going to get him a banking job. Her "promiscuity" wrecks
his chances. Thus despite his self-proclaimed "respect" for "a good honest whore" (Caddy was, one assumes, dishonest) he seeks to destroy the
niece who recalls that tainted body, calling her a whore and "you damn
little slut" (112).

With Quentin II, Jason plays out his revenge against Caddy. He not only
steals the money she sends to her daughter for "things like other girls
have," he loses no chance to brutalize Quentin II in a way that suggests
a sadistic eroticism. Jason is a thoroughgoing misogynist: his attack on
Caddy through Quentin II is an attack on female sexuality. His excessive
attention to Quentin II's boyfriends, her skimpy clothes, her painted face,
and her body suggests barely concealed desire. He constantly reports
how Quentin's "kimono came unfastened, flapping about her shoulder"
or that under her wrap she is "damn near naked" (111). Beating his flim-
sily clad seventeen-year-old niece with a belt seems a rehearsal for a rape.
Clearly Jason's vision of women (except for his mother and the "damn
old nigger" Dilsey) is that they are potential whores who must be controlled by a magisterial phallus. His rage is overtly sexual when he watches
Quentin II go to meet someone, "her hair all gummed and twisted and a
dress that if a woman had come out doors even on Gayoso or Beale street
when I was a young fellow with no more than that to cover her legs and
behind, she'd been thrown in jail. I'll be damned if they dont dress like
they were trying to make every man they passed on the street reach out
and clap his hand on it" (139–40).

He controls the prostitute Lorraine by never telling her when he will see her or how much money he will pay her: he controls Quentin II in a similar fashion by regulating her actions and withholding money. The difference is that he does not have legitimate sexual access to Quentin II. Lacking his father's elegant cynicism or his mother's class-bound pieties, Jason nonetheless sees women as bodies to be legislated and the relations between genders as a war of sexuality to be fought with money and violence. He tries to gain final mastery over Caddy by the quasi-sexual subjugation of her daughter, perpetuating the central place of female sexuality in this drama of Compson downfall.

Sexuality—both his and Caddy's—is at the center of Benjy's section. Without knowing the words for it, Benjy is just as obsessed with her virginity as Jason, Quentin, and Mrs. Compson. However, Caddy's virginity is not, for Benjy, part of an economic or social system. He is a child, signaled to the reader by his holding a narcissus: his need is for a mother, a need only Caddy can fulfill. Before she loses her virginity, still smelling "like trees," he holds her complete attention; when she begins to sleep with men, he feels a loss of her presence as well as her "purity." When the family drives her away, all he has left is her wedding slipper, which he fetishizes, drooling over it. Gwin says that the unvirgin Caddy is "silenced" for "she cannot remake herself in language . . . or throw away her desire" (*Feminine* 46). She becomes not an unmitigated maternal presence (and voice) but an empty object that only speaks loss.

Caddy represents a sexual vocabulary, an erotic symbol system Benjy cannot understand. He is surrounded by sexual activity from which he is excluded yet to which he is a reliable witness. He sees Quentin II and her young man in the swing, triggering memories of her mother, Caddy, in the same swing with one of her lovers. As Benjy weeps from jealousy, Caddy promises to stay away from men, but her desire leads her to "betray" him as she "betrays" the rest of the family. As a child he goes with Caddy to deliver a note to his Uncle Maury's married lover. Through him we see that Jason Compson the elder is an alcoholic trapped in a bleak, passionless marriage with Caroline. He cannot understand his own castration or recognize that he transgressed by frightening a little girl (whom he probably associated with Caddy); nevertheless, he still connects his now-deformed sexuality with Caddy. Seeing his mutilated genitals, he cries, and Luster says, "*Looking for them aint going to do no good. They're gone*" (45).

Gone is what Benjy's keepers are constantly saying about Caddy, just one of the dramas of loss enacted in the novel (Snead 21–23). She is gone away from him. The memory immediately triggered by the sight of his body is of Caddy's muddy drawers. Indeed, it is through Benjy that we receive this central scene, this sort of dumb-show in which Quentin, Caddy, and Versh act out a prophetic drama of their later lives. Seven-year-old Caddy stains her drawers with mud, prefiguring menstruation, the "taint" of female sexuality and pollution. Benjy witnesses Caddy ordering Versh to unbutton her wet dress so she can take it off and Quentin, trying to take control of her body, ordering her not to. Though Benjy does not under-stand the significance of what he sees, he reports Quentin's frightened anger and Caddy's defiance. This explosive scene is diluted by Benjy's un-differentiating consciousness, but the picture of a black boy undressing a white girl in front of her brothers goes to the heart of southern sexual taboos. While Caddy's lovers in later life do not seem to include blacks (the ultimate transgression for a white woman) the very nature of sexu-ality in the South is defined as illicit and "Negro": "*Why must you do like nigger women do in the pasture the ditches the dark woods hot hidden furious in the dark woods*" (56–57). Women and blacks are both Other, marked by race and gender. The "blackness" of sexuality becomes a metaphor for Caddy's life and subsequent fall from ladyhood into exile.

Much has been made of Caddy's "smelling like trees," connecting her to the birch girls of Faulkner's juvenile poetry and the eroticized trees of his symbolist plays. It is evidently her very virginity that causes her to give off that scent, for Benjy records her fall from the tree smell: like Marietta in *The Marionettes* she is transformed from dryad to "flame" by passion. Faulkner says his first "vision" of her, the impetus for the novel, was up a pear tree (Gwyn and Blotner 11, 17, 74). Vegetative metaphors for the feminine are common in Faulkner. Narcissa Benbow is likened to a lily, Belle Mitchell to hothouse grapes, Miss Rosa Coldfield to both an ironic rose and wisteria, the scent of the past. Belle Mitchell, Temple Drake, and her double, Little Belle Mitchell, are, like Caddy, associated with honey-suckle, suggesting a powerful, disruptive female sexuality both enticing and overwhelming.

The feminine vegetative metaphor has a long history in southern writ-ing: it is common for the daughter of the aristocratic family to be "placed" in the plantation garden, a *hortus conclusus* signifying not only the fertile body of the master's land but the forbidden body of the master's daugh-ter. This image of protection, cultivation, and closure is not available to lower-class white women or black women, whose bodies are left unprotected (and undeified) in the rough world. Like many of Faulkner's upper-class white heroines, Caddy is placed in a sort of plantation garden, albeit a mostly ruined one. The Compson Mile was once an ordered, aristocratic space: now it is shrunken and impoverished. Caddy's garden, not so "walled and windless" or high and shut as Narcissa's or Marietta's, opens onto the woods, the location of "negro" sexuality.

Quentin insistently, compulsively, connects Caddy with honeysuckle and thus with the (ruined) plantation garden. Honeysuckle is a disorderly plant, spreading smothering vines bearing flowers with an overwhelming scent. Quentin's section gradually reaches a crescendo of "the smell of honeysuckle," "that damn honeysuckle," "damn that honeysuckle," threatening to suffocate him as the reality of female sexuality immobilizes him. We have clearly come a long way from the static lilies of the antebellum garden, standing aloof and chaste behind the walls of the domain. In Caddy the walls have come tumbling down: the closure and exclusivity that have determined the value of the white woman's body are negated, and her sexuality is freed to both envelop and disrupt the narrative as it envelops and disrupts the Compsons' position as aristocrats.

But reading *The Sound and the Fury* simply as Caddy's exile from ladyhood in a fiction produced out of a society where ladyhood was imperiled is too tidy, too controlled. As I have suggested, the cherished binary of virgin and whore are challenged in her, as the boundaries of desire are constantly breached by the fluidity of relationships within the Compson household. Gender itself becomes liquid, masculine and feminine shifting and recombining in a scandalous solution. I would like to return to the question of Caddy's voice—or perhaps I should say, Caddy's voice/ Quentin's voice: not a graceful expression but a way to insist on the connection. At the risk of reiterating the false advertising in Lacan's 1959 lecture on "Desire and the Interpretation of Desire in *Hamlet*," where he claims he will speak about "that piece of bait named Ophelia" and then goes on to speak mainly of Hamlet instead, it is necessary in discussing that obsession named Caddy to look closely at Quentin. It is, of course, a commonplace to call Quentin the southern Hamlet, the tormented heir to the Compson patrimony—what is left of it—who must confront the reality of "evil" (female sexuality). The status of the family and the bodies of its women are two economies that have slipped from their traditional boundaries. Quentin has no control over the broad expanse of southern history, but he tries to control Compson history, that is, his sister's body, which is for him both an emblem of time and an enfolding *possibility* for an identity, a self. Quentin is not all Hamlet: sometimes he is precipitously near to being Ophelia, caught between the Law of the Father and desire.[5]

Caddy's voice, Caddy's self, proceeds from desire, not masculine discourse: "Resonating from within the dark folds of Quentin's despair, her voice and presence speak the feminine desire that inscribes her woman's body across his male text. Subversively she rises from Quentin's mind to speak her desire for Dalton Ames, for entry into a libidinal economy which allows her to give, to spend herself excessively, to play creatively and productively within that half-light between self and other" (Gwin, *Feminine* 47). Gwin says Caddy "speaks from Quentin *to* Quentin of the feminine within himself—that which he, entangled in a cultural narrative already written for him, can but desire and grieve for" and refers to his "male mind" (48, 50). I quote so much from Gwin's reading of the "Quentin section" because it is helpful in untangling Quentin and Caddy, Self and Other. However, Gwin's opposition of male and female seems too absolute (almost like black and white). Quentin, too, seeks a way out of male discourse; Quentin's discourse is not so fixedly male as Gwin implies. He is not merely a victim of his southern social location, trapped in the historically inscribed "cultural narrative," the last Old South gentleman confronting the New South, but an agent who, at times, seems to transgress *into* the feminine, transforming himself, entering the enveloping pool of feminine discourse.

Quentin's narrative suggests a slippage of gender from the beginning.[6] Shreve is called Quentin's "husband." Quentin mutilates his grandfather's watch—a patriarchal heirloom representing both the Law of the Father and the temporal changes that transform Caddy from child to woman, from virgin to unvirgin. Time is, according to Quentin's father, "the mausoleum of all hope and desire," both a tomb and a womb. Quentin seems to have episodes where he goes *outside* of time: at the beginning of his section the shadow of the window sash appears on the curtains and "then I was in time *again,* hearing the watch" (47; emphasis mine). This space immune from history comes up over and over in Quentin's images of himself and Caddy together in a scene that appears to take place simultaneously when they are children at the branch and young adults, in disjointed recollections (or inventions) of the battle of discourses between his mother and his father, in recurring evocations of Caddy running out of a mirror (as if he, Quentin, sees her as his reflection) in her wedding dress, as well as his projected desire to spend eternity in hell, alone with Caddy, whirling about like Paolo and Francesca in the Inferno: "Nobody else there but her and me. If we could just have done something so dreadful that they would have fled hell except us" (49).

But by breaking the watch, twisting the hands off, Quentin signals his lack of accommodation with patriarchal discourse, with Compson history and linear narrative. The feminine space is not simply owned by Caddy; Quentin creates a feminine space for himself. The mutilation of the watch echoes Benjy's castration and Quentin's projected phallusless self, later in his narrative. Moreover, after he breaks the watch, Quentin begins to *bleed*, "a red smear on the dial," and continues to "bleed" throughout the section. He confuses his blood with Caddy's—"*Oh her blood or my blood Oh*"—and bleeds from his fight with Caddy: "*Where the rain touched my forehead it began to smart my hand came red away streaking off pink in the rain*" (82, 84). When Quentin ineffectually tries to fight Dalton Ames (fainting "like a girl"), he says, "I could hear my blood"; later when he makes Caddy say her lover's name, he "felt the first surge of blood there it surged in strong accelerating beats" (98, 100). This "episode" is juxtaposed with a literally bleeding Quentin after his second failed fight, this time with Gerald Bland. The "bloody rag" Shreve uses to clean Quentin up with suggests menstruation (100). The evocations of blood that saturate Quentin's narrative oscillate between (feminine) loss of virginity and menstruation, with the latter image emerging strongly. Considering that menstruation— "periodic filth"—is the chief marker of the feminine in the masculine discourse, this sets up a violent contrast between the "male" and Quentin. In a sense, Quentin is in the process of becoming the feminine object. He hopes to contain Caddy by becoming her.

It is not a seamless transgression from the masculine into the feminine. According to Quentin, Caddy herself appears at times to appropriate the masculine: he reflects how Caddy "never was a queen or a fairy she was always a king or a giant or a general" (105). Caddy takes on the role of the elder son, sexually assertive, sowing her wild oats while her brother exhibits timidity and inexperience like a (female) virgin. Quentin's one encounter with the "dirty" Natalie in the barn demonstrates his fastidious fear of sexuality while Caddy goes from conquest to conquest.

Quentin is still bound by his situation as the son of the House of Compson, the hollow though still powerful voice of which is represented in his father's utterances. Gwin says that Quentin accepts "his father's discourse of phallic authority" (*Feminine* 50). She sees Quentin as quite invested in a phallic system of authority: the voice that obfuscates the feminine. I would say rather that Quentin is engaged in a debate between phallic and feminine discourses. The father's voice is undoubtedly strong; Quentin frequently tries to appropriate it for himself by constructing a (however perverse) story of sexual conquest: "*I have committed incest I said Father*" (49). Here Quentin is trying to contain Caddy's dangerous body in a *hortus conclusus* of his own language. He even takes on the identity of all Caddy's lovers: "*you thought it was them but it was me listen I fooled you all the time it was me*" (90). This is not only a fantasy, it is an assault on the constant "Father saids" to which Quentin reacts all throughout his section; it is a rebellion— though perhaps a feeble one—against Jason Compson Senior's paternal authority to order the world, which he does with eloquent misogynistic rhetoric: "*they have an affinity for evil for supplying whatever the evil lacks in itself*" and the bankrupt set phrases of the dead Old South, rendered impotent in Quentin's reporting by lack of phallogocentric capitalization: "no compson has ever disappointed a lady" (59, 108). Mr. Compson is the paternal lawgiver, though ineffective himself, the father who speaks the symbolic order to which Quentin is unable to accommodate himself. Quentin is torn between the masculinity that regulates his social location and the pull of the feminine, through which he can approach Caddy.

Quentin's relationship with the phallus itself is troubled: he fantasizes about changing sex. Standing on the bridge, staring into the water, he recounts a story Versh told him "about a man who mutilated himself. He went into the woods and did it with a razor, sitting in a ditch" (71). Critics have tended to read this as a reaching toward asexuality: Matthews posits Quentin's desire for "freedom from differentiation" (*Play* 83), while Snead says, "Quentin equates sexlessness with a linguistic exclusion"—without the phallus there can be no naming (Snead 29). But it isn't an androgyne or eunuch or castrated man Quentin aspires to be, it's a woman: "It's not not having them. It's never to have had them then I could say O That That's Chinese I dont know Chinese" (71). If he never had testicles he could have had a vagina, that *absence* or *creative space* (in Quentin's mind) that defines Caddy; "them," testicles, would then be that male Other as alien as Chinese. If the male is the Other, this logic goes, then Quentin is female. In the water he sees not a man but a nonman, a woman, Little Sister Death, Ophelia. The position of object, passive, desirable, feminine, is what Quentin longs to assume, to be Caddy or to be the focus of her desire as she is the focus of his.

Planning suicide, Quentin attempts to assume the posture of the feminine, identifying Caddy with death. Perversely quoting Saint Francis, he speaks of Little Sister Death; in Faulkner's pseudomedieval romance *Mayday* the Quentinesque Sir Galwyn calls the image he sees in the water, the body he desires above all others, "Little Sister Death." In following her he, of course, kills himself. In a sense Quentin, too, identifies that face in the water, that shadow, as Caddy. They are twinned in a number of ways. Quentin realizes Dalton Ames sees Caddy when he looks at him: "I knew he wasn't thinking of me at all as a potential source of harm but was thinking of her when he looked at me was looking at me through her like through a piece of colored glass" (106). Quentin sees her in mirrors, not himself; he describes water with the flower he associates with her— "I could see the water the color of grey honeysuckle." He even juxtaposes her name with images of death by drowning as his hold on language begins to break down: "I have sold Benjy's pasture and I can be dead in Harvard Caddy said in the caverns and the grottoes of the sea tumbling peacefully to the wavering tides" (106).

Quentin's narrative contains several scenes where he tries to merge with Caddy. His incantation of "*Oh her blood or my blood Oh*," underlines this central confusion of identities; the two elements Caddy and Quentin, "her" and "me," are balanced by the two capitalized *Ohs* at either end of the phrase, walling the two of them off from the world in a closed system like Quentin's favored image of the two of them alone in their own hell. Later, Quentin tries, or at least tells a story to that effect, to make the blood literal in their bonding by holding a knife at Caddy's throat in a failed attempt at a murder-suicide pact or, given that for Quentin he and Caddy ought to be one person, merely, I suppose, a suicide. This is an erotic scene as well, Quentin embracing his sister, crying, recalling the time (so powerfully reported by Benjy in the earlier section) Caddy got her drawers muddy in the creek, prefiguring her "defilement," seemingly confusing the knife with the penis in ambiguous language which becomes more and more liquid until it is difficult to know which Compson is speaking. Quentin's identity flows out like water from a broken glass. The feminine moves in Quentin here: he drops the false phallus, the knife, his and Caddy's voices woven together in a play of mutuality. We hear Caddy's voice but we also hear Quentin's—the one cannot be found without the other. It is still *Quentin* who is allowed to speak; though his voice breaks down into unpunctuated, uncapitalized fragments as his death in the river nears, his is still the subject voice. Paradoxically, his own words detail his flight from words. His attempt to become one with Caddy is nonetheless controlled from his consciousness by his words. We have access to Caddy the way people traditionally have access to women—through their families. We are in danger of becoming voyeurs, watching Caddy as object from the subject position of the narrative, which is active. But I don't think that's the whole story. On the contrary, it is *through* Quentin that we hear Caddy, through him that the feminine can speak. It is a qualified victory, true, for we cannot recover Caddy's voice without his mediation, but his painful negotiation between the masculine and the feminine, his wish to discard the phallus as marker (in which he is at least partially successful), validates both narratives—Quentin's and Caddy's.

Does Quentin truly wish to become one with his mother, to return to the womb? Like everything connected with Quentin, this is contradictory: is it the masculine or the feminine Quentin who wishes to reenter the ultimate feminine space? Marsha Warren suggests that the Compson house is, for Quentin, an extension of his mother's body, "symbolizing her presence, her watching and her judgment" (105). The house is a cold, dark space as unwelcoming as Mrs. Compson herself: the windows symbolize her watchful eyes. One of the images suspended between the real and the imagined in Quentin's discourse underlines the way his mother is, for him, a bounded space:

> When I was little there was a picture in one of our books, a dark place into which a single weak ray of light came slanting upon two faces lifted out of the shadow. *You know what I'd do if I were King?* she never was a queen or a fairy she was always a king or a giant or a general I'd *break that place open and drag them out and I'd whip them good* It was torn out, jagged out. I was glad. I'd have to turn back to it until the dungeon was Mother herself she and Father upward into weak light holding hands and us lost somewhere below even them without even a ray of light. (105)

The two faces trapped in the dark space recall Quentin's recurring image of himself and Caddy in hell; he often constructs them as prisoners, held in darkness, but here he identifies that prison with his mother's body.

It is possible to see Mrs. Compson and Caddy as halves of a whole for Quentin, two sides of the chaste woman/fallen woman binary codified by the South into the rigid "a woman is either a lady or not." In wishing to become Caddy, Quentin wants to become his mother, to reenter the womb. His drowning is a move in that direction, a return to the fluidity of a prebirth state, diffusing his unbounded personality with a feminine element in water. As Elaine Showalter remarks: "Drowning too was associated with the feminine, with female fluidity as opposed to masculine aridity. . . . Water is the profound and organic symbol of the liquid woman whose eyes are so easily drowned in tears, as her body is the repository of blood, amniotic fluid, and milk. A man contemplating this feminine suicide understands it by reaching for what is feminine in himself" (81). In his suicide Quentin not only annihilates the self and returns to the fluidity of the feminine, he also rejects his father's language, which erects boundaries between Caddy, his mother, and himself. He attempts to refuse the masculine order to partake of the feminine. In this sense, Caddy and her mother occupy the same position as objects of desire without voices, without the privileged place in the narrative, to inscribe their desires on the family: they are at the mercy of others' narratives. Both haunt the text, disembodied creatures floating in a world of male language—Mrs. Compson constructed as the woman who detests the body and Caddy constructed as the woman who surrenders to it. Their opposition nonetheless collapses in Quentin's suicide; it silences him, reducing him at last to the position of feminine object in this phallogocentric economy: not Hamlet, in the end, but Ophelia.

Ravishing Belles: Rape and Resistance in Flags in the Dust and Sanctuary

Sanctuary is about rape. Stated baldly, the point seems as obvious as daylight. Yet the novel has frequently been read in such a way that rape becomes a signifier for everything but itself. Readings from O'Donnell's horrified essay in the 1939 Kenyon Review constructing a histrionic allegory—Temple Drake as "Southern Womanhood Corrupted but Undefiled," assaulted "unnaturally" by Popeye as "Modernism"—to Fiedler's exuberant Love and Death (1960) where this "darkest of all Faulkner's books" displays the author's "revulsion from woman's betrayal of her traditionally submissive role," to Duvall's compelling assertion that Sanctuary is "a radical novel," where "male/female unions operate on the paradigms of rape and prostitution," focus on Temple Drake's corncob rape as a symptom of a larger discursive framework (O'Donnell 28; Fiedler, Love and Death 301; Duvall 60).

While I would not deny the interest of any of these readings, I would like to return to Temple Drake's rape—or perhaps I should say rapes, because she is violated even before Popeye wields the corncob and she continues to be violated in various ways up to her courtroom appearance—as worthy of a different kind of consideration. Inspired by Gwin's insistence on "hearing" the voice of Caddy Compson through the obfuscating narratives of her brothers, I try to hear Temple Drake's story unmediated by the masculine voices shouting at and over her. Gwin calls for making "our own texts of Faulkner's world as one which explodes with female creativity and feminine force" (Feminine 21). Temple Drake has a powerful story, an empowering story to tell; in examining the assaults on her body and her mind, we can recover the feminine in Faulkner in a way that honors and enriches it.

For years we were told Sanctuary was about evil in the person of Temple Drake, a woman who "deserved" to be raped.[7] Evil has been read as a Faulknerian code word for female sexuality. Brooks magisterially stated that evil is equivalent to "the true nature of woman," and that knowledge of it constitutes a second Fall from grace—for men (Yoknapatawpha Country 127–28). Fiedler was fascinated by what he calls Faulkner's "sexually insatiable daughters of the aristocracy," the young white ladies whose conditioned repression of their sexuality later ignites a firestorm of "evil," decimating any man foolish enough to have anything to do with them (Love and Death 300). This thorough misreading of Temple Drake can appear to be reinforced by Faulkner himself in Requiem for a Nun, published twenty years later, in which Temple Drake "confesses" to the "crimes" of being raped, imprisoned in a brothel, and, most appallingly, enjoying her force-bloomed sexuality—"because Temple Drake liked evil" (117).

"Evil" suggests a range of failings in the postsuffrage, post-Depression, prohibition, (slowly) urbanizing South. Caddy Compson and Temple Drake must operate in a world filled with sexual and social anxieties. There was the "New Negro" to contend with; there was also the "New Woman." The Sound and the Fury shows, among other things, the difficulty of a young white woman's rejection of ladyhood: gender boundaries blur, and class divisions begin to collapse. In Sanctuary the culture of violence—particularly sexual violence—is used to police sexuality and, to some extent, race. Both these novels were produced at a time when transgressing women had become more visible than before. In addition to the prostitutes (about whom Faulkner would write all of his life) there were suffragists, union organizers, political leaders like Nellie Somerville in Mississippi and Pattie Jacobs in Alabama, and "rebel girl" strikers in the mill towns of Elizabethton and Gastonia (Anne Firor Scott 224–26). On the one hand the Daughters of the Confederacy built monuments to white southern womanhood, and the Saint Cecilia Society, the Piedmont Driving Club, the Crewe of Comus, and various local civic organizations presented debutantes, crowned queens of carnival and maids of cotton, reinscribing old, approved forms of white bourgeois womanhood. At the same time many old, approved forms were disintegrating. Yet the culture seemed determined to enforce distances between men and women, blacks and whites. Lynching and other forms of violence were used as social control as well as the mythologizing of the Old South. Temple Drake lives in a world where violence enforces the official story of an orderly class and race hierarchy. Eric Sundquist thinks "*Sanctuary* is less dependent on Faulkner's native southern traditions than his other major novels" (45). I disagree; *Sanctuary* captures the lynch-mob culture that tried to control deviations from the symbolic order. That the novel does not overtly engage the race question does not make it less grounded in the southern context. The *otherness* of sexuality is present in the otherness of blacks and women themselves. All are potential threats to the careful, always-precarious decorum of the New South. The violence on which class and gender roles are built in the South is exhibited by what happens to Temple Drake, the fallen icon.

In *Speculum de l'autre femme*, Luce Irigaray asks, "But what if the object began to speak?" Temple Drake *does* speak; she does what a select few women in Faulkner's fiction do overtly: she tells her own story. But no one listens—least of all Horace Benbow, a southern gentleman who fails to live up to the chivalric ideal. The story she tells is unbearable for a southern culture that claims to value virginity and innocence above all in its young white women; it is unbearable for a symbolic order that demands dominance over women's bodies. Temple's story tells of victimization, but also of an attempt to take control through the making of her own fiction. What we hear, listening to Temple, is not a story of the masculine confrontation of "evil" in the body of the feminine, but a tangle of rape and (mis)representation obscuring the near-destruction of a woman.

What happens to Temple Drake could be seen as Faulkner's final dismantling of a cultural icon, the Southern Belle. Much of Faulkner's early poetry and fiction, between 1920 and 1934, is concerned with what models of Old South ladyhood do when accosted by the angry New South.[8] *Sanctuary* and Temple Drake's multiple violations grow out of *Flags in the Dust* (completed in 1927), Faulkner's first Yoknapatawpha novel and first appearance of Horace and Narcissa Benbow, Miss Jenny, and Belle Mitchell, the characters who frame and comment on what happens to Temple Drake in *Sanctuary*. *Flags* is also about sexual violence: images of the female body as an enclosed garden, as a vessel, but most of all, as a privileged space that must be penetrated in an attempt (largely futile) to conquer or silence the feminine, are rehearsed here.

In *Flags* Faulkner masks rape in romanticism. Narcissa Benbow is emotionally violated by Bayard Sartoris, foreshadowing her physical loss of virginity: "At the very syllables of his name her instincts brought her upstanding and under arms against him, thus increasing, doubling, the sense of violation by the act of repulsing him and by the necessity for it. And yet, despite her armed sentinels, he still crashed with that hot violence of his through the bastions and thundered at the very inmost citadel of her being" (135). Narcissa is a fortress to be taken in combat, a "sanctuary" to be breached, elsewhere a "walled and windless garden," a *hortus conclusus* whose value in the class, race, and gender hierarchy of the South is dependent on her exclusivity. As her name implies, Narcissa is also a flower in the enclosed garden. Here Faulkner makes ironic use of a plantation-novel convention; as Kolodny has shown, the plantation garden, an enclosed or fenced space of fertile order and beauty, is an erotic, feminized image, while the (privileged, white, chaste) female body represents the integrity and wealth of the southern land (5–25, 115–32). In antebellum plantation romances by William Gilmore Simms, as well as in postbellum plantation romances by Thomas Nelson Page, to give but two examples, the daughter of the Big House occupies a symbolic position as either a white marble statue on a lofty pedestal or a "lily" (or rosebud or magnolia blossom) in the exquisite formal gardens of the estate (Simms 233; Page, *Old South* 146). In *Sanctuary* Narcissa fossilizes into stone "with that serene and stupid impregnability of heroic statuary," but in *Flags* she is still the self-regarding lily, named after a flower, always collecting and obsessively arranging flowers, waiting, in Faulkner's bitter view, merely to be deflowered (110).

Narcissa is a potentially dangerous body: her sexuality is first denied, then "awakened" by the "romantic" rapist Bayard, then, extraordinarily, negated. Like the spring-blooming bulb that is her namesake, Narcissa rises out of the wintry destruction of the Sartorises at the end of the novel with her virginity miraculously restored: "She had been like a lily in a gale which rocked it to its roots in a sort of vacuum, without any actual laying-on of hands. And now the gale had gone on; the lily had forgotten it as its fury died away into fading vibrations of old terrors and dreads, and the stalk recovered and the bell itself was untarnished save by the friction of its own petals. The gale is gone, and though the lily is sad a little with vibrations of ancient fears, it is not sorry" (368). The imagery of "stalk" and "petals" suggests a hymen now "repaired," a solitary vagina: the "bell" (belle) is again pure, the deflowered flower is a whole bud again. Yet there is an uneasy sense that purity is not quite what the lily-belle has returned to, any more than returning Temple to Judge Drake and his sons can repair her torn flesh or her tainted reputation. A knowing woman—yet not a mere wife—Narcissa has become powerful, potentially monstrous. With both Bayards dead, her son an infant, and her brother married to the "dirty" Venus, Belle Mitchell, Narcissa finally gets her wish of living "in a world where there were no men at all," a world completely ruled by her own sanitized reinvention of the feminine, the "ladylike" (138).

If Narcissa is conventionally represented as a flower, she is just as conventionally represented as a vessel. Her brother Horace, one of the controlling masculine voices of the novel, finds himself unable to resolve the images of the female in the sister he apotheosizes and the seductress he goes to bed with. Narcissa objectifies his nostalgia for old-time southern chastity. Horace has never really left the plantation garden; she is, in his apostrophe, "thou still unravished bride of quietude." He makes "one almost perfect vase of clear amber, larger, more richly and chastely serene and which he kept always on his night table and called by his sister's name" (162). He is not alone in seeing her as a vessel: even Miss Jenny compares Narcissa to a "cut-glass pitcher."

So the woman's body is translated from enclosed garden to sexual container, a privileged receptacle accorded symbolic and spiritual significance. Horace defers his anxiety over the female body (particularly Narcissa's) by imaginatively limiting it, defining a woman as a hermetic space, the hortus conclusus or the urn. The Virgin Mary is often called by titles such as Spiritual Vase, Vase of Honor, Tower of Ivory, and so on, all reinforcing the idea that a woman should be closed and empty until she is opened and filled by a male agency, human or divine (Warner 254). Faulkner himself associated women with vessels: in a letter to his great-aunt, written around 1928, he says of a woman (probably Estelle Oldham, later his wife): "I would like to see you taken with her utter charm and intrigued by her utter shallowness. Like a lovely vase" (Brodsky and Hamblin 2.8). To Meta Carpenter, his on-and-off Hollywood lover, he employs a less lyrical metaphor, referring to a woman as "a physical spittoon," (Wilde and Borsten 244).

Belle Mitchell's body is not restricted by any metaphors of virginity, and while Narcissa's name may invoke the lily the angel carries at the Annunciation, Belle's name—perhaps "ironic title" would be a better way of describing it—undermines the edifice of the upper-class southern woman. If Narcissa seems to represent the original story of the stainless vessel, the pure belle of old, Belle represents the counterstory, the secret anxiety about the female body: Belle is the Belle gone bad. Narcissa is nearly incorporeal at times, Belle is all "petulant scented flesh" (168). She is animalistic: Horace speaks of her "tiger-reek." Her sister Joan, who seduces and abandons Horace, is an emanation of Belle: "Carnivorous, he thought. A lady tiger in a tea gown" (292). Joan ridicules his double vision of women, sardonically referring to her presence in Narcissa's boudoir as "desecration" (297). When Horace later thinks of Narcissa, he feels "unclean."

Virginity—shrouded in its sanctified vestments—is as dead as the Old South. The new fantasy of the New South is that even the lily of the plantation garden secretly longs to be defiled even while insisting on her chastity. The community colludes in the polarization of the feminine, where bad women are overtly sexual and good women are asexual. Horace and Narcissa associate sex with "filth": she says of Belle, "She's so dirty!" (192). Certainly Horace could not contemplate sullying a flower-like virgin. But whereas Horace insists on an absolute division between Narcissa and Belle/Joan, Miss Jenny, exempt from sexuality because she is old and belongs to the nostalgically privileged class of Confederate Women (old ladies who have experienced the South's epic period), answers Narcissa's complaints about the sordidness of sexuality by snapping (with faux folksiness), "All women are [dirty], if that's what you mean" (193). Miss Jenny's assertion threatens to collapse the opposition between virgin/whore, Narcissa/Belle, democratizing the carefully hierarchized female body habitually situated in categories of pure or impure. Yet Horace firmly maintains the dichotomy; he can worship his sister's purity without giving up his sexual gratification with Belle. Southern men have always been able to revere the white wife or sister or mother or daughter on the pedestal while they kept mistresses in New Orleans or slipped out back to the Quarters at night.

However, the virgin/whore opposition is radically unstable; the text of *Flags* demonstrates its shakiness in Narcissa's erotic fascination with the suggestive, semiliterate letters written to her by Byron Snopes. Frightened and titillated, she does not destroy them or give them to a father-authority figure like Old Bayard, but keeps them in her dresser drawer tied up with blue ribbon as if they were billets doux. Underneath her serene distaste for the physical, signaled by the white dresses she wears, Narcissa enjoys being validated as a sexual object, being made, as she says, to "feel so filthy" and by a lower-class man, too: the white lower class, like the black, is an official repository of sexuality in the South (59). While it is the aristocratic Bayard who actually deflowers the lily of the plantation garden, the letters—declaring, "I will not hurt you but I am desprate" and "Your lips like cupids bow when the day comes when I will press them to mine"—contain the threat of rape (243–44). Indeed, Byron Snopes does try to rape Minnie Sue Turpin, "babbling a name not hers," in the village of Frenchman's Bend—close to the Old Frenchman Place, where Temple is raped. He is, however, ineffective, and she escapes. Miss Jenny, the designated commentator on the sexual politics of Jefferson, remarks acidly: "Just like a young fool of a woman, to be flattered over a thing like this" (59).

The virgin/whore opposition weakened in *Flags* is thoroughly disabled in *Sanctuary*, where the virgin turns whore and the whore begins to resemble the Madonna. The project of discrediting the Belle, operated on a small scale in *Flags*, intensifies; instead of soiling her fair name in anonymous letters, it is now "written on that lavatory wall!"; instead of threatening her with ravishment by a brooding Byronic hero or an invisible "admirer," all the violence and rage of the symbolic order against the feminine is pornographically inscribed on her body (40). In *Sanctuary* there is no oscillating between constructions of flower and vessel: Temple is the culture's holy of holies, a sacred space whose very name begs for *desecration* (as Narcissa's begs for her *deflowering*), to be looted and pillaged, finally to be destroyed.

Temple Drake is raped over and over again. I state this obvious point so baldly to emphasize its centrality. *Sanctuary* is a text of the destruction of the female mind and body, the acting out of anger against the feminine and final recovery and recapture of a wayward female body. Narcissa the born-again virgin regains power in her widowhood, surrounding herself with younger men and controlling the bourgeois values of her community; Temple leaves the protected spaces where she belongs and is assaulted by the true sexual politics of the South, ownership by men written on her flesh like the slogans and initials written on the body of a gang-rape victim. In the world of *Sanctuary*, all sexual relationships are violent; all family relationships are both violent and sexual; there is nothing that is not perverse or corrupt—no sanctuary, no refuge.

In scene after scene, the male is confronted with the female body, which he wants to contain and control. Horace Benbow, the idolater of his sister's purity and guilty exploiter of his wife's "dirtiness," flees Belle's physical being, manifest in the dripping shrimp he collects off the train for her every Friday. Not only is Friday the day sacred to Venus; the shrimp—wet, pink, smelly—read as if Faulkner has a crude joke about female genitals in mind. The immediate cause of Horace's defection from the marital bed is, as he tells Ruby (herself named after a red gem—not quite *scarlet?*), a "rag with rouge on it," a handkerchief Belle used to wipe off her excess makeup (16). The red stain also represents menstruation, a function of the female body that frightens and disgusts Faulknerian men. The fact of femaleness is what Horace cannot bear, not merely the vulgar specificity of Belle. There is no escape: Horace runs from one enveloping body to an even more complex world of feminine corruption: in temporarily evading Belle, he becomes entangled in another unstable spirit/ flesh opposition when he must negotiate amongst Temple Drake, Ruby Lamar, Belle, Little Belle, and Narcissa. He discovers that if there is no sanctuary, no pure and "unravish'd" *hortus conclusus*, there is also no ignoring the female body. That orifice, thought in the South to be as sacred as the sanctuary of a temple, is the site of decay. As the authoritative male voice in the novel, "seeing" the degeneration all around him, Horace invites us to share his horror. To the feminist reader, however, insistence on the female body as corrupt creates resistance. Rather than being evil, these women are victims, brutalized by their culture and, to some degree, by Faulkner's text. But perhaps *Sanctuary* is best read as Faulkner's attempt to imagine the consequences for the most cherished of southern bodies in a world where the contexts for her protection and veneration were under attack. The class system on which she rested and even the presumption of her purity, given the new sexual freedom, were precarious.

The hermetic, "walled and windless" garden, the appropriate nurturing ground for the southern lady, has become an impossibility in *Sanctuary*. True to her inorganic name, Temple comes not out of the plantation *hortus conclusus* but the college girls' dormitory (though perhaps one could make a case for that as a hothouse). The garden she encounters at the Old Frenchman Place is previolated, the once orderly and imposing plantation house now a "gutted ruin rising gaunt and stark out of a grove of unpruned cedar trees," its "gardens and lawns long since gone back to jungle" (8). Jungle implies lawlessness and has racial overtones (black rapists were commonly compared to beasts in the jungle). Patriarchal control in its ultimate form—the plantation—has collapsed. Patriarchal control over women's bodies has also collapsed: women vote, go to college, and get jobs, and the once-enclosed garden has become a wilderness. This failure of virginity is the "problem" of the novel. The moral weight of virginity, its symbolic relation to the health of the community, its status as a metaphor for absolute good: issues of who should have access to a woman's body, when, and how she should deal with that "sacred space" galvanize the novel.

Narcissa equates sexual inaccessibility with moral elevation; her class, her race, and her community decree chastity—or at least the *appearance* of chastity—to be the highest good for a woman. She condemns Horace for not acknowledging that in Jefferson public morality is intimately related to status; his placing the homeless ex-whore and unwed mother Ruby in the Benbow house is seen not as an act of charity but as an invasion of a sacred space, a family shrine, by a representative of the kind of unregulated sexuality Narcissa most fears. Indeed, Ruby's insertion into the Benbow house is one of the "rapes" of the novel: Narcissa underlines her sense that the house and the garden signify the body by expressing her feelings of violation: "The house where my father and mother and your father and mother, the house where I—I wont have it" (122).

Narcissa's linking of her self with the parental home emphasizes the way she is both product and producer of the bourgeois female community, the "church ladies," who repress their desire. Narcissa denies the flesh but Ruby accepts and uses it, seeing it as her only resource in the patriarchal economy: she even offers herself to a shocked Horace in return for his legal services. The text celebrates Ruby for her very abasement, sexual and social; she is lauded for her subservience to the symbolic order. Not only is she a selfless mother to Lee's baby, she is the "mother" of the parodic family of bootleggers at the Old Frenchman Place.[9] In Ruby,

Faulkner collapses the stories of madonna and magdalen; she is not subject to travesty or rape, because she offers up her own body as sacrifice—it need not be conquered.

Ruby is a vehicle for the presentation of community sexual politics. A significant inversion, the "bad" woman who is really "good," she mounts a radical attack on middle-class southern (typically, in Faulkner's fiction, female-defined) "morality." She is powerless to cope with the hostility of that system, bowing down to the inevitable and vacating the Benbow house when she realizes that her presence causes offense to Narcissa in the same way she accepts Lee Goodwin's physical and verbal abuse. She does not defer to the validity of Narcissa's objections but tries to make life easier for Horace, sacrificing herself for a man. Yet while Ruby is deferential to men, she can be aggressive toward women. Her much-quoted tirade on the official frigidity of "good" women, delivered to Temple at the Old Frenchman Place, locates women in the symbolic order—sexually subjugated to men. Her words, reducing a woman to a kind of sexual addict—"You dont know what it is to be wanted by a real man"—groveling and begging for masculine abuse and penetration, are Temple Drake's first violation: rape by language (63). In the kitchen of the Old Frenchman Place cabin, Ruby and Temple swap stories of restrictive fathers and unsuitable lovers. John N. Duvall sees this as a linking of the two women expressing the similar eroticism of their family patterns and of "the father's desire" (62–65). I should like to focus on the slippage of subjectivity in this passage. Even though she speaks to Temple in the traditionally female space of the kitchen, her child at her feet, Ruby's voice oscillates between feminine and masculine situations. One minute she tells of her father's rage against her lover, echoing (and amplifying) Temple's milder, middle-class version; the next she is abusing Temple as a "doll-faced slut," constructing her rape before the fact, taking on masculine subjectivity to assault her (62).

Temple has already been victimized by male verbal attacks and the intrusive masculine gaze. We have seen how her name insists she is a sacred place; Ruskin, contemplating the home and ideal woman in "Of Queens' Gardens," speaks of a "vestal temple"; he adds, "By her office and place, she is protected from all danger and temptation" (147). But the chivalric code fails: the "Virginia gentleman" Gowan, Temple's supposed "protector," savages her: "Trying to come over me with your innocent ways. . . . You're pretty good, aren't you? Think you can play around all week with any badger-trimmed hick that owns a Ford, and fool me on Saturday, dont you?" (39). Gowan is jealous because a sexual commodity he feels he has the right to control has made herself available to other men, even if only for a car ride. It is possible that had he not been so stupefyingly drunk, he might have tried to rape Temple himself in the woods on the way to Starkeville. When he wrecks the car, Temple finds she is subject to the stares and comments of the men at the Old Frenchman Place. There she is not Miss Temple Drake, the judge's daughter, an object to be venerated, but an object to be penetrated. She is defined by her gender in the crudest sense. Tommy assesses her reproductive potential, seeing her as a piece of land to be plowed (as Judith Sutpen in *Absalom, Absalom!* was compared to a virgin field ready to be planted) saying, "He aint laid no crop by yit, has he?" (43). She tries to act the Belle with Popeye, only to be reduced again to a sexual commodity: "Make your whore lay off me, Jack," he says (53).

Temple expects Ruby, as a woman, to sympathize, to normalize and control the rapacious men outside the kitchen. "You're just like other people. With a little baby," she says, trying to construct Ruby as a young matron with bourgeois values (59). Projecting Ruby as a member of the Junior League fails, so Temple appeals to class, hoping her ladyhood, con-ferred by her father's status as a judge, friend of the governor, will save her. But had Temple read the signs around her—the ruined plantation garden, the wrecked plantation house—she would have realized that the chivalric code is bankrupt at the Old Frenchman Place. Indeed, it is on class terms that Ruby assails her: " 'Honest women. Too good to have any-thing to do with common people. You'll slip out at night with the kids, but just let a man come along.' She turned the meat. 'Take all you can get, and give nothing. "I'm a pure girl. I dont do that." You'll slip out with the kids and burn their gasoline and eat their food but just let a man so much as look at you and you faint away because your father the judge and your four brothers might not like it' " (60). Ruby's onslaught echoes the town boys who angrily mock Temple's repeated "My father's a judge," the talis-manic statement that denies them sexual access to her (31). Just as one of the town boys imitates a female voice (a "lilting falsetto") Ruby takes on a violent, attacking male tone.

Ruby and Temple seem at times to be in a kind of accord, reinforcing each other's life circumscribed by men and their threats of beatings: the story Temple tells about her college life and her family ("I'm on proba-tion and Daddy would just die") is answered by Ruby's darker version:

the family violence in Temple's narrative is exaggerated but in Ruby's it is quite real. Temple's brother Buddy isn't literally going to kill her if he catches her with a drunk man; Ruby's father does hit her and does shoot her lover. Perhaps the actual menace in Ruby's brutal life is what enables her to "cross over," to appropriate the masculine, the rapist's voice that denies woman-to-woman solidarity: "You're just scared of it. And if he is just man enough to call you whore, you'll say Yes Yes" (63). Ruby forces Temple to visualize herself humiliated "naked in the dirt and mire" and whimpering with lust and pain when she meets a "real man," someone who will abuse and violate her. Temple's frightened and fascinated response is all acquiescence: "Yes yes yes," while Ruby scorns her immaturity: "Playing at it" (64). Temple has been taught to say yes all her life, just as she has been taught she will be protected, as an upper-class virgin, by "gentlemen." In her woman's voice, fearful that Lee wants Temple for himself and perhaps feeling some sympathy for Temple, Ruby promises a car to help her escape; but by the end of the chapter she has reneged, saying coldly, "What car?" (67).

Temple is molested by Van and Popeye and menaced by Lee. The more these men terrorize her, the more mechanical, the less human, she becomes. We first see her as nymphlike, her "long legs blonde with running"; by the time of her imprisonment at the Old Frenchman Place, she runs less and less. Finally, she moves from bed to bed, vulnerable, a victim. Her status as a sexual object, raped woman *and* "whore," bodies contained and defined by the bed, is prefigured at the Old Frenchman Place, when Van bursts into her bedroom shouting, "We're bringing you a customer" (77). At the brothel she spends almost all her time in bed, asleep, drunk, or having sex with Red. The association of the bed with stasis, sleep, illness, and death (she has already been likened to an effigy) as well as sex suggest Temple is a parody of the Sleeping Beauty, confined by men to bed. As Hélène Cixous remarks: "Sleeping Beauty is lifted from her bed by a man, because, as we all know, women don't wake up by themselves: a man has to intervene, you understand. She is lifted up by the man who will lay her in her next bed so that she may be confined to bed ever after, just as the fairy tales say" (Cixous, "Castration" 43).

The community demands that Temple belong to one bed or another as sleeping virgin, ruined whore, or corpse. Horizontal, her disruptive body is less powerful, contained by the bed, controlled by father or pimp. For despite the blame heaped upon her as instigator of her own rape, destroyer of men, vampire, and liar, she is only what men have made her. As the designated work of art for the white South, the story of its decline and fall is enacted on the Belle's body. It is appropriate to a world so corrupt and antinatural that she is violated with an artificial penis, the corncob; yet almost all the men in the novel seem like potential rapists, from the town boys who mock the social status that is supposed to protect Temple; to the drunken Gowan Stevens; to Van, Popeye, and Lee at the Old Frenchman Place; to the solid citizens who assess Temple as a "good looker" and "some baby." One even says, "Jeez. I wouldn't have used no cob" (309). The bodies of women are the property of men, to be disposed of as they will. *Sanctuary* is not about ruined innocence but about the sexual violence inherent in a society built on a discourse of rape, defining women as sexual commodities to be exploited.

Temple's efficacy at the Old Frenchman place appears to diminish with every hour she is there. On the trip to Memphis, after she is raped, she exhibits signs of shock; she is described as looking like a sleepwalker, "limp" with "dazed, glassy eyes," nearly catatonic and on the edge of hysteria by turns (142, 145). Like many rape victims in real life, she is morbidly afraid of being seen by someone who knows her and so does not try to escape (something that readers, convinced she *could have* escaped, have pointed to over the years as evidence of her "willingness" to be "corrupted"). She is obsessed with blood, which she thinks is all over her clothes, as if there were an outward sign of her "fall" for all the world to see: a scarlet letter.

Temple is unable to function: she cannot even eat. At Miss Reba's "sporting house" she is put to bed with a large glass of gin and, arguably, remains drunk during her entire stay. Miss Reba "slips" her gin to calm her down, and soon she is begging, demanding it: alcohol softens the horrific edges of the reality. One might even suggest that she becomes an alcoholic; when Horace finds her she asks for a drink, and Miss Reba says, "You already had three since supper" (224). She continues to refuse food, subsisting on the gin she cajoles the maid into bringing her—and a quantity of neat gin would probably have a fairly deadening effect on a skinny teenager. Even in the much-quoted "vampire" scene in the night club where she begs Red (and Popeye) for sex, she is drunk—hardly the calculating slut Fiedler, Brooks, Vickery, and Page make her out to be. Perhaps sex is the only human contact she feels she has. Matthews and Duvall have convincingly argued that she has simply exchanged the control of one father—Judge Drake—for another, Popeye, whom she sometimes calls Daddy and who gives her clothes, locks her up, and controls her body as much as a real father. In any case, it is hard to believe that what Popeye did with his corncob was unchain the hidden nymphomaniac inside Temple so that she could wallow in her "passion" for Red; if anything, Red serves the same function as the corncob. Popeye manipulates him, "whinnying" in impotent arousal over the bedpost as he recreates Temple's rape over and over again.

By the end of the novel when she appears in court, she is deranged. She appears blank, detached: perhaps she is still drunk. This emotional unbalance might explain why she lies about Lee Goodwin's attacking her; to Temple, brutally raped and abused over and over, nearly mad, one man might look as guilty as another; and the courtroom is, after all, "a male space" (Duvall 75). Or perhaps her perjury is a perverse attempt to give power to the woman's voice in a location where the extravagant play of the fantasy rendering of the rape she gives Horace is not allowed. On the witness stand she does not seem an amoral monster of sensuality but no more in control of what is happening to her than when Popeye took her to Memphis. Her eyes are no longer "blankly right and left looking, cool, predatory and discreet," but just blank. She is "gazing like a drugged person," she looks emptied out:

> Her hands lay motionless, palm-up on her lap. Her long blonde legs slanted, lax-ankled, her two motionless slippers with their glittering buckles lay on their sides as though empty. Above the ranked intent faces white and pallid as the floating bellies of dead fish, she sat in an attitude at once detached and cringing, her gaze fixed on something at the back of the room. Her face was quite pale, the two spots of rouge like paper discs pasted on her cheek bones, her mouth painted into a savage and perfect bow, also like something both symbolical and cryptic cut carefully from purple paper and pasted there. (299)

The imagery is of emptiness, of death and artificiality. She is silenced, *absent*: "From a short distance her eyes, the two spots of rouge and her mouth, were like meaningless objects in a small heart-shaped dish" (301). Temple Drake is, if not insane, so divorced from reality, so estranged from her own body that even her features have lost meaning and order.

Temple's resistance in the brothel is muted, her voice barely heard. But from the time of her first rape, what little she *has* said—from being obsessed with her bleeding and fearing someone she knew would see her, to demanding gin with which to anesthetize herself—has been a chilling protest at her disintegration. The reader witnesses not the Angel in the House turning into the devil on the dance floor, but the mental and physical dissolution of a woman who *does* resist, though the text of her resistance, reported to us in chapter 23 through Horace Benbow's suspect, upper-class, "gentlemanly" horror, is often taken as "mere" fiction. But it is a fiction she makes trying to save her life.

The story she tells Horace Benbow at Miss Reba's reveals the extent of her disorientation and retreat into disguise and fantasy. Horace, the masculine subject who tends to force his view on the reader, dismisses what she tells him as "one of those bright, chatty monologues which women carry on when they realize that they have the center of the stage"; he thinks she shows "actual pride" in her ordeal, fictionalizing it, telling the story "as though she were making it up" (226). Obsessed with the purity (and impurity) of young women, Horace finds the "ease" with which Temple tells her terrible tale disgusting: surely a lady would not even be able to form the words to describe such a nightmare—he half believes a lady should not be able to live through such an experience: "Better for her if she were dead tonight" (232).

However, Horace's credentials as an authority on and worshiper of southern ladyhood are impaired by his unadmitted arousal at the thought of Little Belle and his semiviolent erotic dream about a merged Temple/Little Belle where the gender shifts in midsentence along with the orifice that emits a dark fluid. While Horace temporarily occupies a feminine space here as the rape victim, in the original version of *Sanctuary* Horace has another fantasy, this time of assaulting Temple in the courtroom, thinking with "raging pleasure" of "stripping her: This is what a man has killed another over. This, the offspring of respectable people: let them blush for shame" (255).[10] The image recalls Ruby's picture of Temple naked in the dirt, utterly exposed as "merely" a female body, not worth a man's life, not worth suffering over or building chivalric constructs upon.

Horace is handicapped by bad faith and rage against the female body. Thus, he cannot discern that the "naive and impersonal vanity" he condemns in Temple is an attempt to deny the unbearable fact of violation. In her story Temple reconstructs herself into a series of bodies less vulnerable to rape than her own. Temple's gender, like Ruby's and Horace's, is subject to slippage: "You got a boy's name, ain't you?" says Miss Reba while Temple bleeds from her unnatural defloration. Temple is androgynous, yet her body is subject to the abuses particular to women. Her story underlines her vacillating gender. First, she says she tried to "make like" she was a boy; then she conjures up a chastity belt with spikes, "and he wouldn't know till it was too late and I'd jab it into him" (228). In both cases, she imaginatively appropriates a penis; she would not only be safe with a penis, she could "jab" Popeye, taking on the power and authority of a man. Yet as Popeye molests her, putting his hand down her knickers, she changes her fantasy, now constructing herself as a dead bride, then an "old maid" school teacher with "iron-gray hair and spectacles . . . all big up here like women get" (230). While it is curious that Temple envisions the "old maid" as big-breasted—an image of voluptuousness—the picture is of sexual inaccessibility, safety. She changes her mind again, retreating into maleness by constructing herself as an old man with a long white beard, finally growing a penis: "It made a kind of plopping sound. . . . I lay right still to keep from laughing about how surprised he was going to be" (231). After recounting this ludicrous scene she says, incredibly, that she went to sleep: "I couldn't even feel myself jerking in front of his hand, but I could hear the shucks. I didn't wake up until that woman came" (231).

Like Clarissa Harlowe, Temple is raped while unconscious as if to disassociate her body from her self. Her story exposes this dislocation; while "truth" in the form of rape—perhaps the ultimate, basic, biological reality for Faulkner—is being inscribed on her body, she creates an elaborate fiction to displace it, presiding over her own metamorphoses. Her taunting Popeye, "Touch me! You're a coward if you dont. Coward! Coward!" is often read as a desire for sex; but maybe it is part of Temple's "masculine" discourse in her fantasy, the boy's bravado daring another to fight him (229). What Horace Benbow hears as "pride" and "vanity" are actually attempts to decenter herself as the victim of this assault. By telling her story her way, Temple gains a measure of control over something she has not been able to control: the violence done her. By "making it up," she places the horror outside herself. Only in the fiction can she continue to function.

Neither the masculine nor the feminine voice emerges triumphant at the end of Sanctuary. Temple is assaulted once more in the courtroom when the district attorney holds up the bloody corncob like a tumescent phallus while telling Temple's story for her. She does not control her own discourse but appears as a character—even a commodity—in an Old South fantasy about "the most sacred affairs of that most sacred thing in life: womanhood" (298). Having made a valiant bid for autonomy in her protean story, Temple is finally subdued by the phallus. Vacant, nearly speechless, she is passed back to the control of her father and brothers (described as "erect" three times) whose bodies cover hers as they take her away (304–5).[11]

But Horace is drawn back to the vagina. He returns home to Kinston, a town in the Delta, a female space, "flat and rich and foul," reflective of Belle's own body (16). Horace, the champion of purity, of southern chivalry, failed to prevent any of the multiple rapes of the novel; in the end, he himself is menaced by rape. The mob has lynched, perhaps castrated Lee Goodwin: when they see Horace, they threaten, "Do to the lawyer what we did to him. What he did to her. Only we never used a cob. We made him wish we had used a cob" (311). The implication is that Goodwin was somehow raped: the mob voice echoes what the town voice says of Temple: "I wouldnt have used no cob" (309). Horace is finally feminized, his body endangered. The narrative does not reveal how he escapes, but he is next seen locking the back door of his pink-shaded house (suggestive of female genital space) while Belle awaits him in bed. His male subject position has been returned to him, but he seems nonetheless powerless; the competing imperatives of masculine and feminine are left at impasse in *Sanctuary*, the threat of rape enclosing all bodies.

Perhaps the strangest thing about Temple's strange rape and Lee Goodwin's lynching is that nowhere in this world where women's bodies are under threat does a black man appear in his usual role as rapist. Popeye is described as "black," but he is not a black man. Goodwin is white. Red is white. Yet I somehow suspect that while Faulkner consciously wanted to turn away from the South's habitual reading of rape as black (which, of course, he deals with more fully in *Light in August*) the context of spectacular lynchings in 1918, 1920, 1925, and so on in Mississippi, mostly carried out to protect "that most sacred thing in life," white womanhood, is the symbolic underpinning of *Sanctuary*. The way Faulkner writes it, violence becomes less a race than a gender issue. But *Sanctuary* remains a fiction produced out of a world controlled by violence where women were always potential victims.

Helen's Monster Child

Caddy Compson, Narcissa Benbow, and Temple Drake inhabit fictions where there are strict, articulated, traditional parameters for white bourgeois female behavior. They conform to, or rebel against, ladyhood: discourses of class, race, and gender that are the background noise of their lives, that have shaped (or warped) them, even victimized them. Linda Snopes Kohl, though a young woman—a young "lady," even—brought up in the same Jefferson where Narcissa floated in her white dresses, Caddy was ostracized from her own family for having lovers, and Temple considered "ruined," is *not* victimized by the culture of violence that keeps women in their place. She is an avenger. Unique among Faulkner's women, Linda, not a father, husband, or brother, controls and expresses her own body and gets away with it. She is the most powerful of Faulkner's female characters, a radical, a "killer" who does not allow community fictions about the feminine (most specifically Gavin Stevens's fictions about the feminine) to contain and limit her. The world of The Mansion (1959), last but one of Faulkner's novels, is reduced and fragmented: the Old South is found only in traces or else in Hollywood-inspired reinventions like the huge white columns Flem Snopes has stuck on the front of the de Spain house. Linda "perhaps had left the South too young too long ago" to have to be a Belle (358). As Hee Kang, in a Derridian reading of the Snopes trilogy, has said, Linda is "a new configuration of Faulkner's feminine" (129).

Linda is the anti-Belle. Her mother, Eula, was a kind of Olympian parody of the notion of bellehood, a woman so beautiful and so desirable that men practically fainted with desire when they saw her. Eula's profoundly apparent sexuality disrupts the image of the white lady on the pedestal—seamless, cold, untouchable. Her body seemed to signal the opposite. Linda, however, is in control of her body: it is simultaneously sexual and unavailable, though only because she chooses. Her very name begs an ironic reading of her position in regard to white southern womanhood: *belle* means "beautiful," of course; *Linda* means "pretty." Linda seems a name for a Belle, for a *princesse lointaine* like Melisandre Backus, yet Linda is not pretty, not reducible to a single trait, an admired appearance but a person of much complexity, unassimilable into the usual categories used to divide and conquer in the southern symbolic order.

Linda, like Drusilla Hawk, forces a category crisis in Jefferson. Indeed, there is an implied comparison between them when V. K. Ratliff says (quite incorrectly) that Linda is "the first female girl soldier we ever had" (109). It is true that history is not the presence in The Mansion that it is in so many of Faulkner's other novels; in The Mansion the past is almost unavailable. Yet surely Faulkner remembered Drusilla when he was writing

Linda, sending her off to fight for what she believed in, even though Drusilla's cause was reactionary and Linda's liberal. Like Drusilla, Linda slips between masculine and feminine. She cross-dresses in her khaki overalls, and she takes on a masculine job, working in the ship factory in Pascagoula. Yet she feels, and expresses, desire as a woman for Gavin as a man. Her body is a matter for much speculation, especially for Chick Mallison, who thinks she is "too tall to have shape" while also thinking about ways to "get her clothes off her." No committee of middle-class town ladies comes to force her back into what they consider the proper gender, as they did Drusilla. Linda gets away with moving in and out of masculine and feminine, just as she gets away with being a political activist. Her "meddling with the Negroes," trying to improve the lives of Jefferson's blacks under Jim Crow, connects her with another manlike political activist, Miss Joanna Burden (The Mansion 222). But Linda's transgressions into the forbidden territory of a white woman consorting with blacks is not punished by violence the way Joanna Burden's is. A cross is burned on her (Flem's) lawn and "Nigger Lover" graffiti scrawled on the sidewalk. But Linda is uncowed.

Linda is anomalous in Jefferson; in a sense, she is nameless. "Linda" seems incongruous, even ironic. She is not a "pretty girl" any more than she is a sacred space to be defiled or a flower to be deflowered like Temple and Narcissa. Kohl is her dead husband's name, alien and difficult for the Jeffersonians (except Gavin) to pronounce correctly.[12] "Snopes" is a legal fiction: Linda's real father was called McCarron. Linda's inappropriate or unstable names might lead us to read her as another one of Faulkner's fictive women created out of the discourses, the voices that surround her. After all, she does not participate directly in the narrative of The Mansion the way Gavin, Charles, and V. K. Ratliff do. They are the filter through which she is presented; yet she somehow eludes being reduced to their "readings" of her, whether it is Charles seeing her as a mannish body that he would nonetheless like, as he puts it with swaggering undergraduate crudity to his uncle, to "lay"; or V. K., who sees her as a destructive force who will endanger Gavin; or Gavin himself, who sees Linda in some ways as his creation. He gives her books to read, quizzes her on them, plans to send her off to a Seven Sisters college, and, when that fails, seizes the first opportunity (which is Eula's death) to get her out of Jefferson, out of the South, all the way up to Greenwich Village, where she can become a radical and an activist amongst the fashionable Left of the 1930s.

It wasn't, as V. K. says, "jest to train her up and marry her" (137). Gavin's purpose has more to do with an attempt to remake the world according to his dictates—especially to remake women. He could not shape Eula, her mother: she was far more powerful than he. But Gavin (erroneously) sees Linda as a tabula rasa: southern culture, the whole "gentlemanly" tradition Gavin represents, saw young women as blank pages or "blank spaces," as Judith Sutpen is called, to be marked by a man.

So Gavin means to "mark" Linda's mind with his prescribed reading "until somebody would find her and marry her and she would be gone for good," as V. K. says (137). Gavin assumes her passivity: she reads what he gives her; she will be "found" by a man who would want to marry her. If the operative myth for Eula was Venus, Vulcan, and Mars, the operative myth for Gavin must be Pygmalion and Galatea. Gavin thinks he is "making" the perfect woman; yet when she comes to life and comes of age, she has a mind and a will of her own.

Linda is implicitly compared with another one of Gavin's works of art, Melisandre Backus. Before Linda came along, she was Gavin's educational project: "Melisandre was twelve and thirteen and fourteen several years before she vacated for Linda to take her turn in the vacuum, Gavin selecting and ordering the books of poetry to read to Melisandre or anyway supervise and check on" (194). Melisandre is a much more satisfactory objet d'art than Linda, so much so that Gavin marries her instead. There are a number of reasons for this, some of which I will discuss a little later. But perhaps Melisandre was a better creation because of her culturally mandated blankness. She was, as we are told in Knight's Gambit, raised in a "windless and timeless garden," a flower of the plantation, a lady of the Old South whose father was a cliché of a cotton planter sitting on his veranda with his bourbon, reading Latin poetry (233). Melisandre seems an anachronism, a figure of nostalgia for the southern lady as represented by the classical body. Her brush with modernity comes in her reported, not seen, marriage to the New Orleans underworld boss Harriss. Yet he is only a name here, a sort of Riviera Snopes who, like Flem, found the old gentleman's house he acquired insufficiently grand and imposing and proceeded, as Flem did with the de Spain place, to Tara-fy it. The "windless and timeless garden" of Melisandre's childhood recalls the "walled and windless garden" of Narcissa Benbow's childhood and the garden in The Marionettes, the hortus conclusus in which the virgin sits waiting. Melisandre takes us back to the very beginning of Faulkner's career—

even her name is out of the *symboliste* work he admired (and copied) as a young man: Melisande is the heroine of Maeterlinck's 1892 play *Pelléas et Mélisande*.

Perhaps Melisandre is easier for Gavin to marry because she is, like him, a product of the plantation class. Despite her new money, her family is like the Stevenses and the de Spains, the Holstons and the Sartorises: she has not been defiled, nor has she strayed from being a lady. Linda, however, is not a product of a southern ladylike upbringing, despite the books of poetry (doubtless some of the same ones given to Melisandre) Gavin has fed her on. She belongs to a new generation and a new world in which the old class distinctions begin to break down. Perhaps the Snopes in her name is a signal, after all, of her participation in the destruction of the Old South. Of all Faulkner's novels, *The Mansion* has the most sense of the South as part of America and the immense political and social changes that were happening in the thirties, forties, and fifties. Faulkner writes of the KKK, of the Red Scare, of American participation in the Spanish civil war, of growing rights for women, the beginnings of the civil rights movement, and so on. Far more than Joanna Burden, Linda is an activist: her motives, unlike Joanna Burden's, are not travestied as spinsterish Calvinism or sexual repression. While Gavin, Charles, V. K., and the "Faulkner" narrative voice might find her politics anything from bizarre to silly, Linda herself is not punished for having politics in the first place.

It is a commonplace to say that the Nobel Prize brought Faulkner "out" of the South and "in" to the world with an awareness of larger social changes and a sense of commitment to humanity in general. I have been trying to show that Faulkner was engaged with his society and his time all along. It is true, however, that beginning with *Intruder in the Dust* (1949), his fictions take on problems such as segregation and lynching more overtly, perhaps because the social control exerted by the culture of violence and the fiction of racial absolutism was unraveling in a spectacular and obvious way. By 1959 the battle of the Montgomery bus boycott had been fought and won, Martin Luther King, Jr., was president of the Southern Christian Leadership Conference, and the Supreme Court had ordered that public schools be integrated "with all deliberate speed." Autherine Lucy became the first black student at the University of Alabama, and even Mississippians could see that the day when the University of Mississippi—that bastion of Old South iconography where the sports teams are called Rebels, the Confederate battle flag is flown, and the nickname is the same as the senior lady of the plantation, "Ole Miss"—would be integrated soon.

The Lucy case in 1956 was a pivotal moment for the South, both for its sense of panic over integration and for its image in the rest of the world. The public statements Faulkner made about Autherine Lucy and the whole issue of integration between 1955 and 1959 are ambivalent and sometimes contradictory. He expressed sympathy with Lucy herself but not with the NAACP, which he practically accused of conspiring to get her killed by "forcing" her to go back to Tuscaloosa after the university suspended her "for her own good" (Blotner 1591).[13] Faulkner was always suspicious of political activists and particularly unsympathetic toward black organizations such as the SCLC and the NAACP.[14] He gave interviews in which sometimes he argued for tolerance and the inevitability of integration and other times he echoed the "separate but equal" rhetoric the South had armed itself with since Plessy v. Ferguson. In a "background" conversation before appearing on a radio show in 1956, Faulkner maintained that the South's racial problems could be solved if blacks could get a good education in segregated schools, that integration would be successful in a hundred years or so, and that in five hundred years blacks would have been "assimilated" into the white race (Blotner 1592).

Though The Mansion takes place in the thirties and forties, its social concerns place it firmly in the decade that produced it, reflecting Faulkner's vexed attitudes to the compelling debates over race and gender that seized the nation. Linda represents an intersection of southern cultural anxieties: the New Woman who so exercised the crude antifeminism of the thirties, forties, and fifties, the female equivalent of the New Negro—assertive, demanding, and without the constraints of a father or husband to control her; the civil rights activist working for integration; and the communist, theoretically at least dedicated to overthrowing capitalism.

Looking at the ways the novel's narratives present this anti-Belle, Linda the independent woman gets away with her self-determination, perhaps because she officially has a father in whose house she lives, though only because of her acceptance of the fiction of their relationship. Linda the communist gets away with her radicalism, perhaps because the Spanish civil war seemed a romantic cause, a poet's battle, the passion of Ernest Hemingway and Garcia Lorca. This is most interesting, given that in the early fifties, American society was terrorized by the specter of secret communism; here, Faulkner makes gentle fun of both Linda's attempt to find comrades in Jefferson, Mississippi (the two Finns she talks Marx with eventually become, according to Charles, rich capitalists) and of the FBI's ridiculous investigation of her.

Linda's civil rights activism does not fare so well, however. The way Charles describes it fits all too comfortably with Faulkner's gradualist worries over too much talk of equality. In a rather outrageous scene re-invented by Charles, the black high school principal comes to see Gavin and begs him to make Linda "let us alone" (225). She is made out to be a goodhearted but foolish white liberal. Even the racist graffiti, the burning cross, and the repeated combinations of "KOHL COMMUNIST JEW" scrawled on the sidewalk are seen as harmless: perhaps Flem himself did it, Charles suggests, but at least no one would really dare to harm her because she was "the daughter of not just a banker but THE banker" in town (227–28). This seems both condescending and willfully blind, given the many people terrorized and killed even in the short time the civil rights movement had been prominent. But it undoubtedly reflects Faulkner's ambivalence toward the issue of the South, race, and "outside agitators."

After the war Charles can't figure out why Linda would come back to Jefferson, since "there was nothing for [her] to tilt against now" (351). Postwar prosperity has supposedly "solved" the problems on the liberal list: "And as for the Negroes, by now they had a newer and better high school building in Jefferson than the white folks had. . . . double-plus the new social-revolution laws which had abolished not merely hunger and inequality and injustice, but work too" (350–51). This is meant to be con-servative irony directed at antiracist legislation and the welfare state, an attempt to foreclose on any serious discussion of civil rights and social change in the South. Linda cannot change the world. Faulkner's narrative simply ignores both the actuality of the growing civil rights movement in the late forties and the violent racial upheaval in the late fifties to suggest that Linda's agenda no longer exists.

Yet this removal of Linda's political dangerousness does not absolve her of sexual dangerousness. If her nearly ridiculed concerns reflect the social concerns of the time, her sexual autonomy may reflect Faulkner's own liaisons with independent young women like Joan Williams and Jean Stein, young women whom he would attempt to mentor and who would then leave him.[15] Alone of Faulkner's women, Linda "is no longer the ob-ject of exchange in the men's market"; she is a free agent able to choose how to dispose of her body (Kang 132).

Linda makes her desire clear. Her mother, Eula, had once "offered" herself to Gavin because she felt compassion for him and because sex was seen to be as natural as breathing for her. When Linda wants to make love to Gavin she simply says so, yet because he is the transcriber of the conversation he suppresses the operative word: " 'But you can   me,' she said" (238). His shock at hearing her say fuck is similar to the shock felt by Horace Benbow when he hears Temple Drake tell the story of her rape and imprisonment with its paradoxical directness and lacunae. The word sets Linda forever apart from Melisandre Backus and the whole edifice of acceptable white southern female behavior: "*I am old fashioned it still shocks me a little No what shocks is when a woman uses it & is not shocked at all until she realises I am*" (239). Linda's response is, "All right. . . . Dont use any word then" (239).

Gavin is incapable of dealing with mature sexuality. As Ratliff is always pointing out, his interest is best held by adolescent girls with whom he has teacher-pupil relationships. Linda grows up, and so she is spoiled for him. Melisandre, despite her gangster husband and two children, remains curiously the little girl from the old-fashioned plantation. When Gavin is forced to confront Linda's reality as an independent, sexual woman, he either ignores her desire or tries to turn her back into a child. At the end when he has realized that she planned Flem's murder and manipulated him all along, he infantilizes her: "Touching her, learning and knowing not with despair or grief but just sorrow a little, simply supporting her buttocks as you cup the innocent hipless bottom of a child," despite the fact that her lipstick is making his mouth a mess of red—the mark of Venus (424).

Despite Linda's "bald unlovely" word, Gavin fails to understand her, taking refuge in chivalric rhetoric about how they are "the 2 in all the world who can love each other without having to," and again the word fuck is suppressed, leaving a gap in the text. In "Le facteur de la vérité" Derrida suggests that the empty space, the "hole," of discourse represents the feminine, "the metaphor of truth" (441). Hélène Cixous prefers to see the feminine voice as a new language that the woman makes hers, "containing it, taking it in her own mouth, biting that tongue with her very own teeth to invent for herself a language to get inside of" ("Laugh" 257). Linda makes a new language for herself, literally with a voice unlike anyone else's, the "duck quack," as Charles describes it, that sounds so unlovely, so *unfeminine* to Gavin. The new language she makes sets her apart from everyone else but also makes her powerful. She inherits masculine discourse; in a sense she is given it the way Gavin gives her the little pad and pencil to communicate with. The pad has thin ivory leaves "with gold corners, on little gold rings to turn the pages, with a little gold stylus thing to match," a feminine object that Charles sneers at, saying you can write on it then erase your writing "with a handkerchief or a piece of tissue or, in a mere masculine emergency, a little spit on your thumb" (216). Yet what is important about this prissy gift is that Linda can efface Gavin's words with her own; she can control the conversation. She is free.[16]

Linda escapes the shaping (or warping) not only of the masculine voice in general but of the southern voice in particular. Charles points out how she had left the South too young to become socialized by it, to "have formed the Southern female habit-rite of a cavalier's unflagging constancy" (358). He is thoroughly confused by her: on their "dates" she opens car doors for herself and seems to treat him not as a potential sexual partner but simply as a companion. He reads her "difference" as a product of the silent world in which she lives, curiously masculine to him. He says she is "castrate of sound, circumcised from having to hear" (211). She has not heard the behaviors the South expects of women, she has not heard the masculine discourse that would enforce ladyhood on her.

Freed from the dominant language of her culture, Linda can pursue her own power. Instead of being a creature of the fiction Gavin builds around her, she makes him a creature of her own story. She urges Gavin to marry—insists that he marry—and he does marry the acceptable Melisandre Backus, his ladylike work of art. Charles recognizes that Linda had a hand in creating this fiction, as if she "herself had actually invented the whole business: his Uncle Gavin, his Aunt Melisandre, Rose Hill" (357). Freed from the constrictions of middle-class white life in the South, Linda can "write" it for others. She marks Gavin as much as or more than he marked her with his books: he gives her the power to override his language with the ivory pad, and she gives him a gold cigarette lighter with his initials and, most significantly, hers interposed as if she had placed herself inside him, a reversal of the usual narrative of penetration: GLS. In a novel of initials and letters standing for institutions—VK, FBI, KKK, FDR, LLB, IWW, CIO, NRA, POW—GLS signifies Linda's control of the narrative. She follows an alternate story than the one Gavin picks out for her, pursuing her revenge against her "father" Flem for the way he destroyed her mother and tried to circumscribe her, a story Gavin prefers to see as a blank, just as he left the word fuck as a blank. Yet in the end she insists that he know the truth, marking him again with her voice, just as she injected her name into his. Linda escapes the South and its discourses, leaving Gavin and his romantic constructs about women behind.

Linda is a kind of monster, a woman not represented by the classical body that signifies the white woman of the South, nor yet the grotesque body that signifies the black woman. She is even called a monster as the town collectively looks "at Eula Varner's child with a kind of amazement, like at some minute-sized monster" (114). Masterless, fatherless, without a stable name, able to move between genders without being destroyed, Linda testifies to Faulkner's final ability to imagine a woman not shaped by the magisterial contexts of southern culture. In herself, she is revenge for all the titles—Aphrodite, Lilith, Helen—heaped upon her silenced mother.

5 The Night Sister

Poor barren woman.—*William Faulkner,* LIGHT IN AUGUST

The Spinster in the Mind of the South

The unmarried white woman in southern culture inhabits what looks like a small, insignificant corner of the edifice of official virginity. I should stress that in this chapter I am speaking only of white women: unmarried black women occupy a completely different sphere of female sexuality as imagined by the culture. Their blackness is far more important than their marital status. But white women posed a problem for the symbolic order. A woman past marriageable age in the Old South (over thirty), was often relegated to menial family duties, marginalized. Wyatt-Brown remarks that southerners saw the spinster as doubly cursed, deprived of both husband and children, experiencing "a form of social death" (238). It was thought that no southern white woman of any class would choose the "maiden's estate" as it automatically deprived her of status and security, rendering her peripheral to and powerless in her society. According to Mary Anne Ferguson, "With very few exceptions the old maid—a single woman beyond the marriageable age of, say, thirty—has been either pitied or ridiculed in literature. . . . a single woman who remains single in society is seen as queer, frequently thin and emaciated to symbolize her withdrawal from life" (8).

The Old Maid is not an empty vessel the way a young virgin is an empty vessel, expectantly waiting to be "filled" by a man; the unmarried woman's childlessness and manlessness push her to the edge of society. This might seem to make her even less effectual, even more limited by her peripheral place, but in Faulkner's fiction it can be a form of liberation. The spinster evades or reinvents the expressions of the feminine decreed by the symbolic order. Miss Sophonsiba in "Was" is a parody of the Belle with her roan tooth, suffocating perfume, snobbery, and coquetry; yet she sets out to get Buck McCaslin and succeeds. She is travestied by her own brother as the "bear" in "bear country," compared with an animal; still, she "wins" on her own terms.

Faulkner's other unmarried white women exhibit a less comic vision of the single existence. Miss Zilphia Gant, Miss Emily Grierson, Miss Rosa Coldfield, Miss Minnie Cooper, and Miss Joanna Burden—the formal title "Miss" erects a kind of barrier, emphasizing the closed, singular body of the unmarried woman—in some ways reflect and perpetuate the image of the maladjusted, predatory, manless woman judged by her access to or denial of "normal" sexual relations or the possibility of marriage, marginal to the favored definitions of the feminine in the South. Despite this (or because of it, maybe) they are dangerous women literally on the edge, who construct and, to some extent, control fictions that shape their world. By "fictions" I do not mean lies, but stories that speak their own desire, their own sexuality—sometimes their bisexuality.

The precarious, low-status position of the single woman, like so many of Faulkner's other female characters, can create a "category crisis" over sexual and racial definition. Faulkner's spinsters force a "conversation" between two dominant convictions: that superannuated virgins are sexually frustrated—they "need" a man—and that black men rape—particularly white women. Light in August subverts this racist donnée by interrogating the categories of "black man" and "white woman" in a baroque play of sexuality, gender, race, and class. In Absalom, Absalom! the bisexuality of the spinster likewise intersects with the mulatto spaces of the narrative, challenging southern culture's stories about its women. Does heroic virginity—integrity of body and spirit—belong only to women of the pre–Civil War past? Women navigate between the Scylla and Charybdis of absolute purity and absolute promiscuity the way mulattoes and mulattas negotiate the space between blackness and whiteness. The unmarried woman would seem to be safe on her half of the divide, protected by her virginity and her whiteness, but once again, two states not thought capable of existing in the same space begin to tumble toward one another, and the single woman becomes the embodiment of another pressure point in the South's psychosexual disintegration, another dangerous body that rises up to speak.

It is not accidental that Faulkner chooses two relatively powerless but highly mythologized characters from the southern repertoire to dramatize racial and sexual hypocrisy. The conjunction of black man and white woman (especially white virgin) had really been predetermined by the culture's anxiety over the rape of white women by black men. The fear of violent miscegenation, of chaotic "negro" sexuality, and of "social equality" lies behind the program of segregation, the renewed insistence on rigid definition of gender and race roles, and the campaign of lynching that terrorized the South from the late 1870s through to the 1960s. Faulkner's 1930s stories of white women's desire for black men and southern society's murderous responses are fired by what was going on in the South at the time: lynchings in Mississippi occurred practically every year. In 1934, two years after *Light in August* and two years before *Absalom, Absalom!* were published, Claud Neal, accused of raping and murdering Lola Cannidy, a young white girl in Marianna, Florida, was tortured, mutilated, forced to eat his own penis, then hanged. What made this famous case even more troubling is that a preliminary medical examination suggested that Lola Cannidy had not been raped, and a subsequent rumor suggested she'd been having an affair with Neal, a man she'd known all her life (McGovern 46). The psychosexual fears that ignite lynchings spring from myths about race and sexuality, about black men and white women. I will return to the Neal case in the discussion of *Light in August*; for now, it is sufficient to say that Faulkner's fiction in the thirties reflects the climate of racial and sexual terrorism. His work tries to understand and, in a way, contain the terror through a shift in the blame from black man to white woman.

There is an interesting paucity of Old Maids in southern female hagiography, but those there are get the job of telling the histories of their families and their region. The ideology of the plantation rests in their keeping. Thomas Nelson Page's *Red Rock* (1898) celebrates a sinewy old Confederate Woman, Miss Thomasia, much admired for her near-male toughness, yet never masculine. Other characters praise her, saying of her kind, "The mould's broken" (255). She is the curator of family legends, recalling maiden aunts like Miss Rachel in *Waverley*, who indoctrinates her nephew with tales of Waverley chivalry, just as the exemplary Confederate Woman Miss Jenny tells and retells the Sartoris myth to young Bayard in *Flags in the Dust*.

Outside the cult of the Lost Cause, which seeks to absolve women from sexuality, remaining unmarried is nearly always seen as disabling. Strategies for existence as an unmarried woman are not prominent in Victorian culture, especially in the South, where marriage was not only socially desirable but an economic imperative: few "careers" existed for white women. Among young upper-class women marriage was the only legitimate goal, and after marriage, children. Despite the catastrophic immediacy of the Civil War, courting, engagements, weddings, and dynastic alliances occupy the most space in Mary Boykin Chesnut's diary. She spends more time on General Hood's wooing of Sally Preston than she does on any military exploits and economic hardships. There are very few older unmarried women in her pages; since they were socially peripheral, they figured less obviously in Confederate court circles. Virginia Tunstall Clay's lengthy memoir devotes exactly seventeen pages to her life before marriage to C. C. Clay. Maidenhood, even in "belleship," is a state of becoming, not being, a progress toward completion in wifehood. With a husband's name, even a dead husband's, a woman could take on some of his power in the community: she was a filled vessel, a *defined* person.

In southern fiction there was some resistance to the inevitability of marriage if no serious rebellion against it. Augusta Jane Evans's heroine Beulah, in the 1859 novel of that name, works to educate herself, becoming independent as a teacher, wary of losing her freedom to a man. She is brought around, rather abruptly and reluctantly, to marriage in the end, reflecting what Judith Lowder Newton calls the "deformation of the marriage plot" common in nineteenth-century women's writing (78). In novels by men, the marriage plot tends to operate smoothly; spinsters are ridiculed or "converted." Here Beulah resists, even when told to "quit this horrid nonsense about working and being independent" (Evans, *Beulah* 216). As Beulah, finally unhappy and ill in her solitary freedom, surrenders to her former guardian, he says: "Beulah Benton, do you belong to the tyrant Ambition, or do you belong to that tyrant Guy Hartwell?" (500). Her choice is either misery in servitude to an abstract ideal or "fulfillment" in servitude to a man. A single woman is an anomaly: she must be "owned" by one side or another: moreover, she must be silenced. Beulah, and Edna in Evans's 1867 novel *St. Elmo*, cease writing in submission to their husbands.

Evans's wartime novel *Macaria* (1864) is one of the few that depict a life outside of marriage for young women. Of course, it is by necessity, not choice: all the young men die fighting for the "holy cause." The subtitle "Altars of Sacrifice" indicates the self-denial demanded of the southern woman. Irene and Electra end up not absorbed into marriage and dependent upon husbands but subservient to an equally masculine ideology: an idealized national spirit. Brides of the Dixie Christ, they reside together in a celibacy celebrated as patriotic, not perverse. They consign their identities to the male war myth, sitting "mute and resigned at the foot of the Red Dripping Altar of Patriotism" (326). Though they are able to "speak" through their art, they simply chant the masculine ideology of patriotism.

Marriage as a goal, an indication of "participation" in life, remained strong in the southern sensibility, even among feminist writers like Ellen Glasgow. Molly, the independent heroine of *The Miller of Old Church* (1911), declares she does not want to marry. The earthy Mrs. Bottom tells her, "A single woman's a terrible lonesome body, Molly," but it takes her sudden understanding of the genuine Old Maid of the novel, Miss Kesiah, to bring Molly to the truth of her need for conjugal love and a proper horror of being an un(re)productive body, a childless virgin (119). Molly sees in Miss Kesiah an "expression of useless knowledge and regret, as though she realized that she had missed the essential thing and that it was life, after all, that had been to blame for it. For a minute only the look lasted for Kesiah was a closed soul and the smallest revelation of herself was like the agony of travail" (338). The creation of a self is compared to childbirth, the "womanly" act Miss Kesiah will never know. Despite Glasgow's critical view of marriage, the "closed soul" (and closed body) is not presented as a better alternative.

Women who almost reject marriage (and men), then do not, are seen to be "saved." But there are always some women who are not "chosen." They are constructed as pathetic, sometimes weak. Louisa May Alcott sums up the popular attitude:

> Don't laugh at the spinsters, dear girls, for often very tender, tragical romances are hidden away in the hearts that beat so quietly under the sober gowns, and many silent sacrifices of youth, health, ambition, love itself, make the faded faces beautiful in God's sight. Even the sad, sour sisters should be kindly dealt with, because they have missed the sweetest part of life, if for no other reason; and, looking

at them with compassion, not contempt, girls in their gloom should remember that they too may miss the blossom time.[1]

In other words, some of those spinsters *have* received a measure of definition in their possible "tragical romances" with long lost men, but because they have missed the imprint of marriage, "the sweetest part of life," they are necessarily pitiable, their feminine "value" diminished.

Like masterless slaves, unmarried women can be perceived as a threat to the conventional order: "When women reject these roles, refusing to direct their primary attention toward a man, his home, and his children, they are often stigmatized. A woman who does not seek her identity through association with a male seems to threaten the social value system" (Duberman 20).

In the South any challenge white women and blacks might have made to the representations that imprisoned them was thwarted by the way these two powerless groups were made out to be natural enemies. There evolved a peculiar response to this threat to plantation ideology, a way of psychically punishing especially single women that became a major theme in postbellum writing. As southern culture had always encouraged the displacement of white women's sexuality onto black women, at a crucial moment in history it also encouraged the displacement of white men's sexuality onto black men. Where before the war only a few proslavery polemicists raised the specter of the black slave rapist (generally in response to the Denmark Vesey and Nat Turner rebellions), now free black men were pictured as animals lusting concertedly and undeviatingly after white women. Southern sexual anxiety shifted somewhat from the black female harem on the plantation (though black women were still sexually exploited by white men) to the lone freedman lurking in the night. The culture swiftly erected new stories about black sexual atrocities, then created ways—the Ku Klux Klan, founded in 1866, for example—of dealing with them.

The uncomfortable fact was that manless white women and masterless blacks now inhabited the South. The preponderance of the two groups antebellum southern patriarchy had expended a great deal of energy to contain posed a serious menace to the symbolic (and social) order. Representing the two as absolute enemies became central to a racist mythology that operates even now. George Fitzhugh in *Sociology for the South* (1854) had declared: "Women, like children, have but one right, and that is the right to protection" (214). But the men, the instruments of "protection," were dead, and the women were living alone: the fabric of southern society was shredded, and paranoia increased. The emancipated black man turned into the "bad nigger," the rapist who became an emblem of the anarchic forces at work in the Reconstruction South, a terrifying indication of the shaky state of southern patriarchy. Rape replaced war as the new terror visited on the South and its women, especially its single women.

White women's inaccessibility symbolically reinforced the sense of an inviolate land. The white woman with no man (husband, father, son, brother) to protect her was, according to plantation ideology, at risk of becoming an object of black vengeance, of experiencing individually what the land had experienced collectively: rape was the habitual metaphor for the "invasion" of the South. This served southern nationalism in Reconstruction and the later buildup of legal segregation. It is no coincidence that James McGovern, writing of the Claud Neal case, found that the local people talking of the Battle of Marianna and how Union troops, including the Eighty-second and Eighty-sixth Negro regiments, "took" the town connected that "rape" with what happened to Lola Cannidy (McGovern 18).

The Ku Klux Klan novels of Thomas Dixon, Jr., *The Leopard's Spots* (1902), *The Clansman* (1905), and *The Traitor* (1907), reflect, in the most lurid manner, the postbellum obsession with black ravishment of white virgins. In *The Leopard's Spots*, Flora Camp, daughter of a lame Confederate veteran, is attacked by a black man and found in the woods by her father, who had previously insisted that he would rather see his child dead than "polluted" by a "nigger beast" (a common white male sentiment of the time, expressed everywhere from pulpits to the Senate floor in Washington). She has been raped: "Down her little white bare leg was still running fresh and warm the tiniest scarlet thread of blood" (371).

There is some dynamic connection in the popular mind between these perceived polar opposites: the lustful black man and the remote white virgin. The image of the white lady is constantly intertwined with the theory of racial separation. The imperative of her protection was used to support the lynchings that went on all over the South from the 1880s and into the twentieth century. The white woman represented the one absolute possession of the white man no black could approach with impunity. In the breakdown of all other social institutions and taboos, the final fall into degeneracy was signaled by this almost inevitable clash of sexual territory between freed blacks and psychically deposed whites. There were race riots in Atlanta in 1906; John Temple Graves, a Georgia aristocrat, responded that it was justifiable to lynch an infinite number of blacks, innocent or not, to protect sacred southern womanhood (Williamson, *Crucible* 214–20).[2]

At the time of the Scottsboro case and just after the peak point of lynchings in the South, Faulkner was working on some of his most complex fiction, particularly dealing with the white fear of rape. Faulkner grew up in the atmosphere of Dixon's hate-soaked novels (*The Clansman* was part of his Oxford library), as well as of the rapid rise of lynching and the racist rhetoric of Benjamin Ryan Tillman, senator from South Carolina, who constantly reiterated his famous nightmare scenario of black men with "breasts pulsating with the desire to sate their passions on white maidens and wives" (Williamson, *Crucible* 116–17). In an unsettling conjunction of feminism and racism, Rebecca Latimer Felton, the first woman to become a United States senator (appointed in 1922 when Tom Watson of Georgia died), saw white women victimized by white men's neglect of them, leading to black men's aggression. She said that a thousand blacks a week should be lynched "if it becomes necessary" (Williamson, *Crucible* 128). Though her picture of women robbed of their "dearest possession" by "drunken, ravening human beasts" is similar to Dixon's fantasies of black rape, she places the blame on white men of power for not taking responsibility. The southern social order was served by the inability of southern feminists to see blacks as an equally oppressed underclass. Black women were constructed as nymphomaniacs seducing white men; black men were constructed as rapists attacking white women. White culture loaded its sexual terrors onto blacks and, in dividing, conquered.

Until the first few decades of the twentieth century the predominant story cast the white woman as victim and the black man as aggressor, seeking to muddy the racial "purity" of the ruling classes with his mulatto children (a curious mirror image of when white men had mulatto children by slave women who were denied rights to their children or even their bodies), seeking to insinuate or force himself into the closed garden of the southern patriarchy. A potent and urgent dissonance results when the sexually frustrated manless white woman is thrown against the politically frustrated masterless black man. In white men's rush to "protect" female property from the black rapist, both white women and black men are rendered impotent. The fear of rape serves southern racism and white male dominance: if women have to be protected and black men intimidated, the southern social order remains intact.

Faulkner approaches the unmarried, unregulated woman by casting her against a discourse of rape yet allowing her, through her own story-telling, to negotiate a bisexual space that, while not always protecting her from violation, is a strategy to evade masculine domination. The spinster never gets out of her own fiction alive: she is silenced, but she does not give up without a fight, and without disabling the plantation ideology.

"Long Embattled in Virginity": Sexuality and Story

Contrary to the marginal representations of the Old Maid in southern culture, Faulkner provides in his fiction a wide range of unmarried white women, all busily subverting convention. Unmarried women seem at first to betray yet another set of troubled oppositions. They are either bearers of sexless aristocratic virtue or victims of repressed sexuality. Miss Worsham in "Go Down, Moses," and her later avatar Miss Habersham in Intruder in the Dust, show Old South heroinism residing in the spare form of the town spinster, affirmation not only of the suppression of the female body but the triumph of paternalism. Miss Worsham in "Go Down, Moses," acts in the grand plantation manner, so much admired in romances: her "people" remain loyal to her, and she takes care of them. Miss Worsham asserts the white fantasy of southern race relations when she says of Molly Beauchamp, "We grew up as sisters would," (375). In Intruder in the Dust (1949) Miss Worsham, renamed Miss Habersham, acts the aristocratic liberal, determined to protect one of "her people," Molly's husband, Lucas Beauchamp. The people of Jefferson repeat over and over again that Miss Habersham is a "lady"; covered by that talismanic word, she need not pander to bourgeois notions of ladylike (that is, passive) behavior when Lucas Beauchamp is charged with murder. She behaves instead as a Confederate Woman, validated by her age, race, and class, and the community's nostalgia.[3]

Miss Habersham's domain objectifies her status as an historical icon: "old big decaying houses of Jefferson's long-ago foundation set like Miss Habersham's deep in shaggy untended lawns of old trees and root-bound scented and flowering shrubs whose very names most people under fifty no longer knew and which even when children lived in them seemed still to be spellbound by the shades of old women still spinsters and widows waiting even seventy-five years later for the slow telegraph to bring them news of Tennessee and Virginia and Pennsylvania battles" (119–20). The integrity of those old, chaste gardens surrounding those old, chaste (because associated with the Arcadian South) houses, expresses spatially the custom and ceremony of Miss Habersham's blameless life. She speaks a lost language, knowing the names of the old trees; she is a witness to an unspoken past.

If Miss Habersham/Worsham represents a community celebration of the sexless Confederate Woman, elsewhere Faulkner's fiction demonstrates an opposing unease with the unmarried woman as a sexual outlaw, a "neurotic" or "repressed" woman whose inability to take her place in the sexual economy has embittered her. Emily Grierson, Zilphia Gant, and Rosa Coldfield are "read" by their communities as women driven almost insane from lack of sexual satisfaction, fulfilling the stereotype of the frustrated old maid, so racked by a desire she cannot express that she turns to violence or, worse still, *storytelling*. These manless women, supposedly crazed by virginity, appropriate the masculine. As with the Belle, the unmarried woman can inhabit and speak out of a bisexual space negotiating both feminine desire and masculine power, both feminine and masculine voices.

Miss Emily Grierson in "A Rose for Emily" ought to be a Miss Habersham, a Confederate Woman propping up the heroic verities. She is upper class, if living in genteel poverty, indulged in her eccentricities by the town because she is perceived, like Miss Habersham, as a relic of its own supposedly noble past. Yet Miss Emily harbors a covert sexuality that destabilizes not only the integrity of the spinster lady but the whole edifice of southern history and class.

Faulkner wrote "A Rose" some time in early 1930 (the story was published in the Forum in April 1930), at a time when sexuality warped, thwarted, and fascinated him: the white woman's burden.[4] For the Freudianized Faulkner, the denial or misdirection of the middle- to upper-class white woman's sexuality becomes the obsessive focus of her being. Where class absolves the Confederate Woman from desire, it implicates the spinster in repression and destruction. Class is the reason for Miss Emily's spinsterhood. Her father does not lock her up physically (as happens in "Miss Zilphia Gant"), but he does lock her into a rigid Old South concept of ladyhood, elevating her out of reach of the young men of

Jefferson. Miss Emily's handicap, stemming from her being, the narrator reiterates, "Grierson," as if that were a synonym for *royal*, leads her finally to defy conventional community sexual standards for her gender and her rank. Like her "heavily lightsome" house, Miss Emily is constructed of improbable stories: she is "dear, inescapable, impervious, tranquil, and perverse" (*Collected Stories* 128). Miss Emily is a sort of community icon but, as the choric narrator (clearly masculine) emphasizes, the townspeople desire a demonstrable "link between the gross, teeming world and the high and mighty Griersons" (122).

Miss Emily has been taught to repress "gross" physicality, buying into her culture's insistence that white ladies be spirit not body, angel not whore. But perhaps the "perverse" is the key term here: in Miss Emily, the unspoken comes to be spoken, the suppressed story asserts itself. Her house, once the grandest in town, develops a terrible smell, a sort of advertisement that she has "fallen"; she herself becomes ruled by her desire and her anger, not the code of Old South old maidhood. The rancid odor of the princely Grierson home reflects her "perverse" liaison with Homer Barron, "a Northerner, a day-laborer," who will not allow her to confine him in marriage: his class and his regional origin make their affair doubly antagonistic to the symbolic order. Miss Emily poisons her lover and sleeps with his corpse (the source of the smell) as unconcerned with committing murder and necrophilia as she is with refusing a postal address. Her house, with its musty unused rooms and locked doors—a prison and a mausoleum—signifies how she has pretended to conform to the Old South code of chastity, all the while reveling in her deviancy. The house, like Miss Emily's body, is simultaneously a shrine to her father's narrow values, with everything left in its nineteenth-century place, and a denial of Grierson sexual decorum, with the dead lover's corpse enclosed in an inner chamber.

Homer Barron's body in the upstairs room is at once an image of a love dead in the womb and an indicator of Miss Emily's determination to retain her moment of power over both time and the male world. Her obsession with confounding time is a quotation of Miss Havisham in Dickens's *Great Expectations* (1861), whose dusty room with "no glimpse of daylight" and antique wedding clothes signify her grim attempt at withdrawal from the mutable world and her dessicated sexuality. When the Jeffersonians break into Miss Emily's sealed chamber after her death, they find a similar "room decked and furnished as for a bridal," a dark, decomposing tableau (*Collected Stories* 129). Their entry into her house signifies a kind of violation of her own body: she is "exposed" before their rapacious, judgmental gaze. Since the masculine collective voice controls the narrative, they see not Miss Emily's triumph over her father but entrapment and entombment, recalling the terror of the powerful female body in Poe's claustrophobic romances: heroes locked in windowless rooms, in coffins, in the airless holds of ships. The vagina here is not a perfect vessel or an enclosed garden but a prison cell.

Miss Emily is an interrogation, a parody, and a celebration of the Confederate Woman. She is a murderess and a necrophiliac, but above all she is a lady. After her death the narrator seems more proud of her eccentricity than damning of her crime (Homer Barron was a *Yankee*). There are no Union soldiers to shoot off the front porch so Miss Emily poisons one in her bed: she should be a heroine of the culture. Her sexuality is the location of vast anxiety, however, insofar as it is an attempt to usurp masculine autonomy, to retain in her house, as the nymphomaniac tries to retain in her body, the body of the man. Miss Emily's house, like Miss Havisham's, is an emblem of her sterile body. She keeps her lover's clothes lying around in the "bridal" room "as if they had just been removed," as Miss Havisham has one wedding slipper on and one off, pausing for decades at the catastrophic moment caused by a faithless man, forever preserved yet poised on the edge of destruction. Dickens calls up a picture of "bodies buried in ancient times, which fall to powder in the moment of being distinctly seen" (57). The object of Miss Emily's desire, the putrid form "inextricable from the bed in which he lay," is rendered powerless, yet still an inscription on (or penetration of) the feminine womb-room. Both Homer Barron and Miss Emily are destroyed by her deviance, her perversity; the opposing stories of her "Griersonness" and her sexuality move in constant, unsettling dissonance.

The discursive connection of a house or a room with a woman's body also informs "Miss Zilphia Gant," written in late 1928. Zilphia's mother, Mrs. Gant, boils with sexual rage, seeking out her adulterous husband and his lover with "the pertinacity of a Fate, the serene imperviousness of a vestal out of a violated temple," killing them in cold blood, then imprisoning her daughter in a back room in order to separate her from sexuality altogether (*Uncollected Stories* 370). When Mrs. Gant kills her husband and his lover, she is transformed from female avenger to patriarch, as if her appropriation of male power through murder with a male weapon—a gun—has ungendered her. With her daughter she is a puritanical father, regarding her solely in terms of her potential for sexual misconduct. The narrative insists on Mrs. Gant's masculinity: she plots her husband's murder "with the capability of a man," beats the half-wit begging for money as if she were man, even turns physically male: "a woman who for twelve years had been growing into the outward semblance of a man until now at forty there was a faint shadow of a moustache at the corner of her mouth" (370, 373). Mrs. Gant divorces herself from the community of women, especially those concerned with Zilphia's "social development," calling them "bitches." She plays the domineering head of the house while her daughter becomes hyperfeminine, that is, meek, passive, scared, submitting to incarceration and beatings, being herself called "you bitch," even undergoing a kind of rape, made to "strip naked and stand cringing before her [mother] while the savage light fell through the bars" as her body is inspected for the damning signs of puberty. Taking on masculinity allows Mrs. Gant to control her child's body, to inspect her like an object, to lock her up, defining Zilphia as a dangerous body to be contained.

Zilphia does rebel against the Law of the Father by meeting a nameless boy in the woods and escaping from her mother long enough to develop some relationship with a housepainter. She even goes through a marriage ceremony with him. Yet her desire for him cannot withstand the ferocious emotional control her mother exercises over her. The marriage is never consummated: the housepainter leaves town while she remains in the narrow imprisoning space inside the house, letting herself be locked up once more in Mrs. Gant's sterile tower. Even her mother's death while sitting on the porch, the shotgun on her lap like an artificial penis, does not free Zilphia. She lives on the disorientating edge of "hysteria," having erotic hallucinations and dreams, imagining herself the bride in newspaper wedding reports, writing to agony columns, and trying to will herself pregnant through masturbation, a vicious parody of the Immaculate Conception. Where the smell of honeysuckle signals luxuriant sexuality in Flags in the Dust, The Unvanquished, and most notably The Sound and the Fury, here the mock orange outside Zilphia's window, its name suggesting both lies and ridicule, becomes the aroma of her perversity. Mock orange gives off the "faintest suggestion of turpentine," a toxic, antisensual smell associated with the housepainter and his brushcleaner, that heralds Zilphia's violent masturbation: "She would think about Christ, whispering, 'Mary did it without a man. She did it'; or, rousing, furious, her hands clenched at her sides, the covers flung back and her opened thighs tossing, she would violate her ineradicable virginity again and again with something evoked out of the darkness immemorial and philoprogenitive: 'I will conceive! I'll make myself conceive!' " (379).

Zilphia's desire propels her to order her life according to a series of fictions—she is a bride, then the Virgin Mary, then the new wife of the housepainter. Frustrated as Mrs. Gant was enraged, Zilphia sends a private detective to find the remarried housepainter and his wife, demonstrating that "deadly female intuition" and "undeviating conviction for sin" which the Faulknerian male theorizer of the feminine subscribes to (370). She imagines herself experiencing their sexual life once removed in "ecstasies the more racking for being vicarious and transcendant of the actual flesh" (380). She does not need to murder them: they conveniently die, leaving Zilphia to take their daughter away to become the immaculately conceived child of her fantasies. She enters a new fiction at this point—or rather she returns to an old one, becoming a mother, indeed an avatar of her own mother. The descriptions of Mrs. Gant in her black dress and oil-cloth sewing apron, "her bosom festooned with threaded needles," and the descriptions of Zilphia with "glints of needles in her black bosom and the gossamer random festooning of the thread" are nearly identical (371, 381).

The original family structure is replicated: the child is called Zilphia and she, too, is imprisoned, or at least overprotected: Miss Zilphia walks her to school, and she becomes the latest denizen of the barred back room where Miss Zilphia was kept. This is obviously sinister, reminiscent of Poe's "Morella," where the dead mother lives on in the daughter. Zilphia never commands the "masculine" power of her dead mother: she never has a real child or a real gun, never kills, she inhabits a paler fiction of her earlier life the needles stuck in her bodice slender metaphors for the penetration she will never experience. Yet Miss Zilphia, while devalued in a sexual economy demanding definition in marriage and self-annihilation in motherhood, has achieved a sort of victory; she fulfills her fiction. "Mary did it without a man," and so does she. By identifying herself with the Virgin Mary (though the needles in her bodice suggest Saint Sebastian, himself often depicted as androgynous) she perversely appropriates the most elevated image for a southern white woman, yet is not silenced by it. Her desire and her anger (read from a masculine point of view as frustration) allow her to create and control her little family. Like Emily

Grierson, Zilphia is marginalized by the symbolic order yet subverts it in revenge.

The rose in "A Rose for Emily" is a tribute to Emily Grierson's eccentric life and a funeral flower for her death: it is also an erotic symbol, the sign of feminine desire. Miss Rosa Coldfield in *Absalom, Absalom!* is a rose of a different color, her name neither tribute nor grave offering but ironic comment on the flowering in her of outraged articulacy and angry desire. Miss Rosa's surname suggests sterility, a "cold field," not the bounded virgin pasture represented by Judith Sutpen or the lush garden represented by Belle Mitchell. Yet barrenness is only part of her story, seeing her the way Mr. Compson would, as a "frustrated," "insulted old maid," ignoring her anger and her forceful sexuality. The woman unintegrated into the patriarchal community, her desire uncontained in a social structure, threatens the symbolic order. "All margins are dangerous," remarks Mary Douglas (121). Miss Rosa—like Emily Grierson and Zilphia Gant— is a dangerous body. The community constructs the stories of "repression," "disappointment," and "virginity" to circumscribe them; ironically enough, their overflowing, insistent desire empowers them. Miss Rosa's very marginalization becomes a means to challenge masculine stories about the South, about history, and about her own "embattled virginity."

Like Zilphia Gant, Rosa Coldfield creates and inhabits her own fiction, drawn out of rage and desire. Yet, as Matthews points out, her and Mr. Compson's tellings "are usually dismissed by critics as varieties of irrelevance" (*Play* 122). Vickery calls her narrative a "rank melodrama" (87). While it is true that Miss Rosa makes her story out of a gothic discourse, it is more useful to read her, as Gwin suggests, *hysterically*, from the perilous eloquence of her sexuality (72). What might be called melodramatic is actually the speaking of her desire and her fury at the way her desire has been devalued.

Other narrators try to contextualize and contain her stories. Mr. Compson, defining for his son "the Southern Lady," calls Miss Rosa a sort of "vampire" feeding off the lives of her sister Ellen and her niece Judith at Sutpen's Hundred (86). Miss Rosa, however, takes on the gothic language that defines her as some kind of supernatural being, as ghost or vampire or fury (the male narrator's approximation of the female Other) and pours her literary consciousness into "writing" the Sutpen story as an elaborate gothic fiction, a traditionally female-dominated genre. The death of Bon is revealed across "*the upraised and unfinished wedding dress*"; Henry and

Judith are "*two accursed children*" (135). Miss Rosa's language is so compelling that Shreve later parodies it with his references to Sutpen as a demon, an ogre, and Beelzebub, but he does not manage to trivialize it. Indeed, he reinforces *her* version of Sutpen gothicness.

Rosa is also the gothic heroine, usurping the place that might seem to belong to Ellen as wife of the "demon" or Judith as center of the incest-miscegenation triangle and beloved of both Henry and Charles. Miss Rosa is the quester who ventures into the unknown, stuck first in her father's dark loveless house then transported to the backwoods castle of the Sutpens with their "wild negroes" and curses. She is subject to the sexual menace of Thomas Sutpen, and she uncovers the family "secret." Miss Rosa acts as heroine of her own story, and her voice is given authority, at least for a while, not just as the persecuted maiden but as an inquisitor, interrogating the masculine versions of the story. She inhabits marginalized spaces that are nonetheless disruptive—her "virgin" body; her dark, shut house. The play of room/womb/tomb is activated in her narrative, which is both hysterical—coming from the charged space of feminine desire—and deathly, leading to her own destruction: "And so Rosa's narrative desire, her need to speak not only her own sexuality in a culture which denies it but also the madness of that denial, fuels *Absalom* even as it devours her" (Gwin, *Feminine* 66). Rosa's story expresses her desire, but she cannot escape her cultural context. How is Rosa situated as an unmarried woman in the South? How does the masculine discourse in the novel attempt to silence her?

Like Emily Grierson and Zilphia Gant in their shut inner rooms, Miss Rosa's officially repressed sexuality is expressed spatially. On the first page of *Absalom, Absalom!*, she sits in "a dim hot airless room with the blinds all closed and fastened for forty-three summers" (7). Her enclosure is voluntary rather than enforced enclosure (her father does not lock her up; indeed, in a sense, she locks *him* up) but it seems as hermetic as the back room of the Gants' sewing shop or upstairs at the Grierson house: a sterile space to match the sterile space of the Old Maid's body. Rosa shares with Miss Emily and Miss Zilphia a subversive self, manifest in what the men who write her (as opposed to how she writes herself) see as her "warped" sexuality and rage.

Her project as the county's "poetess laureate" has been to form an artificial past out of Lost Cause rhetoric. She has self-consciously created a functioning story to inhabit in a community that seeks to limit her. But she has a private narrative, not of the heroic Confederate dead but of the destruction of southern women by southern men. She negotiates between fictions, living a public life as a writer of Old South propaganda and a private life exposing the miscegenation and violence of the Old South. She is a secret agent against the Law of the Father, skulking in the shadows of Goodhue Coldfield's pleasureless house, both a woman disguised as a child and a child disguised as a woman. Goodhue Coldfield, like Miss Emily's father and Miss Zilphia's masculinized mother, defines women according to their potential for sexual mischief. But prisoners of such an extreme fiction sometimes escape: Miss Rosa's nameless maiden aunt, long playing the spinster's role of raising someone else's child (Rosa) and even arranging someone else's wedding (Ellen's), eventually runs away with a horse trader. Miss Rosa, in her role as dutiful daughter, feeds her pacifist father when he hides during the war, even though she despises him. Her "schoolgirl's poetry about the also-dead" allows her to take on a literary voice, a passive, "feminine" form of speech. Women in the South have often resorted to literature as a way to rebel while maintaining their position as ladies, as evidenced by the diary of Mary Boykin Chesnut, the essays of Louisa McCord, or the fiction of Augusta Jane Evans. Yet while Rosa's poetry challenges her father's politics, it also reinforces the dominant plantation culture, the culture that betrays her and seeks to silence her. It is a disguise—perhaps a form of ventriloquism.

Voice is critical in *Absalom, Absalom!*. Of the five voices that put together the sometimes competing, sometimes intersecting stories, four are men (Mr. Compson, Quentin, Shreve, and Faulkner himself). Their voices construct Miss Rosa as an actor within the stories; her voice constructs herself both within the story and as author of the story. Her version works against the men's writing of her as a ghost, "also-dead," an outraged spinster, a fury, an innocent, or some other kind of female stereotype. Mr. Compson, the novel's chief theorist of the feminine, calls her "a breathing indictment, ubiquitous and even transferable, of the entire male principle (that principle which had left the aunt a virgin at thirty-five)" (59–60). In other words, she stands outside the sexual economy: she informs against it. Because she has not been part of a sexual traffic in women, he condescendingly writes her off as a "man-hating" old maid. The masculine voices also construct Miss Rosa oppositionally as a child and an old lady, physically tiny, her maturation arrested by the war. She is likewise perpetually virginal *and* sexual. Mr. Compson, Shreve, Quentin (and Faulkner, the invisible narrator) cannot reconcile the contradictions in her story and so try reducing her to the archetypal Old Maid, fixated on the cavalier behavior of Thomas Sutpen toward her. Mr. Compson speaks of her "lonely thwarted old female flesh embattled for forty-three years in the old insult, the old unforgiving outraged and betrayed" (14).

Rosa's gender position, however, is unstable and liable to slippage. In telling Sutpen's story, she employs the discourse of rape. The rapist Sutpen "*tore violently a plantation*" out of the untouched land or "dragged house and gardens out of virgin swamp, and plowed and planted his land with seed cotton which General Compson had loaned him" (9, 40). The "insult" Sutpen offers Rosa is a reduction of her worth to the basest object position as a breeder: "In this world, blacks, women, and poor whites, insofar as they represent only their economic value as labor, might as well signify beasts as humans" (Snead 106). At other times, however, Rosa takes on a masculine subject position. If Sutpen penetrates the land, Rosa penetrates the fragile shells of self, "entering" the stories of Judith, Ellen, and even Charles Bon. Snead, in his helpful unpacking of the "merging" and "seepage" in the novel, reminds us that "all the major male characters in the novel" become feminized by what Faulkner describes as "some hiatus of passive and hopeless despair" (Snead 111; *Absalom* 197). This particularly applies to Charles Bon, who, though Rosa thinks of him as her male dream lover, also seems to her to have the "delicacy" of a woman (see chapter 3): "One cannot be certain whether Ellen, Judith and Rosa love him more because he is a man or because he resembles a woman" (Snead 111). Rosa herself declares that she should be read "not as a woman, a girl, but as the man which I perhaps should have been" and soon after describes herself as "androgynous" (144, 146).

At a crucial moment, Rosa aligns herself with the symbolic order that separates whiteness from blackness when she says to Clytie, "*Take your hand off me, nigger!*" (140). She temporarily joins the enemy; but this retreat into class and racial imperatives is fragile, and touch explodes the hierarchy of white over black: "*There is something in the touch of flesh with flesh which abrogates, cuts sharp and straight across the devious intricate channels of decorous ordering, which enemies as well as lovers know because it makes them both—touch and touch of that which is the citadel of the central I-Am's private own*" (139). Physical contact with Clytie catapults them into a mulatto space, neither black nor white, and, in a sense, makes them lovers as well, neither male nor female. Rosa and Clytie are both masculine and feminine and so disrupt the "*eggshell shibboleth of caste and color too*" (139).

The contradictions and gaps in the representation of Miss Rosa—white, yet with a scandalous comprehension of her black "sister" Clytie; female, yet sometimes taking on a male position—define her paradoxically: she inhabits a charged, creative, *bisexual* domain. Snead points out, "Rosa is 15 or 16 when her world of men virtually vanishes" (104). This is an important observation, but I would add to it that the world of *women* is also absent. Rosa must fashion herself in the evocative, dark, womblike space of her father's house as she sews those awkward garments she wears. Conventional femininity never fits her, just as her dresses hang badly on her body. Yet she is not mannish in a stereotypical, cryptolesbian manner. Miss Rosa inhabits a much richer fiction, constructing herself not just as a perpetual preadolescent but as a wielder of imagination. She is both masculine and feminine in speaking her desire. Her sexuality is ignored or denied by the men who speak of her; yet she speaks openly of her longings in the "summer of wisteria," when she was fourteen. She says she is "not more child than woman but even as less than any female flesh" (144). She is not merely "androgynous" but an "advocate," both a victim of Sutpen, who she says "insults" her, and his conqueror in fiction. She denies that there was any sexual attachment in her dealings with Sutpen, her "nothusband": "I had not lost him because I never owned him: a certain segment of rotten mud walked into my life, spoke that to me which I had never heard before and never shall again, then walked out; that was all. I never owned him; certainly not in that sewer sense" (171).

One reading of this is that Miss Rosa here rejects the erotic—as Old Maids are held to do. As a member of a class to whom chastity is an important marker of self, she is scandalized at the way Sutpen transgresses the boundaries of decorum, speaking the unspeakable, telling his desire, which for her makes him lower than excrement. The "sewer sense" refers to a sexuality Miss Rosa defines as a devaluation of herself. She would rather see herself as part of a moral order and class structure, a potential upholder of the plantation system, a woman to be married, or at least loved, and thus given status, moreover a woman whose voice is *heard*. She insists on her story: *she wants it told,* Quentin thinks. It is her masterpiece, her roman à clef revenge against the world that has marginalized her.

Throughout *Absalom, Absalom!,* Miss Rosa's voice operates *against* the male narrators, correcting, amplifying, denying their vision of her as passive, weak. Quentin Compson becomes not just the audience for her story but its victim. His father thinks she wants him because his grandfather knew Colonel Sutpen and thus sees the Compson family as implicated in the "curse," and because she, being a lady, needs an appropriate escort, "a man, a gentleman, yet one still young enough to do what she wants, do it the way she wants it done" (12). Critics have read Quentin as being in the forefront of her story, the masculine legitimizer, yet he is for her only a conduit. It is not just that she "*wants it told*," implying a detached agency; it is because she wants it inscribed on the person most likely to be affected by it—she wants to mark as she has been marked. Quentin is confused by his father's romantic notions when he thinks Miss Rosa tells her story "*so that people whom she will never see and whose names she will never hear and who have never heard her name nor seen her face will read it and know at last why God let us lose the War: that only through the blood of our men and the tears of our women could He stay this demon and efface his name and lineage from the earth*" (11).

But even as the potential writer of this Great Southern Novel, Miss Rosa still sees Quentin as a vehicle facilitating her quest for authenticity. She "impregnates" him with the story, in a way using him as Sutpen would have used her. Gwin observes that "for the symbolic order to assert itself over the unrepresentable, it must silence its difference within" (*Feminine* 103). Miss Rosa is silenced, "constituted, objectified by Quentin's male imagination" (*Feminine* 64). In a sense, this is true; indeed, Faulkner's fiction shows a world prepared to celebrate the already-silenced, contained woman and to annihilate the woman who insists on speaking. Joanna Burden's transgression into masculine articulacy poses a danger to the symbolic order: she is destroyed. Before Drusilla Hawk is married, storytelling is part of her soldierlike virtue, yet when she is reduced to "womanhood" at the end of "An Odor of Verbena," she disappears into hysterical unintelligibility. I would argue that though Miss Rosa dies, allowing Shreve and Quentin to take over her narrative, travestying and even *racially* reducing her in the way Shreve misnames her "Aunt Rosa" (the title of an old black woman in southern culture), she first gets her chance to speak. The insistent story with which she marks Quentin will deny him sleep for the rest of his short life. His exclamation "I dont hate it! I dont hate it!" is, at least in part, a response to what she has insisted that he know. Miss Rosa's power is in her ability to control the narrative as effectively as the other narrators.

Miss Rosa is both victimized and powerful in the oxymoronic way Faulkner likes to make his characters. The requirements of her culture confine Miss Rosa in certain modes of behavior, restricting her ability to create herself as something other than the Old Maid, the marginal woman of the stereotype. Yet her ability to "write" herself and her story allows her to push at the limits of her community-defined role, even to transgress into spheres of masculinity. In inventing Miss Rosa for the mid-1930s South, Faulkner partakes of elements of the conventional representation of the Confederate Old Maid. Yet he also allows her to subvert them. I wonder if Miss Rosa is as she is because of the way that some women were beginning to tell stories about the South that were not like Daughters of the Confederacy poetry. Though *Absalom, Absalom!*, unlike *Light in August*, is not overtly about lynching, both novels are concerned with the threat of a "black" man to the sexual integrity of a white woman. This was a central social issue in the South at the time Faulkner was writing. Jessie Daniel Ames and her organization, the Association of Southern Women for the Prevention of Lynching, began to question the white/black binary, this source of vast social paranoia. Miss Rosa is no reforming clubwoman out to improve relations with the Negro (though her Methodist background would make her a candidate for some of the more progressive groups such as the Home Mission Society or the National American Women's Suffrage Association), yet Faulkner invented her at a time when women were openly questioning their places on the pedestal as well as the arrangement of southern society.

The Racial Politics of Rape: Light in August

In *Light in August* (1932), as in *Absalom, Absalom!*, a kind of textual bisexuality intersects textual mulattoism in the crucial issue of feminine desire. Joanna Burden, like Rosa Coldfield a manless woman, attempts to speak her desire and runs afoul of southern society's hierarchies of white over black, male over female, maternity over childlessness. As in so much of Faulkner's fiction, however, those hierarchies are unstable, always collapsing in on each other, penetrating each other. The narrative of Joanna Burden and Joe Christmas is framed in the discourse not only of rape— as we've seen in *Sanctuary*, *Flags in the Dust*, and *Absalom, Absalom!*—but also of a black man raping a white woman, perhaps the most profound psychic assault on the southern sense of integrity, and lynching, the response of southern culture to what it defines as the worst of sins. Of course, we don't know Joe Christmas is literally a black man: Faulkner's fiction seeks to expose the crudity of the community's insistence that he must be to fit their story of how the black Other "violates" the sacred body of a white woman. That Joanna Burden, previously tainted with "blackness" and "Yankeeness," only becomes fully a "white woman" in the eyes of Jeffersonians when she is found murdered (and, they assume, raped) is one of the central ironies of the novel.

The juxtaposition of a white woman and a black man produced a frenzied attempt by southern society to control the merest possibility of miscegenation, or even of minimal racial and gender transgression. Trudier Harris calls lynching a "ritual" to purge the community of pollution and evil, "exorcising blackness." In the thirties the South was racked by internal debate and external violence: lynchings occurred at the same time that Jessie Daniel Ames and her Association of Southern Women for the Prevention of Lynching were organizing in every state of the old Confederacy. Rhetoric on both sides was hot—spheres of race, class, and gender were a political issue. South Carolina Governor Cole L. Blease founded his 1930 reelection campaign on a defense of lynching, neatly summing up the unreconstructed southern understanding of participatory democracy: "Whenever the Constitution comes between me and the virtue of the white women of the South, I say to hell with the Constitution!" (Hall 195). *Light in August* is one of Faulkner's most pointed responses to the turmoil in the South. In this novel Faulkner anatomizes the community's central secret anxiety: the desire of a white woman for a man defined (by the community) as black.

The old southern story says that all black men want to rape white women; Faulkner inverts this, suggesting that white women desire black men. Two forbidden bodies come together in a moment of pure subversion, imperiling two of the South's solid sustaining fictions: that black men are rampagingly sexual and that white women are immutably chaste. In Faulkner's dismantling of the "rape theme," the women who long most deeply for union with the Other, represented by black men, are those officially deprived of their sexuality, the Old Maids.

A year or so before *Light in August* was finished, Faulkner wrote a short story about the dynamics of lynching. "Dry September" (1930) explores the intersection of race and gender as an indictment of white ladyhood; here the black man is a victim, not a criminal; the white woman is a manipulative parody of a Belle, not a victim. No one imprisons Miss Minnie Cooper in a locked room or dark house, but she is trapped in her fantasies and obsessed with class. Miss Minnie, with her "slender nervous body" and "hard vivacity," looks both boyish (like Temple Drake) and ultrafeminine. Her smallness and frilly voile dresses make her out to be a sort of arrested child (like Miss Rosa), epicene and immature; yet her sheer underclothes suggest a covert eroticism. She evades the reality of her isolation from the community, drinking whiskey, fashioning a fiction to inhabit where she is a romantic heroine "irresistible" to men. Miss Minnie is addicted to the cinema: I wonder if D. W. Griffiths's *Birth of a Nation* (based on the Ku Klux Klan novels of Thomas Dixon), in which innocent white virgins are preyed upon by "bad niggers," is the sort of film Faulkner imagines her seeing.

Her lack of community validation in marriage (the assured married daughters of her old friends now call her "aunty" as if she were an old black woman, reducing her status the way Shreve reduced Rosa Coldfield's) leads her to accuse an innocent black man of assault. "Something about Miss Minnie Cooper and a Negro" rouses the white men of the town to a lynching fury. Chivalry (a "wronged" lady is always right) is aligned with racial hatred; behind the reverence for white women lurks racial paranoia. Hawkshaw the barber, on the other hand, has no illusions about Sacred White Womanhood. He subscribes to the theory that spinsters imagine rapists behind every azalea bush, suggesting that Miss Minnie's complaint is really the fantasy of a repressed virgin: "I leave it to you fellows if them ladies that get old without getting married dont have notions that a man cant—" he trails off (*Collected Stories* 170).

The men of the town reduce Will Mays and Minnie Cooper to their mythic states as black man–rapist and white lady–victim in their rage to punish the very concept of a "free nigger." "Are you going to let the black sons get away with it until one of them actually does it?" asks McLendon with curious logic (172). Miss Minnie's chastity is not the issue; her credibility is very low anyway. The white men of the town are more interested in maintaining the power structure in which they "protect" women and terrorize blacks.

Behind the horror of the supposed attack lurks a titillated interest in rape: even more important is the fascination with sex between a white woman and a black man (which, according to the prevalent equations of black man = sexual depravity, white woman = asexuality, *had* to be rape). The threat of black sexual potency excites the white people of the town: "You reckon he really done it to her?" they whisper (173). Miss Minnie's friends revel vicariously in her story, demanding the details as if it were a piece of pornography: "When you have had time to get over the shock, you must tell us what happened. What he said and did; everything" (180). Miss Minnie has taken on a new status as a woman who has experienced the ultimate forbidden, the pairing of bodies southern patriarchy has decreed forever antithetical. And the town—like the community in *Sanctuary*—participates in the discourse of rape.

Miss Minnie becomes the heroine of her own story, manipulating community sexual and racial anxieties to control her fiction, asserting her desirability by constructing a story where a man simply "could not help himself." She wields power through her story, for the black man is lynched; she asserts efficacy only in pain and chastity only in violation. She insists on her purity by asserting the robbing of it. In the expression of her desire, disguised by the rape story, she elevates herself and destroys another. In the end, however, the narrative is ranged against her, the very title of the story a dismissal of her fiction of attractiveness and importance. She is useless and old, a "Dry September," a body with no purpose whose desire momentarily galvanizes and kills, then is erased.

The question of the dry female body "not any good any more," that is, not suitable for bearing children any more, impels the narrative of *Light in August* in which the appropriate feminine is defined as motherhood. The inarticulate (in the male-centered discourse of Jefferson) fecundity of Lena Grove is celebrated, while the protean bisexuality of Joanna Burden is destroyed. The fictions of the spinster and the black rapist collide, destroying two people struggling to break free of the boundaries of race, gender, class, and sexuality, yet who finally reduce each other to the roles of white woman and black man. As in so much of Faulkner's work, the violent hierarchies of male/female, white/black, angel/whore, and now heterosexual/homosexual collapse into one another, creating dangerous marginal voices that the narratives both give play to and finally work to silence. Lena Grove, Byron Bunch, Gail Hightower, Joanna Burden, and Joe Christmas pose a threat to the official gender and racial structure of Jefferson (and the South) and must be satisfactorily limited.

As in *Absalom, Absalom!*, the mulatto space and the bisexual space are in full play in *Light in August*. As Snead remarks, the central figure is "a man both masculine and feminine, both black and white, a 'tragic mulatto,' an American double-being who breaks all the semiotic codes of society" (81). The novel declares itself an exploration of perilous gender territory from the beginning: Joe Christmas often feels powerless in his relationship with Joanna Burden, "like she was the man and I was the woman," while Joanna Burden is constantly described as "manlike." Lena Grove is heavily pregnant yet the "unravish'd bride" of Keats's urn. Two of the novel's "country women" are practically described as cross-dressed men: Mrs. Armstid looks "manhard" with a face like "those of generals who have been defeated in battle" and Mrs. McEachern appears "without sex demarcation at all save the neat screw of greying hair and the skirt" (18, 182). Jefferson teems with childless, dysfunctional marriages. Feminized, passive Gail Hightower cannot meet his wife's sexual needs; the unloving McEacherns must adopt a child; Byron Bunch is, in the beginning, apparently without gender. The sexual atmosphere is distrustful at best and often vicious. Mr. McEachern despises the "soft," the feminine; Doc Hines talks of "womanfilth." Joe Christmas beats rather than sleeps with the black girl the other boys use as a sexual receptacle. He himself has no history, no defined race, no stable gender; he inhabits the tormented territory of the mulatto, the feminine, the homoerotic—all intolerable in Jefferson's social order.

Light in August is rich in homoerotic pairings, simultaneously suggestive and violent, including Joe Christmas and Lucas Burch in the cabin on the Burden land; Joe Christmas and Mr. McEachern, obsessed with each other and treating with contempt the "feminine" in Mrs. McEachern; Byron Bunch and Gail Hightower, both evading the world with poetry and religiosity; Gail Hightower and Joe Christmas; and finally Joe Christmas and Joanna Burden. The feminine is travestied or brutalized in these pairings; only in Lena Grove's creativity, forced to the periphery of the community yet a focal event, is the feminine positive. The community insists on restoring the symbolic order by celebrating a woman's "confinement" (in every sense) in childbirth, just as it acts to remarginalize or destroy those "outsiders" who temporarily capture the imagination of Jefferson. Joanna Burden and Joe Christmas are victims of the necessity to clarify gender and race roles in the community, as Lena Grove becomes the fertile presiding goddess of an apparently restored order. However, despite the insisted-upon "correctness" of maternity and the abhorrent barrenness and perversity identified in Joanna Burden, the reassertion of the urn's perfection in the timeless life cycle of copulation, birth, and death, Light in August hints at a subterranean potential for chaos: sexuality, race, gender, history, even class gone liquid, all hierarchies erased.

In Joanna Burden, the hierarchies that marginalize her, "a Yankee, a lover of negroes," appear intact, at least for a while. She lurks on the edges of Jefferson, speaking only with blacks, allowing only blacks in her house, identifying herself scandalously with the forbidden and despised, for which the community punishes her in its longtime ostracism of her family. Only after her death is she accorded community status as a "white lady," appropriately helpless. As in "A Rose for Emily," "Miss Zilphia Gant," and *Absalom, Absalom!* the empty, cold, claustrophobic house signifies the body of the spinster in a sexual economy where the female body is appropriately "completed" by a man, then by a fetus. This is a gothic strategy; the stories of Poe employ architecture to reveal profound anxiety about the female body constructed in the House of Usher's tomb-like frigidity or Rowena/Ligeia's womblike bridal chamber. But whether the edifice expresses the virgin, the bride, or the mother, it is *not*, in the end, empty, not simply a vacancy to be filled by the male but "pregnant" with something Other, haunted by something monstrous. In *Absalom, Absalom!* Miss Rosa utters the essential sentence of the gothic plot; "There is something in that house": the Old Maid, and the house that defines her, always have secrets—the outlaw Henry Sutpen, the dead day laborer, the "black" lover.

Both Joanna Burden and her house are sealed containers to be broken into: though the kitchen door is unlocked, Joe Christmas feels he must come in through a window, just as he feels Joanna herself must be penetrated by force. Yet the simple story of the maiden lady raped by a drifter is full of contradictions: though a man assaults her in apparently heterosexual fashion, inscribing on her body her powerlessness in a male sexual economy, the rendering of the story works at the same time to undercut both her "feminine" victimization and her femaleness. The phrase "almost manlike" appears over and over again in describing her; her face is "unfeminine," "prominently boned, long, a little thin, almost manlike" (291). Her first sexual experience with Joe Christmas is a "hard and manlike surrender," and her voice, as she tells him the story of her family, sounds "steady, interminable, pitched almost like the voice of a man" (264–65). She displays no fear of violation; she does not seem bothered when she discovers Christmas in her kitchen one night and does not run when he, uninvited, enters her room to rape her. Much of her being seems profoundly "unfeminine": the "mantrained muscles and the mantrained habit of thinking born of heritage and environment which he had to fight up to the final instant" (221–22). Joanna's body verges on the parapet of gender: she is *almost* a man, yet she is also a woman.

Joe Christmas thinks that "*she has nothing under her clothes so that it could have happened*" (263). Joe Christmas does not have to bear the guilt of rape because he tells himself his victim does not possess the requisite genitalia. But "it," the rape, does happen, though in a bisexual space that does not allow it to be reduced to male over female, penetration and reception. Cixous defines the bisexual as "a 'dual' or even multiple subject, who is not afraid to recognize in him or herself the presence of both sexes, not afraid to open him or herself up to the presence of the other, to the circulation of multiple drives and desires" (Suleiman 16). Joe Christmas may not acknowledge in himself "the presence of both sexes," yet the narrative implies they are there. I suggest that he "reads" Joanna Burden according to his desire for both a woman and a man; perhaps Joanna Burden's own desire is also masculine and feminine. The bisexual space they maneuver within allows them—initially—to be all things to each other. Later on that creative liquidity solidifies: Joe Christmas becomes a black rapist and Joanna Burden a white victim. Their fluid desires are arrested and parodied.

Still, in the first instance, Joanna Burden refuses to be only a woman at the critical moment; she refuses even to be ravished as Christmas, coming from a culture that cannot separate sexuality and violence, assumes women are ravished, that is, half-willingly, ritually. She thinks as well as fights (real women presumably simply feel and surrender). She exhibits "no coyness of obvious desire and intention to succumb at last. It was as if he struggled physically with another man for an object of no actual value to either, and for which they struggled on principle alone" (258). The rape is uncomfortably viewed by Joe Christmas as a bonding ceremony, not an assertion of his alleged male superiority or even an erotic episode. In this passage Joanna is virtually a man. She has become a *subject* fighting over "an object," that is, the feminine itself. The shadowy female body not owned by *either* combatant at this moment is the valueless object, the conduit for masculine communication, perhaps the apex of the homoerotic triangle. Yet rape demonstrates women's powerlessness even while women are supposed to "like" it, even to secretly assist in it. A little later in Joe's reading of their encounter, gender again comes unglued; the homoerotic structure collapses into pornographic fantasy. Joanna is a woman now: "She did not resist at all. It was almost as if she were helping him with small changes of position of limbs when the ultimate need for help arose" (259). Joanna's slide from masculine to feminine is swift and vertiginous: she is both equal and vanquished, both the Self-same and the Other. Like Temple Drake in her fantasies about growing a penis before she can be raped, Joanna Burden acts as both a body that cannot be raped and a body that is raped. But where Temple Drake makes her own fiction in attempt to become impenetrable, Joe Christmas, not Joanna, controls this story. It is *his* desire that makes her both male and female.

Attempting to solidify himself as "masculine," he must feminize her, subordinate her, saying "I'll show you! I'll show the bitch!" as he tears at her clothes and expects, wants, her to despise him. But she is not sufficiently defined as "female" at this point to allow him to construct this rape story in the way he wants. Worse still, her masculinity forces Joe Christmas to acknowledge, to some extent, his "femininity": " 'It was like I was the woman and she was the man.' But that was not right, either. Because she had resisted to the very last. But it was not woman resistance, that resistance which, if really meant, cannot be overcome by any man for the reason that the woman observes no rules of physical combat. But she had resisted fair" (258–59).

Here is another story that can't be nailed down. The confusion between Joanna Burden's male and female aspects reflects the confusion of both gender and race in Joe Christmas. The insisted-upon opposites, man/woman, black/white, prove volatile. The implication that women want to be raped further muddies the issue: they could not be physically overcome otherwise. This places the blame on women as instigators of their own sexual subordination. So Joanna Burden both desires her defloration and fights like a man to avoid it, both aids in her rape and takes a masculine role to stop it.

Before returning to the issue of Joe Christmas's femininity, it is worth considering that the rape is also a homoerotic rape. Joanna's erotic appeal for Joe is sometimes located in her masculinity. I do not necessarily suggest that he sodomized her, though his refusal to believe she possesses a vagina calls the actual sexual act into question. Joe prefers Joanna because of her masculinity, though he eventually "reduces" her to femininity to win the power struggle they engage in. Despising women, he is initially attracted to her because she is not a "womanly" woman. Joanna, unlike the prostitute Bobbie, is not associated with the awfulness of menstruation, though Bobbie's "boy's name" (like Temple Drake's) disrupts her essential womanliness. It might seem that in his vomiting over the fact of menstruation represented by Bobbie, like his violent response to the fact of blackness represented by the unnamed girl in the barn, he radically rejects the feminine. In Joanna he finds a kind of Self-same, as well as an Other. They can be read as halves of a whole; even their names, Joe and Joanna, are versions of each other, both incomplete and paradoxical bodies struggling for definition.

Joe and Joanna are paired both heterosexually and homosexually, the homosexual being one of the text's multiple renderings of desire. Gail Hightower also has a place in this continuum. Byron suggests Hightower give Joe an alibi for Joanna's murder: "You could say he was here with you that night. Every night when Brown said he watched him go up to the big house and go in it. Folks would believe you" (430). It is easier for the community to accept Christmas—now firmly constructed as a black man— as Hightower's lover than Joanna Burden's.[5] Brooks reads Christmas's misogyny as "a latent tendency" toward homosexuality without identifying a possible object of his desire (*Yoknapatawpha Country* 56). Pressing these suggestive readings allows for seeing Joe's (and Joanna's) sexuality/sexualities as unfixed, and so *outside* the South's symbolic order, at least for a time.

Joe and Joanna are most equal, most fluid, least locked into categories of class, gender, sexuality, and race at the beginning of their relationship. Later, Joe takes on the trappings of *maleness* and *blackness* to a greater degree, while Joanna becomes feminized and impotent. But in the beginning, they struggle over power as much as over sex. As we have seen, they exchange genders at some points, perpetually pitted against one another for control of the relationship. This is a war no one wins. Joe tries to enforce the gender hierarchy on Joanna's body in penetrating it, every encounter an attempt to "despoil her virginity each time anew," yet she refuses to be an orifice to be used (257). He cannot conquer her body ("*I dreamed it. It didn't happen*") and feels she reduces him to the status he has tried to reduce her to by contemptuously placing food in the kitchen "for the nigger" and leaving the door unlocked, as if she had nothing to fear from him (261). *Which* door is significant: she bolts the front door but leaves the back door open. Back doors are for blacks, "poor white trash," and servants. In *Absalom, Absalom!* Thomas Sutpen is humiliated by the southern class system when a black butler tells him to go to the back door of a Virginia plantation house. Given the connections between Joanna's house and Joanna's body, the back door is perhaps further suggestion of the homoerotic aspect to the liaison as well as the racial power struggle. Thadious Davis sees the early stages of the affair, when Joe acts "the woman" to Joanna's man, as implying "the relationship that has existed between the Negro and the white South. . . . Unable to express his manhood, he has assumed external behavior patterns which the dominant culture associates with the female" (139).

Davis also shows how "black life in the novel is closely associated with the female" (139). While Joe (and the symbolic order with which he is in constant, strained negotiation) conflates the "hot wet primogenitive Female" with the black, he also struggles against this stereotyping of gender and race (126). In Snead's phrase, "Christmas is the sign of resistance to fixed signs" (88). He appropriates both white and black male versions of power in hatred of blacks, hatred of domesticity (which he associates with women and weakness) and hatred of women. His response to the unlocked back door is to come in through the window and smash the dishes set out on the table for him. He refuses food and cuts off buttons because a "woman's hand" has touched them. Sexuality equals violence for him: he tells a white woman he slept with once that he was "a nigger," then beats her because she does not display disgust. He hits instead of rapes the black girl in the barn, but his first sexual encounter with Bobbie resembles rape: he rips her dress, half carrying and half dragging her into the woods.

In Joanna Burden, Joe Christmas confronts both his black and feminine (powerless) selves, as well as his homosexual self. All three are unacceptable to him; he must construct her as the enemy to be destroyed. Joanna's deviation from femininity, called her "manlikeness," is partially constituted in language: she tells the story of her abolitionist family's violent mission in Yoknapatawpha not in the elliptical, narcissist manner that Miss Rosa speaks her rage and desire in *Absalom, Absalom!*, but in a linear, "masculine" narrative. Later, her speech names him black ("Negro! Negro! Negro!") and finally attempts to subjugate him in her guilt-ridden calvinist "burden." After the initial play of their multifarious desires and positions where they struggled for control, their "equality" begins to disintegrate. Joanna makes a fiction and tries to force Joe to inhabit it; Joe tries to recover his masculine subjectivity by "making a woman," an object, out of Joanna. In *Intruder in the Dust*, the white people want to "make a nigger" out of Lucas Beauchamp; in *Light in August* Percy Grimm "makes a nigger" out of Joe Christmas, but not before Joanna Burden does. It is a state he does not resist: when he tells her one of his parents "was part nigger," she replies, "How do you know that?" and he says, "I dont know it" (279–80).

Why does Joe masochistically define himself as black, taking the lowliest position he can in southern society? Is it part of his identification with or disgust for the feminine? Even when acting out the story of the "nigger rapist," Joe is marginalized. White heterosexual masculinity is the one category he cannot situate himself in. Two excluded, despised bodies come together, in what he refers to as "the second phase," to subvert the old rape theme of black man and white woman. What Faulkner explores from the point of view of a white spinster's unjust accusations in "Dry September," he approaches through the apparently fulfilled fantasy of interracial sex in Light in August. Yet this is part of Joanna Burden's fiction: no longer a masculine narrative but a parody of feminine desire. They cast themselves as prey and beast, white virgin and "bad nigger." The suggestion of Joe's blackness excites Joanna, moving her from "the first phase," as Joe sees it, of masculine disdain—when their relationship is at its most fluid, incorporating homosexual and heterosexual desire and a liquidity of gender—to the "nymphomaniacal" state most critics focus on. There are actually three stages in her destruction, as represented by Joe. While he does not "write" her story in the way the narrators in Absalom, Absalom! write the Sutpen novel(s), he "reports" on her behavior and so shapes the story of how his victim/lover/partner/Other meets her final (fragmented) feminization.

In the second stage Joanna is no longer masculine; she is a parody of femininity, Miss Minnie Cooper all over again, desiring a black man's body. She plays rape. Joe Christmas colludes in the story of mingled romance and assault, becoming the "negro" ravisher. She directs her fiction, chattering to him about her day and making him tell about his day every night in bed, leaving notes in a secret place directing him to come to her at different times and locations, playing cupiditous hide and seek, this time ripping up her own clothes. Most interestingly, she speaks her now-exaggerated sexuality in "the forbidden wordsymbols" revealing "an insatiable appetite for the sound of them on his tongue and on her own" (283). Joe seems almost incidental to what seems, by now, a species of autoeroticism, feeling "shocked" at her slide into these grotesque "avatar[s] of a woman in love" (284). "This is not my life. I dont belong here" he thinks. As Rosa Coldfield's story of multiple desires leaves Quentin behind, as Minnie Cooper's and Zilphia Gant's fictions use men as characters only to be controlled, the liaison in *Light in August* becomes more Joanna's and less Joe's.

The narrative reinforces this sense of her degenerating into mere "feminine" heterosexuality. She has become "filthy," neurotic, evidently on the edge of mental collapse: "Within six months she was completely corrupted." "The sewer ran only by night" (281). This excremental image of female sexuality echoes Tertullian's description of a woman as a temple built over a sewer. Joanna revels in the story of her own uncleanliness; Joe fears he will drown in her "bottomless morass" (285). She objectifies the sewer, pregnant not with their child but with "that rotten richness ready to flow into putrefaction at a touch, like something growing in a swamp" (287). But Joe, her violator and coconspirator, is not blamed for her corruption; when he says she is more like the man and he like the woman, he inverts not the mere physical details of their affair but the accepted view of rape as well. Joanna, rather than being "ruined" by her liaison with him, gathers corruption "from the air itself" and begins "to corrupt him" (285). The nature of this corruption is not explained, but perhaps it is fixity in a role. Joe here seems a unified subject, not the multiple being he was earlier, crossing genders, races, and sexualities. He is masculine and heterosexual, and appears to have accepted (for this moment) the "blackness" with which Joanna has marked him. He sees her contest in her own doubleness the masculine and feminine selves battling for dominance:

> He stayed, watching the two creatures that struggled in one body like two moongleamed shapes struggling drowning in alternate throes upon the surface of a thick black pool beneath the last moon. Now it would be that still, cold, contained figure of the first phase who, even though lost and damned, remained somehow impervious and impregnable; then it would be the other, the second one, who in furious denial of that impregnability strove to drown in the black abyss of its own creating that physical purity which had been preserved too long now even to be lost. (286)

The narrative accords Joe Christmas pride of place as the victim, his sexuality called well-adjusted "as a life of healthy and normal sin usually is." Joanna's sexuality is perverse by contrast. Her sexuality is associated with that "thick black pool," the "sewer" he thinks he has fallen into. These might be seen as images of menstruation, recalling the "liquid, deathcolored and foul" that comes from the visionary cracked urns in the forest that make Joe vomit when he finds out the messy truth of female biology (209). Likewise the blackness relates to his possible "black blood"; even while Joe seems to work to fix his position relative to Joanna, her story opposes his and destabilizes it.

When she enters what Joe constructs as the third stage, Joanna's femaleness is further fixed in the most fundamental of roles: mother. "She had begun to get fat" as if she were pregnant or at least growing "womanly" in body instead of hard and angular (286). Of course, she is a travesty of a mother as she was a travesty of a nubile woman. Her menopausal pregnancy parodies Lena Grove's real one, her "praying" perversely recalls Mrs. McEachern. Joe begins to rebel against her fiction: "*She wants to be married*" (290). She wants to take control. This misogynist wisdom often emanates from the mouths of men in Faulkner's fiction. Gavin Stevens, in *Intruder in the Dust*, tells his nephew that women "want to be married" more than anything else. Even Lena Grove wants to be married. According to the community, women do not wish physical communion so much as social validation. In Joanna's case she wants power over Joe, either in a domestic arrangement or by becoming another adopted mother, sending him off to a black college to better himself. Joanna changes the direction and genre of her fiction from the masochistic-romantic story of the black rapist, where Joe is written as a cross between Romeo and Gus in *The Clansman*, to a liberal drama of uplifting the race in the manner of T. S. Stribling's *Birthright* or Charles Chesnutt's "passing" novels, in which she assumes the dominant character of white Friend to the Negro.

Joe, however, resists this new fiction. While Joanna's histrionic passions "shocked" and confused him, their relationship at least gave him a powerful role as the sexual intruder. In the "third phase," Joanna turns herself into a domineering mother, making him an abusive child. They are no longer bed partners: "You're not any good any more," Joe says, calling her an old woman, beating her for becoming menopausal. Where before she was "manlike," then "nymphomaniacal" and "rotten" with desire, Joanna now represents the dried-up body of the spinster, "useless" in a male sexual economy. Like Zilphia Gant, she gets a child without pregnancy but does not count on the child's rage against her. What is often called Joe's misogyny is hatred of the mother's body. He despises the nurturing of Mrs. McEachern, seeing in it "feminine" weakness. He is most successfully violent against Joanna when she is most maternal: cooking him food, planning his future for him, even trying to save his soul.

The single woman, though marginalized, is not allowed to opt out of the sexual economy. Joanna Burden is menopausal, childless, manless: "not any good any more." Her dissonant storymaking, the fictions—subversive retellings of the rape theme or the "nigger-loving Yankee" drama—she makes to control her own world, present a challenge to the symbolic order and must be silenced. As she becomes more and more the pious nag of a "mother," another female parody, Joe becomes more and more the "bad nigger," the instrument (though victim himself) of southern society's need to contain the feminine. Which of the two "moongleamed shapes" that are his vision of Joanna does Joe kill: the feminine caricature whose body with its thirty extra pounds advertises sexual receptivity or the masculine mirror image with whom he engaged in a homoerotic affair? In the third phase, Joe goes to her bedroom summoned by notes no longer "evocative of unspoken promise, of rich and unmentionable delights," not for sex—she has begun to say no—but for her attempts to convince him to enter the (black) bourgeoisie by going to college, running her affairs, becoming a husband of sorts, perhaps more a son and heir. He responds by hitting and cursing her with the words he previously used to arouse her.

Joanna's doubleness manifests itself physically now with her face "prominently boned, long, a little thin, almost manlike: in contrast to it her plump body was more richly and softly animal than ever" (291). She wants to reduce Joe's doubleness just as he wants to reduce her to an "old woman" who hasn't "got any baby" (304). The multiplicity that once seemed creative in their relationship is now terrifying. In their final scene together, the ambivalence, the lack of fixity of signs, is almost dizzying. The "no" with which Joanna refuses sex becomes the "no" with which Joe refuses to pray. Joanna asks God to absolve her of her sins of the flesh, but the prayer itself is obscene: "When it was necessary to use the symbol-words which he had taught her, she used them, spoke them forthright and without hesitation, talking to God as if He were a man in the room with two other men" (308). Here Joanna is "she" but also one of the "two other men" present. Joe refuses to light the lamp, yet he lights it; he finds Joanna wearing her nightdress sitting in bed, yet she does not want sex from him but death; it sounds as though she wants him to kill her, yet she tries to kill him (309–10).

The stories don't add up; they can't, uttered in this bisexual, mulatto, double space inside the Burden place, the nonplantation house of the unvirginal spinster where she entertained her racially ambiguous lover.

When Joe and Joanna face each other over the bed that has been the site of rape and pleasure, of protean expressions of desire, gender, and race, they each have a weapon; she points the old cap-and-ball revolver at him while he holds the razor. The gun is a "white" weapon, masculine, for defending property, probably used by elder Burdens to protect blacks from whites or themselves from the likes of the Sartorises; the straight razor is a "black" weapon, a street-fighting or quiet murdering instrument: Jesus in "That Evening Sun" means to murder his wife, Nancy, with a razor. But the gun fails to fire, and Joe Christmas becomes again the black rapist, acting out the stereotypical assault and murder on the isolated, manless virgin.

The community accepts the murder, so neatly does it fit into the dominant story of the "nigger beast" preying on white female flesh. They see not a complex relationship but "an anonymous negro crime committed not by a negro but by Negro and who knew, believed, and hoped that she had been ravished too: at least once before her throat was cut and at least once afterward" (315–16). Like Temple Drake at Lee Goodwin's trial, Joanna's body is subjected to the rapacious gaze of the community. In cutting her throat, Joe gives Joanna another orifice, *refeminizing* her, yet silencing her forever. Joanna only achieves the status of "white lady" in death, her body both violated by their titillated gaze—they assume that she, like Miss Minnie Cooper, has known the ultimate forbidden, sex with a black man—the presumed stain of "dishonor" washed away by her blood.

John Duvall thinks it's wrong to define this as murder, lest we "tacitly affirm that woman is victim—and that we unknowingly participate in the crowd's hope that she has been raped—and that the death of a woman . . . is somehow special, more important than that of a man" (24). While the object of this argument is to "place Joanna on equal ground . . . with Joe" and to "give her an agency" so as not to reduce her to "passive object," Joanna is a victim. In the end Joe destroys her, erases her body, the multifarious symbol of his desire. The contradictions she represented became intolerable: any agency she might have had is denied her. Joe has made a "woman" of her.

But the rapacious community makes a woman of Joe as well—both a woman and a "nigger." Where he played "Negro" with Joanna to arouse her sexually, now he has to play "Negro" for the whole community. He seems to have tried to reduce his own varietous selves into one: black-man. He behaves as grossly as any "nigger beast" from the lurid imaginations of Klan apologists and white supremacist politicians, exposing himself to passing cars as though the sight of his penis will finally inscribe his maleness on the world: " 'White bastards!' he shouted. 'That's not the first of your bitches that ever saw . . .' " (118). However, his maleness, like his blackness, is unstable: the narrative and several characters within it (such as Gavin Stevens) speak through a discourse of black and white blood. Black blood is particularly evocative and associated with menstruation— the tree urns run with foul, dark fluid. When Percy Grimm, constructing Joe as both black rapist and homosexual—"Has every preacher and old maid in Jefferson taken their pants down to the yellowbellied son of a bitch?"—castrates him, it is almost like a revelation (512). As Joe dies, "from out the slashed garments about his hips and loins the pent black blood seemed to rush like a released breath. It seemed to rush out of his pale body like the rush of sparks from a rising rocket" (513).

While I will not, as Aristotle did, define a woman as a mutilated man, Joe Christmas is "feminized" here, robbed of his signifying genitals, emblematized in that "black blood" which *sounds* like a racial reduction when it might really represent his feminine self, menstruating. In *Sanctuary* Horace Benbow has a vision of Temple/Little Belle with "something black and furious . . . roaring out of her pale body" (234). This "black blood" suggests both menstruation and ejaculation; the ejaculatory nature of Joe's death is suggested by the "rising rocket." In the end Joe incorporates both white and black, both male and female, both the ability to menstruate and to ejaculate, and is present yet erased; the myriad play of self and desire is obliterated in the face of the community need for conformity and unity, for the hierarchies of white/black, male/female to remain undisturbed.

The South used lynching as a means of category control to insist that transgressions could not take place unchallenged. Faulkner wrote *Light in August* in the midst of a culture that both lynched and debated lynching. Ida B. Wells said in her journal, the *Memphis Free Speech* (1892), that it's a "lie that Negro men rape white women," and that behind many lynchings was actually an interracial love affair.[6] White Jefferson must believe that Joe, a black man, raped and killed Joanna, a white woman. Otherwise, racial and sexual anarchy would threaten. Jessie Daniel Ames became accustomed to attacks on the Association of Southern Women for the Prevention of Lynching that suggested that the members were monsters who unnaturally craved sex with black men. Ames responded that she found it odd that "only segregation and the law against intermarriage keep white women from preferring the arms of Negro men" (Hall 154). What if white women secretly wanted black men? The social order of the South could not bear that attack on its categorical absolutes. It was an unexpressed anxiety in the west Florida lynching of Claud Neal for Lola Cannidy's murder in 1934: it could have been, a rumor said, that Claud and Lola had been lovers. This story was quickly suppressed in favor of one that stressed that she had been "brutally" raped, as Faulkner would say, "not by a negro but by Negro"; Claud Neal was the sacrifice to community order.

Gail Hightower, Joanna Burden, and Joe Christmas are destroyed by a rapacious social order that demands their reduction to single, circumscribed categories of being. The other outsider, Lena Grove, escapes. She triumphs over the patriarchal order by wearing her sexuality and fecundity overtly, without the layers of social denial that warp others' sexual relations. In her wandering, she represents the unfettered feminine, not constructing her desire in erotic racial play or articulating it in obscene "symbolwords" like Joanna Burden, but expressing it through her body. Gail Hightower, jealous of her hold on Byron, puts it rather reductively: "That will be her life, her destiny. The good stock peopling in tranquil obedience to it the good earth; from these hearty loins without hurry or haste descending mother and daughter. But by Byron engendered next. Poor boy" (448). Nonetheless, Lena is not penalized for her sexuality. She walks out of the wreckage in Jefferson with her body intact, still the perfect urn, still the "unravished bride," still "unbroken" (Clarke 400).[7] The less perfect vessel, Joanna Burden, and her shadow/lover/child, Joe Christmas, pay for their play in blood spilling from unspeaking orifices.

6 | Mothers and Motherhood

Oh blessed tie! uniting mother and child. Earth cannot, and Heaven will

not break it.—Mary H. Eastman, AUNT PHILLIS' CABIN

Dixie Madonna: The White Southern Mother

In *Gone with the Wind*, Scarlett O'Hara confuses her mother with the Virgin Mary; when she prays she imagines Ellen Robillard O'Hara instead of the Queen of Heaven, secretly according the Virgin's titles Health of the Sick, Seat of Wisdom, Refuge of Sinners, and Mystical Rose to her ever-suffering, ever-loving mother (60, 70). The Virgin as the conduit through which passes the masculine deity or, more important, as the vessel that, for a while, *contains* the Word made flesh, is the model for representing the white mother of the antebellum South. Her body provides white heirs to the property; her chastity guarantees racial purity. White supremacy is situated in her, as is the perpetuation of the class system and the plantation structure. Yet she is paradoxically asexual for all that she bears children. Like the Virgin, she remains intact, an unbroken vessel. Her husband barely dares approach her sexually: "He stood before her in dumb, half-amazed admiration, as he might before the inscrutable vision of a superior being. What she really was, was known only to God" (Page, *Old South* 155). And Julia Kristeva reminds us that "of the virginal body we are entitled only to the ear, the tears and the breasts. . . . the female sexual organ has been transformed into an innocent shell" (108).

The madonna-mother's body is central to the plantation world, yet mystified. In John Pendleton Kennedy's *Swallow Barn* (1832) the Meriwether estate is presided over by a fecund mistress whose only utterance comes in childbearing: "She is a fruitful vessel, and seldom fails in her annual tribute to the honors of the family" (40). Children make up Mrs. Meriwether's contribution to the wealth of the plantation: she gives them in "tribute" to a feudal overlord, her husband, whose name distinguishes the family "honors." In her designation as fruitful, Mrs. Meriwether is connected to the land and its economy. In her ability to produce a crop, she fulfills the role the Belles, those "virgin fields" and "untouched lands," are brought up to.

The physical body of the mother, and the biological bond with her children as the defining feature of white motherhood, are displaced in favor of a spiritual image of the matriarch. She becomes not just the mother of a few privileged white children (apparently by means of parthenogenesis) but the mother of the entire plantation: "'A planter's wife has little occasion for romance,' said Mrs. Weston; 'her duties are too many and too important. She must care for the health and comfort of her family, and of her servants. After all, a hundred servants are like so many children to look after'" (Eastman 256). This vision of white plantation motherhood assumes that adult black slaves occupy the position of children directed by the wife of their owner; not only does it destroy the idea of the discrete black family, it expands the white family to dominate all with the white woman as figurehead, a symbol of the owner's power, mediating between the lowly and the master as the Virgin intercedes for souls with God the Father. She is singular, the source of moral instruction, grace, goodness, represented by the classical body on the pedestal. But she is also powerless:

> This recognition of the desire of uniqueness is immediately checked by the postulate that uniqueness is achieved only by way of exacerbated masochism: an actual woman worthy of the feminine ideal embodied in inaccessible perfection by the Virgin could not be anything other than a nun or a martyr; if married, she would have to lead a life that would free her from her "earthly" condition by confining her to the uttermost sphere of sublimation, alienated by her own body. (Kristeva 115)

While northern and English writers also produced pious fictions of maternal perfection, in the South the construction of white motherhood served an important ideological purpose in reinforcing the patriarchal structure of the plantation. Perhaps more important, angelic motherhood papered over the fissures in sexual decorum on the plantation. The insistence on the white mother's innate goodness and morality betrays a profound anxiety about the coherence of the family, both the ruling white family and the extended slave "family." Sarah Gayle, an Alabama slaveholding woman, places the mother next to God: "I never think of woman's character as it should be but, my mother my dear mother, rises up in all her excellence, all her native purity. It did not need the precepts of men to make her all she should be her heart was the handywork 'of the Creator'" (Fox-Genovese 10). Indeed, the precepts of slaveholding men often had little to do with "native purity"; Sarah Gayle tells of a slaveholder whose "child and his grand-child have one mother" (Fox-Genovese 9). Mary Chesnut talks of white mothers "pure as angels" surrounded by the slave "concubines" their husbands keep "like patriarchs of old" (29–31).

Slaveholding women like Gayle and Chesnut glorify white motherhood as all that is opposite to the sexual anarchy and license they see around them. Of course, the official version of southern motherhood does not even admit of such knowledge; fictional representations of mothers in southern writings place the angelic mother in a setting not at odds with her virtue but worthy of it. Like the southern land itself, or the Virgin Mary, the antebellum southern mother is inwardly pure, spiritually inviolate, no matter how great the menace of Yankee invaders, black rapists, looters, or carpetbaggers. In the prewar order, she resides at the center of the plantation myth, the madonna of the Big House, who, as a "true woman," used her influence to instill bravery and chivalry in her sons, modesty and chastity in her daughters. The home was spiritualized and all disruptive passions banished as the wife and mother became more and more invested with all goodness, incapable of committing any of the seven deadly sins, particularly immune from lust. Sir William Acton's *The Functions and Disorders of the Reproductive Organs* (1857) says of "good" women:

> Love of home, children, and domestic duties, are the only passions they feel.
>
> As a general rule, a modest woman seldom desires any sexual gratification for herself. She submits to her husband, but only to please him; and, but for the desire of maternity, would far rather be relieved from his attentions. (Trudgill 56)

Dr. John Kellogg's *Plain Facts for Old and Young* (1881) characterizes sexual drives as dangerous, to be employed (sparingly) for procreation only (Degler 254, 250, 253). These assertions reveal deep confusion over female sexuality and its power; for a woman to be "modest" she must be asexual, yet all her energies must be directed toward becoming pregnant. The Galenic gynecology of the Middle Ages and the Renaissance asserted that a woman could conceive only if she had an orgasm (which was defined as "heat"); orgasmic women in Victorian times were often thought to be "insane," sometimes subjected to clitoridectomies, and generally condemned as whores.[1] Anything that diverted sexuality from conception was immoral. The pietizing of motherhood reinforced this rigid containment of the female body exclusively as a vessel for the nurturing of babies. The self was suppressed: "She must learn to control herself, to subdue her own passions; she must set her children an example of meekness and of equanimity . . . never let her manifest irritated feeling or give utterance to an angry expression" (Rich 62–64).

The southern model of motherhood incorporated these strategies of containment, veiled in a rhetoric of worship: "We live in a civilization in which the *consecrated* (religious or secular) representation of femininity is subsumed under maternity" (Kristeva 100). Children defined a woman's existence; it was a southern gynecologist, J. Marion Simms of Alabama, who recommended that a patient who found intercourse "painful" have sex while unconscious on chloroform so that she might conceive (Degler 257). Lack of children was a stigma: Mary Chesnut records how Colonel Chesnut, her father-in-law, flaunts his wife's fecundity and that of their children and grandchildren, in the face of his childless daughter-in-law: "Old Mr. C. said today 'Wife, you must feel that you have not been useless in your day and generation. You have twenty-seven great-grandchildren.' . . . [[Me a childless wretch . . . Colonel Chesnut, a man who rarely wounds me. . . . And what of me, God help me—no good have I done myself or anyone else with this I boast so of, the power to make myself loved" (32).

The vision of the mother as the Virgin Mary appears not just in Scarlett O'Hara's imagination: W. J. Cash lists "the pitiful Mother of God" in his catalog of white southern archetypes (86). The ideal mother inhabits the plantation garden, a fertile but hermetic setting she shares with her virgin daughters (Kolodny 67, 72).

The Edenic plantation ruled over by the exemplary mother-goddess is depicted in a vast array of romances before and after the war. The novels of William Gilmore Simms and Caroline Gilman evoke a pastoral, maternal setting. The integrity of southern motherhood was held up as a counterargument to the widely assumed southern decadence during the slavery-abolition debate. Stowe accepts the universal motherhood of the plantation mistress up to a point: *Uncle Tom's Cabin* shows Mrs. Shelby feeling appropriate distress when some of her slave "children" are sold away. But the sickly and narcissistic Marie St. Clare, ancestress of generations of neurasthenic ladies of the Big House, does not care even for her white child. In the responses to *Uncle Tom's Cabin*, however, the southern mother is perfect. In *The Black Gauntlet* she is semidivine; the mother of the plantation master Mr. Wyndham is called "a ministering angel"; when she dies it is declared, "They had never seen her angry in all her life" (55). Later in the novel, this "sainted mother" acts as a kindly ambassador to God in heaven, interceding for her foolish son who has married a frivolous and nonmaternal woman.

The southern mother becomes a saint on earth through sacrifice: in the postwar novels the sacrifice is often put in terms not only of the children but also of the Lost Cause. In *The Clansman* Marion Lenoir's mother, in jumping off a cliff with her daughter, not only eradicates the "stain" of her child's rape, she also responds to the chaotic Reconstruction hell of free and freely attacking blacks in the way most appropriate to a white southern mother: resigning from the scene in sympathy with her "ruined" daughter, she takes her purpose and identity from her child. In Ellen Glasgow's *Virginia* (1913) Virginia Pendleton's mother is Christ-like, living "not in her own joys and sorrows but in those of others" (25). She is not person but role: "She doesn't seem to have any life at all until you see her with Virginia's children" (191). Indeed, she does not, nor can she, live without the other shaping force in her existence, her husband. After his death she fades gracefully: "She had gone through life without giving trouble, and she gave none at the end" (297).

In the 1930s and 1940s a few writers still affirmed the ideal. Stark Young's *So Red the Rose* (1934) could have been written half a century before, so neatly does it fit into the pious view of southern motherhood and so adamantly does it insist on Confederate Woman virtue for all its mothers— and, by extension, the contemporary white mothers of the South. Young took part in the wars of southern representation in the thirties, battling with images from mass culture and literature (Erskine Caldwell, T. S. Stribling, and William Faulkner were on the "other side") that suggested white southern womanhood had fallen very far from the pedestal. In later fiction the white southern mother ceases to embody feminine perfection, becoming conversely the scapegoat for its transgressions and excesses, linked, like the Belle, with the South's decline in the morally reduced twentieth century. Even *Gone with the Wind* with its exemplary Ellen Robillard, the "great lady" and self-denying mother who haunts the novel, reproaching Scarlett from beyond the grave for her every crime against Old South sanctity, or the saintly Melanie Wilkes, who so resolutely fulfills her goal of childbearing that she dies from it, places these figures in the irretrievable past. The entrepreneurial, selfish, antimaternal Scarlett, unwilling to define herself either through a husband or through children, represents the future.

White women writers often interrogate the "perfect" southern mother. Kate Chopin's *The Awakening* (1899) poses a serious debate between the madonna, who would annihilate herself for her children, and a woman who begins to see that she has a discrete self that cannot be denied. The private demands of sexuality and autonomy are weighed against the social demands that a white woman play her role; Edna Pontellier fails in her husband's eyes: "He reproached his wife with her inattention, her habitual neglect of the children. If it was not a mother's place to look after children, whose on earth was it?" (885). Glasgow, in *The Miller of Old Church* (1911), a less benign view of the southern mother than *Virginia*, does not dismiss marriage and reproduction—as they are not dismissed in *The Awakening*—yet she critiques the spurious "motherly" values that produce the clinging Mrs. Gay: "She dominated not by force, but by sentiment, that she had surrendered all rights in order to grasp more effectively at privilege" (72). Mrs. Gay insists on her place in the saccharine hagiography of motherhood. She is "sensitive"; indeed, she, like Marie St. Clare, gains power through invalidism, lying on a sofa all day, not selfless but self-obsessed. Estranged from her body, she nonetheless uses its supposed weakness to manipulate her family.

Lillian Smith insists that the white southern mother is a victim; in her 1949 autobiographical *Killers of the Dream*, a generation of impotent women silently acquiesce in their husbands' sexual profligacy and their children's demands as they stand still on their pedestals, participating in their own fossilization: "The majority of southern women convinced themselves that God had ordained that they be deprived of pleasure" (137). Frances Newman, however, constructs the ideal as a false idol to be knocked off her pedestal. In *The Hard-boiled Virgin* the *haute bourgeoise* southern mother merely mandates "good taste" for her children. Katharine Faraday's class-obsessed parent, for example, "thought that a taste for flowers was a necessary quality of all Southern ladies" and had "heard in her cradle that a nation which would prefer a Lincoln to a Breckenridge was unlikely to return to the conviction that elegance is the greatest of all human virtues" (188, 17).

The representation and critique of the white mother in Faulkner's fictions is similarly class-based; as with Belles, upper-class white women are most punished for their fall from the ideal. Just as loss of virginity seems less a catastrophe with larger cultural and social implications for Dewey Dell Bundren than for Temple Drake, the twentieth-century southern wasteland implicates not lower-class mothers such as Lena Grove but decadent descendants of Confederate Women such as Caroline Compson. Faulkner's narratives indict white women for being sexual without being maternal or being asexual and therefore incapable of nurturing children. Faulkner's work reflects the struggle over the sentimental ideal of white motherhood in a twentieth-century South that seemed unable to support such an angelic being. How can the devil on the dance floor become the Angel in the House? Does the post-Confederate, postsuffrage woman still accept her silencing?

Faulkner told Loïc Bouvard in a 1952 interview, "The most important thing is that man continues to create just as woman continues to give birth" (Meriwether and Millgate 73). His black mothers are, as we have seen, often a reproach to the white middle- and upper-class mother: Dilsey, Molly, Elnora, and Louvinia demonstrate the self-sacrificing ascendancy of black women over their white counterparts. Caroline Compson and Addie Bundren belie the stereotype of the supreme nurturer at the heart of every southern home, and Laverne Shumann and Charlotte Rittenmeyer abandon the children who are supposed to be the defining light of their existences. Eula Varner and Temple Drake are forced by their society to act out dramas of expiation. The white mother in Faulkner's fiction betrays much anxiety about the place of childbearing and child rearing in the modern woman's life: these women reveal an alternating romanticism and rage.

Sally R. Page claims that for Faulkner, "woman's purpose is the bearing of children and in her submission to that process she achieves serenity and virtue" (93). This is far too simple a reading. Even in Faulkner's later novels, when motherhood can seem a reforming force, only the minor figure Margaret Mallison gains "serenity and virtue"; born-again mothers like Eula Varner and Temple Drake die or are eternally silenced. Southern culture wants to "solve" the female body by declaring it dangerous or anomalous unless defined by a man or a child; women who resist this confinement are destroyed. Faulkner may not call up the Virgin Mary, Margaret Mitchell's image of the perfect mother, but he evokes the vessel that, unless "filled" by the masculine, contains only empty—meaning-less—space.

Absent Bodies and Overflowing Wombs

Faulkner's first experiments in prose reveal an obsession with child-bearing as experience and metaphor. In "Elmer," the unfinished novel begun in 1925, the title character's earliest memories are of his mother's body, particularly her breasts. Despite the nurture and feeding implied by Elmer's recollection, she is no madonna but a restless, "passionate, indomitable woman" who continually forces her weak husband and children to move around. Elmer's "true" mother is his androgynous sister Jo-Addie: she provides the selfless comfort Elmer cannot get from his biological mother. The relationship between Elmer and Jo-Addie, as well as between Jo-Addie and their mother, anticipates the estranged affections in The Sound and the Fury, where Quentin is "mothered" by his sister Caddy (even her name is similar to Jo-Addie's) and simultaneously fascinated and repelled by the dark womb spaces he associates with his mother.

If Jo-Addie partakes both of the masculine (her boyish body antici-pates the garçon vierge in so much of Faulkner's fiction of the twenties and thirties) and of the maternal, Elmer himself appropriates the feminine; he is a painter who describes artistic production as "brooding maternity" in which the "pregnant" paint strives to deliver that "in which was yet wombed his heart's desire." Throughout his career Faulkner intertwined birthing images with declarations of the artist's function. But he assigned gender roles to "creativity"; as he stated in his interview with Loïc Bou-vard, men make art, women make babies. In his fiction women who take on the role of producer of art rather than producer of offspring, either overtly like Charlotte Rittenmeyer, who makes sculptures, or covertly, like Addie Bundren (who usurps "masculine" discourse by actively con-trolling her story through language), are punished or silenced.[2] Maternal roles in "Elmer," as in much of Faulkner's early prose, are displaced; real mothers are absent or antimaternal.[3] Mrs. Monson, "a brusque woman with cold eyes," mother of Elmer's "unattainable star," Myrtle, ruthlessly runs her daughter's life (*Uncollected Stories* 613). In *Soldiers' Pay* the "mother" is Margaret Powers, whose decidedly "powerful" sexuality is suppressed in favor of nurturing motherless men: Cadet Lowe, Joe Gilligan, and the wounded soldier Donald Mahon. Though she marries the paralyzed Mahon (instead of the virile Gilligan), their relationship is of mother to helpless infant: charity replaces desire.

Mosquitoes has no mothers at all, just aunts, spinsters, boyish virgins, and incipient earth goddesses waiting to get pregnant. This lack of a genuine maternal presence never stops men in the novel from pontificating on the role of the mother, however. Dawson Fairchild invokes the "old biology" that governs the creativity proper to women and pities men who must create through "perversion" instead of the natural process of copulation, conception, and birth: "Creation, reproduction from within. . . . Is the dominating impulse in the world feminine, after all as aboriginal peoples believe? . . . There is a kind of spider or something. The female is the larger, and when the male goes to her he goes to death: she devours him during the act of conception" (267). The passage (over)dramatically expresses the essentialist idea that women's reproductive capacity governs their identities. Most men in Faulkner's fictions conservatively view the female body as a container for gestation and instrument of nurture. They endorse something called "the female principle," described as if it were a deified vagina or giant cave in which men get fatally lost. In *Light in August* it is the "lightless hot wet primogenitive Female"; in *Absalom, Absalom!* it comes from "the hot equatorial groin of the world"; in *The Wild Palms* it is simply that which causes men to be "doomed and lost." Properly utilized in motherhood, this dangerous space, with its power to engulf, is filled and validated.

It is not until *The Sound and the Fury* (1929) that Faulkner confronts the decay of the perfect southern mother. Caroline Bascomb Compson is a bitter rebuke and devastating response to the plantation angel-mother. Dilsey acts as the authentic mother of the Compson family. Some critics have suggested that this accurately reflects the state of affairs in the Murry Falkner–Maud Butler household, where Maud held aloof from her children emotionally, leaving Mammy Callie to provide love and attention (Sensibar 50–53). Whatever the biographical connection between Falkner

home life and the declining Compson family, the portrait of Caroline indicts the white mother for psychological cruelty, snobbery, and moral
and emotional vacancy. Quentin thinks to himself with despairing accuracy, "If I'd just had a mother so I could say Mother Mother" (213). Mrs. Compson,
like Narcissa Benbow, focuses on appearances and role-playing. Class is
her defining principle. She scolds Caddy for carrying Benjy around and
possibly injuring her back: "All of our women have prided themselves on
their carriage. Do you want to look like a washerwoman" (77).[4]

The four narrators in *The Sound and the Fury* give a changing and refracted
view of Caddy and Dilsey: each sees according to his need. The curious
thing about the rendering of Mrs. Compson is the way her portrayal varies
only slightly from voice to voice. Benjy "reports" her concern with family
pride and status: she originally called him after her brother but changed
his name when she found out he was retarded and so not deserving of
the accolade of a Bascomb name. Quentin's fragments, punctuated by
his father's generalizations, show his mother condemning her daughter's
"bad blood," while Jason records his mother's refusal to take any money
from Caddy, though they are rather poor, because she is a "fallen woman."

In short, Caroline Compson defines herself in terms of the role of lady.
She is not an individual but an extension of the Bascombs, a family point-
edly not of the elevated rank of the Compsons—middle class perhaps,
but not aristocrats, about which she is sensitive. She blames her lack of
power over her children on her husband's perceived snobbery: "*How can I
control any of them when you have always taught them to have no respect for me and my
wishes I know you look down on my people*" (118). Control is Caroline Compson's
ruling passion. She wishes to order her children and her life to suit some
vision of the proper upper-class southern home (a spurious vision), but
history catches up with her: the Compson lands are sold off, the house is
crumbling, her husband is an alcoholic, her brother a sponger, her eldest
son a suicide, her youngest son an idiot, her favorite son an avaricious
miser, and her daughter unmarried and pregnant. To add insult to injury,
these tragedies are laid at her feet: Quentin's *cri de coeur* sums it all up: if
he, if they all, only had a mother. Mrs. Compson's portrayal reflects punishment of white mothers for their weakness and narcissism: "I am not
one of those women who can stand things" (7). Dilsey, the black mother,
can "stand things," can "endure," but her mistress keeps to her bed in a
crisis, signifying the absence of the white woman's body while Dilsey is
perpetually and helpfully present.

The neurasthenic mother is an important figure in the mind of the South, perhaps stemming from the exaggerated Victorian notion of feminine delicacy. Middle-class society in the nineteenth century assumed that women were always ill.[5] For some of Faulkner's mothers, illness is aggression. Ellen Sutpen takes to her bed over the disappointment of her daughter's nonengagement to Charles Bon. Mrs. Compson rules her world from her bed; she appears impotent, weak, and fragile, yet the household revolves around her whims. That bed is the focus of her world: later in life she leaves it only to struggle ostentatiously to family meals in order to further impose her ideas about "position" and "place" on the ragged remnant of the Compsons and to visit her dead in the Jefferson cemetery. Surely the bed once had positive associations: the conception and birth of the Compson children, what Faulkner would see as the orderly and natural direction of a healthy female sexuality. Now it marks a location of coldness and denial. Inverting its erotic associations, Caddy seems to carry out her sexual liaisons everywhere but in a bed.

Mrs. Compson is generally reviled by critics for her cold unmaternal behavior and blamed for warping her children. Joan Williams, however, sees her as much maligned, preferring to blame Mr. Compson and the Mississippi class system with its restrictive rules and roles for women. Williams has a point: Jason Compson the elder is like Mr. Bennett in *Pride and Prejudice*, a clever, literate, but largely uninvolved parent; and the limits of possibility for the southern "lady" of Caroline Compson's day might have embittered her.[6] Certainly Caroline Compson is a product of the southern patriarchy that has, as her husband remarks in *Absalom, Absalom!*, turned its ladies into ghosts. The culture encouraged her to be fragile, chaste, and submissive, the guardian of family status and fruitful vessel for the production of family heirs. In her rage Caroline Compson takes these rules of ladyhood to extremes: she is hypochondriac, prurient, manipulative, snobbish, and, now that she has "given" her husband heirs, sexually unresponsive. Within the confines of her culture, it is as close as she can come to asserting a self.

The text appears to set up Caroline and Caddy as extreme responses to sexuality; it can seem as crude as Caddy = life, birth, sexuality, self-sacrificial motherhood, while Caroline = death, coldness, sterility, selfishness. Caroline Compson is constantly associated with death and dying. In one of the first recollections in Benjy's section, she prepares to visit the cemetery to brood over the graves of her husband and son. The

Caddy/Caroline binary proves, however, to be illusory. They appear to have opposite attitudes to sexuality; but in both, at least as they are constructed by Mr. Compson, Jason, Benjy, and Quentin, sexuality is tied to death. Jason recalls Caroline catching Caddy in an adolescent sexual encounter: "All next day she went around the house in a black dress and a veil and even Father couldnt get her to say a word except crying and saying her little daughter was dead" (286). The scent of honeysuckle announces Caddy, but Caroline smells of camphor like a closed-up house or a mothproof closet. She is already a sort of preembalmed corpse. Indeed, she signifies the empty womb, the cold body, while Caddy signifies the warmth and life. But Caddy is also Quentin's Little Sister Death. John T. Irwin's interpretation of Quentin's desire to merge with his sister clarifies the connection: "Quentin's love of death incorporates his incestuous love for his sister precisely because his sister, as a substitute for Quentin's mother, is synonymous with death" (153). The object of Quentin's desire, Caddy, blurs into his absent mother ("if I just had a mother"); the beloved body of the sister in which Quentin wishes to lose himself becomes the constricting body of the mother: "The dungeon was Mother herself" (173). By drowning, Quentin does, in a sense, achieve the sister/mother's body, returning to the feminine he craves. Caroline Compson, the dungeon/womb, meets the erotic through Caddy, her avatar, who only *seems* to be her opposite.

Addie Bundren not only is associated with death, but she is dead throughout most of the novel of which she forms, paradoxically, the dynamic epicenter. The connection between sexuality and death in this novel is as explosive as in The Sound and the Fury; indeed, As I Lay Dying can be read as the "poor white trash" version of The Sound and the Fury. The distant mother/sexual daughter binary works (ostensibly) in Addie and Dewey Dell, Addie wielding power even from her sickbed, Dewey Dell pregnant and unmarried. Whereas the Compson house objectifies the mother's body in The Sound and the Fury (see chapter 4), the coffin expresses the womb in As I Lay Dying. In both novels, the "problem" of the female body must be worked out; in both novels, the feminine destroys at least one of the family. But whereas, at the end of The Sound and the Fury, the feminine is contained in the maternal self-sacrifice of Dilsey, it remains an at-large threat in As I Lay Dying: Addie is dead but not gone.

Like Caroline Compson, Addie rules her family from her bed; then she directs them from her coffin. She is the central obsession of the Bundren family and the novel, in this way like Caddy Compson, a personality powerful in its (apparent) absence. Like Caroline Compson, she rejects the role of self-sacrificing mother. Dominating her family even from a nailed-up coffin is part of her struggle for a voice, for a self. "I would be I" she says. But the movement of the narration and the project of the narrators is to silence her, to finally bury her.

Unlike Caroline Compson, Addie does not create her self according to the dictates of "ladyhood." Also unlike Caroline, her voice is directly heard. Most tellers of tales in Faulkner are men or single old women. Mothers tell their stories through their children; words are officially the province of men (or the "manlike"). Addie, however, seizes language for her own purposes; she speaks the forbidden. She speaks the body in claiming language is irrelevant: "That was when I learned that words are no good; that words dont fit even what they are trying to say at," (163). Language is seen as a male preserve. Men compose most of the speakers of the novel: Darl, Anse, Jewel, Cash, and so on; or, in Cora Tull's case, a spokeswoman for the patriarchy; or, in Dewey Dell's case, nearly inarticulate. Addie is both constructed by others' words and the constructor of her family. The children constitute a kind of *logos* for her: they are her creations, and Anse is only the incidental provider of the seed. She says, "My children were of me alone, of the wild blood boiling along the earth, of me and all that lived; of none and of all" (167). Cleanth Brooks is on to something when he describes her as a "masculinized woman," according her "masculine" qualities, in contrast to Anse's "feminine" passivity; but he simply reinscribes the false "given" that motherhood is transcendent when he says: "She is completely feminine to the extent that she expresses herself in and through her children. She has fulfilled herself in breeding up and nurturing the children whom she is forcing to become heroes" (*Yoknapatawpha Country* 148). In Addie's section there is no sense that she is "fulfilled": she is simply ready to die. She is, if anything, a challenge to the idea that children are a woman's sole "fulfilling" end and purpose. Addie does not bring up and "nurture" her children into heroic action; she just exacts a promise that extends her control of them beyond death. She cares little for them as individuals; she values them only as she rules them. By making them, and Anse, bend to her will, she both takes revenge on them for invading the singleness of her being and witnesses her power over them just as the bloody welts on the schoolchildren increased her power: "Now you are aware of me! Now I am something in your secret and selfish life, who have marked your blood with my own for ever and ever" (162).

Addie is often seen as a kind of goddess, a figure encompassing birth and death, as André Bleikasten points out, the "queen bee," genetrix, dark Demeter, Medea (76). She is, as is common in southern writing, identified with the land: those natural forces bedeviling the Bundrens' "underworld" journey to bring her to burial almost seem to be attracted by her corpse. She is land-as-ambivalent-mother, both violent and creative: "the focus for both personalized and transpersonalized (or culturally shared) expressions of filial homage and erotic desire" (Kolodny 22). Addie elicits both desire in her children's jealousy over her attentions and homage in their obedience to traverse an often-hostile landscape at her command.

She inspires different, but almost equally intense, feelings in each of her children. Jewel, her "love child," has a fierce, exclusive, almost erotic attachment to her. He fantasizes about being perpetually alone with her, like Quentin's vision of living with Caddy safely isolated in hell, "just me and her on a high hill" (15). To Vardaman his mother's identity in death is unstable: she seems to become a kind of sacramental food, a fish he sees the night she dies, "Cooked and et. Cooked and et" (55). Addie is both sacrifice and goddess to be placated, sacred fish to be eaten and precipitator of disaster, fire or flood, on her family's archetypal journey. Communicating enigmatically with her children even in death, she typifies, in many ways, the engulfing mother. Adrienne Rich says this figure threatens her (male) offspring: "She is first of all the Mother who has to be possessed, reduced, controlled, lest she swallow him back into her dark caves or stare him into stone" (112). The mother is the ultimate powerful body, the womb that threatens the child with annihilation. As I Lay Dying works itself out as a containment the mother's body and silencing of her voice.

At the heart of the novel is a debate between the voice of the feminine and the rule of the patriarchy spoken by a female. Cora Tull speaks the Christian view of the family, the Law of the Father. Seeing the dying Addie, she says, "The eternal and the everlasting salvation and grace is not upon her" (8). In other words, Addie will not submit. Cora asserts that a wife and mother becomes an extension of her husband and children. She expresses horror at the Bundrens' plan to go forty miles to bury Addie: "A woman's place is with her husband and children, alive or dead" (22). Self is not a meaningful idea for her. Her third and most important section, juxtaposed with Addie's single monologue, attacks Addie for demanding a voice, a power almost equivalent to God (the Father): "It is out of your vanity that you would judge sin and salvation in the Lord's place" (159).

Cora spouts the party line: women find fulfillment in subsuming themselves in their husbands and children, remaining silent. Addie, however, is a Faustian woman: she demands knowledge, power, and autonomy. With her rage she sadistically "marks" her pupils, weakening them, reducing them to the powerless "feminine" state. Her anger produces children: "When I knew that I had Cash, I knew that living was terrible and that this was the answer to it" (163). Her children are not the focus of her life but a validation of her power. Far from exemplifying the role of selfless wife and mother Cora outlines for her, Addie's isolation increases. She sees Anse as "dead," sees her vaginal space, "where I used to be a virgin," as creatively blank and her children both as possessions and as interruptions to the tedious process of living "to get ready to stay dead a long time" (161). Snead reads Addie as emptying herself of Anse's name (and being) and replacing it "with a white space, Reverend Whitfield ('white field'), the tabula rasa that has, amazingly, made her pregnant. . . . The 'white field'—punning on the name of the usurping lover—is replaced on page 82 with the white space of Addie's coffin" (51). However, I see the blank space as a tabula rasa only from the point of view of the masculine text that requires words on the page for meaning. The wordless space of Addie's vagina—as well as the dead space of her coffin—resonate with messages. Gwin reads Addie's evocation of "the shape of my body where I used to be a virgin" as Addie's defiant I: "From inside the coffin in which patriarchy has sealed her, Addie Bundren rethinks subjectivity as a female space" (Feminine 154). Addie's voice resides in that enigmatic space.

As I Lay Dying can be read as conflicting stories about motherhood. There is a similar debate in Kate Chopin's The Awakening where Adèle Ratignolle, a "faultless madonna," ever pregnant, discusses the role of the mother with her friend Edna Pontellier, who, despite her two children, is "not a mother-woman" (888). Adèle Ratignolle's personality is subsumed into that of her children: "A woman who would give up her life for her children could do no more than that—your Bible tells you so. I'm sure I couldn't do more than that" (929). Here again, the Law of the Father, "your Bible," combats the law of desire; Edna, like Addie, puts herself first: "She would never sacrifice herself for her children or for anyone else" (929). Edna insists on a self: "I would give up the unessential; I would give my money, I would give my life for my children; but I wouldn't give myself" (929).

Addie is, at the very least, a refutation of sentimental motherhood. To her, children are never, as they are to Cora, "the sweetest thing I ever saw" but creatures with "little dirty snuffling" noses (20, 161). Cora speaks of duty, Addie speaks only of the radical power of pain, as in Emily Dickinson's poem:

> I like a look of Agony
> Because I know it's true.

Roles are empty; language is paradoxically both liberating and illusory: "When he was born I knew that motherhood was invented by someone who had to have a word for it because the ones that had the children didn't care whether there was a word for it or not. I knew that fear was invented by someone that had never had the fear; pride, who never had the pride" (163–64).

Addie identifies language as a male invention—they are the ones who didn't have the children. Moreover, motherhood is a male construct, designed to contain women in an unreal role. Addie's subversive act in appropriating language while at the same time distancing herself from it marks another bid for freedom from the Law of the Father. Her sexual rebellion attacks the Law of the Father through its opposite, the Law of Desire. As she usurps the male privilege of self-expression, she removes her body from the male economy that would control it as "wife" and "mother," and she commits adultery. Like Hester Prynne, she accepts responsibility for her passion. And her lover, Whitfield (as a minister of the church the most prominent representative of the Law of the Father and the obvious choice for Addie's partner in crime), like Dimmesdale, fears confession. Addie's affair with Whitfield parallels that of Hester and Dimmesdale, producing instead of a Pearl, a Jewel. And though Addie calls her adultery "sin," it is the expiation, the suffering, that matters to her: "And so when Cora Tull would tell me I was not a true mother, I would think how words go straight up in a thin line, quick and harmless, and how terribly doing goes along the earth, clinging to it, so that after a while the two lines are too far apart for the same person to straddle from one to the other" (165). According to Addie's version of the Law of Desire, doing and being cancel out words: the Law of the Father. According to the conventional representation of motherhood, Addie is not a "true mother": she is the antithesis of self-sacrifice. To Addie, motherhood is divorced from selfhood. The irony is that Addie must represent herself in language, in a text, and so she implicates herself in the very system from which she has tried to defect. As her powerful body is nailed in the box, her powerful voice is co-opted by the masculine. The coffin, the focus of fear and desire for her family, the objectification of the womb, is finally buried in the most traditionally "feminine" element, earth. Addie is defeated by the definition of femaleness that she resisted all her life.

In contrast to her mother, Addie's daughter, Dewey Dell, does not attempt a rebellion against the Law of the Father. Dewey Dell's very name locates her identity in her vagina, marking her as a vessel for creation, defining her through "old biology." In a Donne-like conceit, Darl connects her to the radical principle of procreation: "her leg coming long from beneath her tightening dress: that lever which moves the world; one of that caliper which measures the length and breadth of life" (97–98). The child Dewey Dell carries in her womb circumscribes her. Rather than being a seductive or terrifying space, Dewey Dell's womb is fruitful: she does not challenge the conventional definition of the feminine but fulfills it. Nor does she usurp language for subversive purposes. She speaks in the most rudimentary fashion. Her consciousness, such as it is, looks inward toward the life growing in her. She says: "I feel my body, my bones and flesh beginning to part and open upon the alone and the process of coming unalone is terrible" (59). Addie, too, felt that the process of gestation and birth was "terrible," but she declared her independence in words while Dewey Dell submits to the inevitable (163).

Dewey Dell is acutely aware of the process of gestation, but the act that produces the embryo does not seem to have much of an impression on her. She can barely articulate her body, and then in archetypal "feminine" terms: "I feel like a wet seed wild in the hot blind earth" (61). The narrative burlesques her pathetic attempt to get an abortifacient pill from a lecherous druggist; nothing seriously challenges her surrender to fertility. She is all body as Darl is all language.

Lena Grove in *Light in August* is perhaps the least problematic of the women Leslie Fiedler famously designated "the peasant wench as earth goddess" (*Love and Death* 300). Like Dewey Dell, she is nearly inarticulate; she accepts the dictates of her body. Her "closeness to nature" is admired by critics who do not examine what they mean by "nature." Sally R. Page says: "Lena Grove is Faulkner's most fascinating portrayal of a woman fulfilling her natural destiny. It is with the understanding of Faulkner's view of women offered by his earlier works—the initial despair in the face of the failure of the virginal ideal and the subsequent devotion to woman as the nourisher and sustainer of life—that his portrait of Lena Grove can best be comprehended as a wholly favorable one" (140). The symbolic order defines Lena (and Dewey Dell) as born to get pregnant.

Gail Hightower, like Horace Benbow and Gavin Stevens, sees Lena as an affirmation of life. At the same time, Hightower worries over Lena's unvirgin state. In his romantic attempt to contain the feminine, he subscribes to the idea that a woman should have only one "mate." He tells Byron it is "not fair that you should sacrifice yourself to a woman who has chosen once and now wishes to renege that choice. It's not right. It's not just. God didn't intend it so when He made marriage. Made it? Women made marriage" (347). It is as if a woman's self is negated by the man who impregnates her. Lena is not an "unravished bride." Nature's joke is on both Hightower and Byron. Fecundity simply invalidates virginity as a cultural ideal.

Eula Varner in The Hamlet (1940) is another emanation of the soil, another insistent female body, more sexually potent than Lena, a backwoods Venus at the very sight of whom men go weak with lust. She, too, is born to get pregnant: one of the major plot lines of the novel deals with working out this biological necessity. Like Lena and Dewey Dell, the sexual act itself is not particularly interesting or notable. It is only the nervy daughters of the upper classes for whom the loss of virginity is anything more than a minor transition: Eula comes home from her defloration as calmly as if she'd been for an afternoon drive, quietly changing "the dress which had her own blood on it" (159). Her illicit pregnancy is a matter of interest to her only in that she "dont feel good" (162). She exhibits no shame, no social pressure, none of the status-conscious outrage that sends her brother Jody roaring off vowing revenge. Her own mother seems annoyed only at the fuss caused in the house, and her father, when he finally learns of it, shrugs it off, unsurprised and unagitated, though he is the traditional defender of a virgin daughter's "honor."

The Varner family display, in comic form, two competing philosophies about female sexuality. To Jody with his bourgeois aspirations, Eula is an appendage of the family, an indication of its integrity. His grandiose posturing over her "sin" and threats of vengeance farcically recall the tragic situation in The Sound and the Fury. Both Quentin Compson and Jody allow a sense of family pride to be invested in their sisters' bodies. Jody vainly tries to tame Eula's luxuriant sexuality by making her wear corsets. She lives "in sullen bemusement, with a weary wisdom heired of all mammalian maturity, to the enlarging of her own organs," while her brother, like a cross between Quentin Compson in his pathological obsession with virginity and Jason Compson with his cynical conviction that all women are sluts, is terrified that the men of the village are itching to despoil Eula's, and therefore the Varner family's, good name. Though Jody, "erudition's champion," tries to civilize Eula through learning, he is not at all concerned with the quality of her mind: she embodies a disruptive force he wants contained.

Eula is a bawdy story come to life. Her body is a slapstick comedy routine out of a fabliau, irrepressible breasts breaking out here, incorrigible buttocks thrusting out there, while her enraged puritan of a brother tries to dilute this fertility idol "out of old the Dionysic times" who, in the supreme farce, ends up married to an impotent man half her size (107). Her woman's body (even at age thirteen) will not be ignored or confined in the garments or the roles Jody's patriarchal order lays out for her. Even locked into marriage, she disrupts town decorum.

Like black women, lower-class white women have more to do with the grotesque body than the classical body of the Confederate Woman. Eula and Dewey Dell exemplify the protuberant, multiplicitous, open, insistent "lower" body whose sexuality is not hidden under marble constraints or confined to the small space of the pedestal. Pregnancy and childbirth are, according to the narratives they inhabit, natural. Women of a more elevated social class in Faulkner's fiction do not surrender to their biological destiny with such facile alacrity. Faulkner's narratives are not as heavy-handed in portraying the bucolic baby machine with her absent-minded sexuality as are those of Erskine Caldwell, whose novels *Tobacco Road* (1932) and *God's Little Acre* (1933) made a national dirty joke of the "poor white trash" nymphomaniac. Nonetheless, in Dewey Dell, Lena, and Eula, Faulkner contributes to the South's stock of sexual imagery. In the twenties, thirties, forties, and still later, the drawling, revealingly dressed Daisy Mae figure with her double entendres and overdeveloped body became, no less than the highborn belle, part of the popular culture of the twentieth century.[7] The overbodied young white woman was not, however, usually a joke on sentimental motherhood. Faulkner exposes the ideological underpinnings of the eroticized South by showing how Dewey Dell's, Lena's, and Eula's voices are effaced while their bodies are overemphasized.

Writing the Womb: Laverne Shumann and Charlotte Rittenmeyer

Laverne Shumann and Charlotte Rittenmeyer are mothers with insistent bodies that signify their desire. They are verbally articulate as well. In common with so many of Faulkner's women, their bodies—and their stories—destabilize the South's gender binary. The essentially absent (lady's) body represents Caroline Compson, and the all-too-present (peasant's) body represents Lena, Dewey Dell, and Eula, but Laverne Shumann and Charlotte Rittenmeyer's bodies veer precipitously between feminine and masculine, transgressing gender boundaries until the symbolic order contains them as well, either in the appropriate feminine of self-sacrifice or what Gwin calls the "patriarchal" coffin.

These women are assaulted by narratives determined to silence them, despite their valiant efforts to escape. *Pylon* (1935) experiments with voice and form—not surprising considering Faulkner wrote it in the middle of composing *Absalom, Absalom!* in 1934. Though it concerns stunt flying at the opening of an airport in "New Valois," and despite its modern setting and slangy Eliotian style, it is curiously like *Absalom, Absalom!*, obsessed with questions of paternity, sexual fidelity and family integrity.[8] As in *Absalom, Absalom!*, the narrative deals with an erotic triangle, or perhaps an erotic *parenthesis* (see chapter 1) with the woman occupying the volatile space in between the two male elements that would define her, thus: ( ).

Laverne is the matrix of a vexed set of apparent binaries: both the Faulknerian earth goddess with her "mealcolored . . . strong pallid Iowacorn-colored hair" and a rather unfeminine body, both wife and mistress, both *femme couverte*—safely contained in the parentheses—and dangerous body, leaving the earth, which Faulkner's fictions, like southern culture, identify as feminine, to fly—a metaphor for appropriating masculine sexual license (22). She is threatening in her gender ambivalence: she appears "a woman, not tall and not thin, looking almost like a man in the greasy coverall" as she works on airplanes, yet she can swiftly "disguise" herself as female by putting on a skirt and stockings, conventional trappings of feminine attractiveness, to play lover or mother (24). In a sense, she is cross-dressing as a woman, causing a category crisis embodied in the boy who has apparently two fathers, or no father, and a manlike mother. Laverne's shifting gender attributes challenge the symbolic order; the movement of the narrative is to regulate her, to reduce her to being the sexual partner of one man and to being the "mother" in a conventionally structured family.

Like Lena and Eula, Laverne takes conception, pregnancy, and childbirth casually, as though the fecundity itself were all that mattered. Like Fairchild's universal woman in *Mosquitoes*, Laverne seems neither to know nor to care whose son Jack is. And like Faulkner's peasant mothers, she bears him as absentmindedly as an animal: "And so the kid was born on an unrolled parachute in a hangar in California, he got dropped already running like a colt or a calf from the fuselage of an airplane" (48). Laverne and the two potential fathers flip a coin to determine "official" paternity. She marries the winner, Roger, so that proprieties, about which none of them care, are nominally upheld. At least so the reporter, making a story out of these exciting and dangerous characters who have so thoroughly seduced him, tells us.

Millgate connects Laverne with Lena and Eula. He says their names are "near anagrams of each other" and that they are "earth-mother figures, symbols of continuity, permanence, and rebirth" (142). However, Laverne is more troubling in the way she slips between genders and desires. Despite her cosmetic links with Lena and Eula, her sexuality is quite unlike theirs in its ferocity and violence, tied in with the ferocity and violence of her life. She effectively rapes Roger Shumann in a plane before her first parachute jump, one of Faulkner's more creative juxtapositions of sex and death and attacks on conventional male and female roles. She comes to him in the cockpit while he pilots the plane "clawing blindly and furiously not at the belt across his thighs but at the fly of his trousers, he realized that she had no undergarment, pants" (195). Presumably postorgasm, she jumps, dressed only in stockings, dress, and parachute, skirt blowing up in a more revealing version of the classic Marilyn Monroe over-the-steam-grate pose, an erotic dream come true for a young man on the ground watching "the ultimate shape of his jaded desires fall upon him out of the sky, not merely naked but clothed in the very traditional symbology—the ruined dress with which she was trying wildly to cover her loins, and the parachute harness—of female bondage" (196–97).

The bottomless parachute jump is a pornographic scene, a male fantasy of the receptive female that comes out of nowhere, legs spread, as well as a quasi-comic rendition of the power of lust which Faulkner uses to mock-heroic effect in *The Hamlet*. Here, desire is destructive: Laverne is the punch line of a crude joke, but she is also threatening in her sexual aggression and masculine. She cannot be dismissed as mindlessly concupiscent;

she must be made to conform instead. Duvall argues that the "*ménage à trois* disrupts the patriarchal order represented by bourgeois marriage" and that Roger Shumann "subverts patriarchal values by accepting a woman whose sexuality breaches cultural limits," but he does not take into account the end of the novel when this small revolt against the symbolic order is quashed (82, 83). With Roger dead, Laverne is transformed from gender-breaching archadulteress to reformed magdalen, grimly abandoning her child, Jack, to his (official, at least) grandparents, speaking the words of the self-sacrificing mother: " 'Yes,' she said. 'I have to do it' " (308). In the end she is shrunken, no longer a pornographic image from the sky but a *mater dolorosa*, brought into conformity of a sort, the "loose woman" facing up to both the economic and moral responsibilities of maternity, her sexual and social independence abrogated once and for all.

In *The Wild Palms* (1939) the magdalen is not reformed but annihilated; the dangerous female body is not redeemed in motherhood but destroyed. Charlotte Rittenmeyer's abandonment of her husband and children seems at first an iconoclastic bid for freedom and individuality, a triumph of the creative self, a vindication of desire. Yet the intolerable incongruity of a woman who tries to break free of motherhood, domesticity, sexual submission, even the womb itself, must be punished. Charlotte suffers a painful, messy, sordid, and significantly "female" death in a failed abortion. Charlotte's counterpart, the nameless woman in the counternarrative "Old Man," on the other hand, is celebrated as the animated womb from which life pours and through which women receive validation.

The contrapuntal chapters and cyclical structure of *The Wild Palms* emphasize the debate between life-affirming and life-denying forces. Judy Reese suggests in an unpublished essay on *The Wild Palms*, "Womb/Woman as Text," that the two plots correspond to "the menstrual/miscarriage phase of the womb in blood imagery as well as the swollen, water-retentive state of pregnancy and childbirth" (2–3). Gwin's analysis of the novel focuses on the feminine properties of flooding: "As Faulkner himself well knew, a river—particularly the Mississippi River—reproduces itself by flooding, creating new flows. In this way land and water cross-fertilize each other" (*Feminine* 125). She goes on to say the novel "explores the expansive powers of female desire" (127). Flooding and containment are alternating strategies in *The Wild Palms*, each representing a way of writing the feminine.

The "Wild Palms" narrative opens with Charlotte's uncontrollable

bleeding from her botched abortion, a vicious parody both of menstruation and of the loss of virginity. The "Old Man" narrative opens with an
evocation of the great Mississippi flood of 1927. The latter narrative produces a child and a vindication of fertility, while the former ends with a
woman lying dead and her lover masturbating in prison, futile and sterile
(McHaney 172–73). Harry Wilbourne and Charlotte Rittenmeyer commit
crimes against nature, that is, against gender categories. The novel immediately suggests a series of gender reversals. As in Pylon, the woman of
the piece wears man's clothes, while the man, her submissive worship-
per and ineffectual protector, is "feminized" by his passivity and fear. The
masculinity of the Gulf Coast doctor's wife, Miss Martha, echoes this, her
hardness contrasting with the doctor's "thick soft woman's hands" (2).
Blurring of gender roles intensifies in the opening "Old Man" chapter:
the first convict is stereotypically manly, tall and lean and a reader of
"male" pulp detective fiction, while the second convict is described as
"short and plump," nearly "hairless," and "white." Along with these traditional female attributes, he wears "a long apron like a woman" and does
"women's work" cooking and sweeping (21–23).

The realm of the novel overflows with ambivalent sexualities and genders. At the mining camp in Utah, the couple there, the Buckners, wear
identical clothes and are called Bill and Buck. Cross-dressing in Faulkner's
fiction leads to dangerous undifferentiation that the culture always seeks
to correct. Drusilla Hawk insists on appropriating masculine violence
even when she returns to skirts; Temple Drake with her boyish attributes
cannot escape rape; and Charlotte, with her trousers "just exactly too little
for her in just exactly the right places," is forced to be a woman as she
bleeds from the womb. When women transgress by taking on masculine
power, their bodies are no longer sacrosanct vessels of purity or creation
but instruments with which to punish them.

Charlotte is perverse. Ellen Douglas remarks: "Charlotte Rittenmeyer,
in the terms that Faulkner presents men, is a man in disguise. Or rather,
perhaps more accurately, she is that always androgynous creature, the
artist" (Fowler and Abadie, Faulkner and Women 59). But as a woman artist, she is, as Karen Ramsay Johnson says, "multiply unnatural" (6). Her
lack of definition is alarming: one is tempted to see in her relationship
with Harry a revisiting of the homoeroticism and/or gender switching of
Joanna Burden and Joe Christmas, where the woman is "like" the man
and the man "like" the woman, where the power is located perversely

in the woman. Charlotte's male disguise seems a good one: she calls herself "Charley" when Harry first meets her. Like Laverne in *Pylon*, she is a sexual aggressor: as Gail Mortimer points out, she takes the lead with the monkish Harry, regulating and initiating their lovemaking (124). Sometimes she disguises herself as a "true woman," but her few attempts at approximating the role of wife fail. In Chicago she goes domestic and takes to cooking, arranging flowers, and covering their flat in chintz; later the same day, she acts sexually masterful with Harry, saying, "Get your clothes off" (85). For Charlotte, gender role-playing reveals a shakily imposed social condition. In her fluffy apron she exhibits "a quality not only female but profoundly feminine" and completely out of character: Charlotte is "female," but she, like Laverne, is also unsettlingly masculine. At the lake she practically rapes Harry: "This time she came straight and got into the cot with him, as heedless of the hard and painful elbow as she would have been on her own account if the positions had been reversed, as she was of the painful hand which grasped his hair and shook his head with savage impatience" (107).

Harry is sexually and emotionally cowed by her. He associates her with Lilith, who, in Hebrew legend, was cast out of Eden because she would not assume a submissive sexual posture; Charlotte calls Harry "Adam" in the false paradise of their lake cottage (100–101). Charlotte's volatile sexuality is her motivating force: Harry is her victim. He is shy, reticent and uncertain compared to Charlotte's swaggering virility. She works with her hands, sculpting while he takes on a female persona to write "women's" confession fiction: "If I had only a mother's love to guard me on that fatal day—" or "I had the body and desires of a woman, yet in knowledge and experience of the world I was but a child" (112). In some ways, it is easy for him to assume that victim's, that virgin's voice. He is the penetrated partner, the passive, the powerless. His description of the loss of virginity underlines Charlotte's power as the engulfing woman: "Surrender volition, hope, all—the darkness, the falling, the thunder of solitude, the shock, the death, the moment when, stopped physically by the ponderable clay, you yet feel all your life rush out of you into the pervading immemorial blind receptive matrix, the hot fluid blind foundation—grave-womb or womb-grave, it's all one" (128).

Harry means matrix both in its sense as uterus and as mother: motherhood is the (womb) space in which the novel operates. It is no accident that his "women's" fiction laments the lack of mother-love as its tragic burden. His sexual experiences with Charlotte constitute a return to the mother's womb and a kind of death by drowning. Charlotte's ambivalence frightens him: she is both the female sexual principle and, as Harry keeps pointing out, "a better man than I am" (123).

Charlotte's counterpoint character, the nameless woman in the flood, looks not at all "feminine": she hasn't the chance to dress up in a frivolous apron like Charlotte's; she wears "unlaced man's brogues," a badge of the "poor white trash." But she, like Charlotte, is ultimately defined by the functions of her uterus. To the Tall Convict, she "had ceased to be a human being and . . . had become instead one single, inert, monstrous sentient womb" (150). The difference is that her womb serves the symbolic order: it is filled, it produces a child, and she, unlike Charlotte, does not resist this "essential" female function. Her very namelessness underscores her lack of individual importance in the process: she is an emblem of the maternal.

The birth and the flood are closely paralleled in "Old Man," as the dam breaks and the nameless woman's water breaks. The convict fears both the rising Mississippi and the woman's labor; the feminine element surrounds him, threatening to engulf him. He cannot tell "whether the river had become lost in a drowned world or the world had become drowned in one limitless river." The "monstrous womb" seems to have taken charge and reordered the world with literal feminine fluidity.

The womb rules "Wild Palms" narrative as well. Harry obsessively makes a calendar based on Charlotte's body. Her periods regulate time: days "vanish" into a "timeless void" (82). The natural menstrual bleeding becomes the mortal bleeding of the failed abortion; in both cases, Harry is subject to the functions (or dysfunctions) of Charlotte's body, controlled by "where women bleed." While the two daughters Charlotte abandoned back in New Orleans have little impact on Charlotte and her actions, her other "children," the homunculi she sculpts, again emphasize her powerful womb, though not her maternal feelings. Initially Harry assumes that Charlotte could not desert her children. But she dismisses the conventional notion: not that she does not care for them but that they, and their feelings, are secondary to her design (a Sutpenesque word); her credo goes "love and suffering are the same thing and . . . the value of love is the sum of what you have to pay for it and any time you get it cheap you have cheated yourself" (43).

Charlotte's art and Charlotte's sexuality intertwine: both celebrate desire and the integrity of the self, not the annihilation of the self in a social or gender role. Yet her sculptures parody feminine creativity: that is, babies. Her puppets of historical and fictional characters signify the grotesqueness of her own situation, sexually and socially askew. She makes a venereally diseased Falstaff, a cheap and sluttish Roxanne, and so on. According to the dominant order, her art, as Thomas L. McHaney points out, is "perverted" (74). The narrative "solves" the problem of the woman artist by constructing her art as deviant, as figures that mock women's "true" creative function in birth, almost like a series of miscarriages—perhaps aborted fetuses. Charlotte's statues are born out of a defiant womb; she struggles to be true to her desire yet her world defines her as artist manqué, woman manqué, even man manqué. She says, "I like bitching, and making things with my hands" instead of accepting the limits of her class and her gender and her "appropriate" medium, her woman's body.

Charlotte is condemned to die for refusing the destiny ordained for her as a woman. McHaney says, "She cannot flee the price Nature demands of her" (160). *Nature* here means the hierarchies of male/female, madonna/magdalen that Charlotte means to confuse and confound. McHaney relates Charlotte's downfall to an excess of volition: Faulkner may have been influenced by Schopenhauer's *The World as Will and Idea*, which locates the source of all human misery in desire, in the will (McHaney 46–69). Charlotte acts on her desire, she is a dangerous body the social order needs to contain while the nameless woman who has surrendered to the (literally) fluid forces of life, the flood and the waters of her womb, flourishes. Faulkner might have also known Schopenhauer's *Parerga and Paralipomena* (1851) in which he explains that women exist solely for propagation. Women do not have intellects or a sense of justice. They are not even aesthetically pleasing after the birth of a child or two. The nameless woman affirms the primacy of maternity and the fertility of all the ages by having her baby on an Indian mound—life emphasized by earth and water. Charlotte dies in an agony of fiery pain, in a hospital where reminders of the womb she tried to deny stare up at Harry from the linoleum floor, which is "like wombs into which human beings fled before something of suffering but mostly of terror, to surrender in little monastic cells all the burden of lust and desire and pride, even that of functional independence, to become as embryos" (299).

In a sense, Charlotte is killed by her own body. In a pitiless patriarchy, it is a fitting death for a woman who put her body's pleasure before anything else, who insisted on control of her body herself, not channeled through a man. The Wild Palms is perhaps Faulkner's most profound expression of men's need to "penetrate" and contain the female body. After he finished the novel, he told his publisher it "was written just as if I had sat on the one side of a wall and the paper was on the other and my hand with the pen thrust through the wall and writing not only on invisible paper but in pitch dark too, so that I could not even know if the pen still wrote on paper or not" (Fowler and Abadie 1985, 16). The writer wields what Gilbert and Gubar have famously called "the metaphorical penis," breaking through the hymen of discourse, returning to the abysmal and threatening dark of the womb, filling that volatile creative space with the masculine. But he is also the abortionist, thrusting the sharp instrument into the womb. In either case, the teller of the story controls the story, controls the frightening female body. At the end of "Wild Palms," Harry has destroyed Charlotte by ineptly piercing her womb with a sharp instrument. He has, intentionally or no, inscribed on (in) her body the symbolic order. The doctor thinks of him as a man who "*has proof on the body of love and of passion and of life that he is not dead*" (17).

Charlotte, however, is dead, and Harry is left to remember her, to finally take charge of the story. His decision not to commit suicide or to run but instead to rot in prison, covered by the romantic credo "*between grief and nothing I will take grief*," is seen as heroic and affirmative. This image is subverted, however, by the fact that Harry is masturbating (punning on the wild "palms," hands) recalling Charlotte's "body, the broad thighs, the hands that liked bitching and making things. It seemed so little, so little to want, to ask. *With all the old graveyard-creeping, the old wrinkled withered defeated clinging not even to the defeat but just to an old habit—the wheezing lungs, the troublesome guts incapable of pleasure.* But after all memory could still live in the old wheezing entrails: and now it did stand to his hand, incontrovertible and plain, serene, the palm clashing and murmuring" (227). Finally the penis asserts itself in a novel that had been controlled by the womb; in his imagination, Harry can at last gain power over Charlotte's body, though he, like the convict, returns to another womb, a cell, in the officially (and comfortingly) womanless existence of the prison. Separate for the length of the novel, the "Wild Palms" and "Old Man" narratives meet in this retreat from the feminine.

The original title of the novel was "If I Forget Thee, Jerusalem," from Psalm 137. It was removed against Faulkner's wishes (McHaney xiii). The psalm is one of the songs of Babylonian captivity: Jerusalem the good mother must be remembered in "a strange land." Verses 8 and 9 of the psalm speak of the revenge against the evil mother Babylon: "O daughter of Babylon who art to be destroyed; happy shall he be, that rewardeth thee as thou hast served us. Happy shall he be that taketh and dasheth thy little ones against the stones."

The bad mother is punished by killing her children; in Faulkner's novel, the bad mother is punished by being killed herself. The attempt by a woman to declare her body her own, not a sacred vessel to be filled with children, cannot be tolerated. The bad mother can be reformed if she, like Laverne Shumann, accepts her procreative role; if she does not, like Addie Bundren or Charlotte Rittenmeyer, she will be defused, contained, and finally buried.

Altars of Sacrifice: "Redeeming" Eula and Temple

In *The Town* (1957) and *Requiem for a Nun* (1951), two of Yoknapatawpha's most sexually transgressive women appear to be redeemed for the pantheon of self-immolating mothers. Revising the "devouring" or "absent" or "promiscuous" mother of the earlier fiction parallels what Betty Friedan has called "the feminine mystique," the dependent yet morally secure domesticated woman, the ideal mother of the 1950s, a return to the Victorian paragon: "The feminine mystique says that the highest value and the only commitment for women is the fulfillment of their own femininity . . . sexual passivity, male domination and nurturing maternal love" (43). In what Richard Moreland calls Faulkner's "revisionary repetitions" of earlier narrative concerns, the continuations of Eula's and Temple's stories suggest a preoccupation with reimposing conventional representations of the masculine and the feminine (237). This impulse is limited; we have seen how Linda Snopes Kohl disrupts class, gender, and even regional categories, making conformity to the conservative southern pattern quite problematic. Yet Faulkner's attention to the issue of mothers and their sacrifices for children in *The Town* and *Requiem for a Nun* reflects some of the concerns of the society around him (and in America in general) over the place of the maternal. The popular icon of the fifties mother is familiar and deceptive: Mrs. Cleaver, the dispenser of food and unquestioning love, was challenged by the fear of the dominant, emasculating female, the all-powerful "mom." Again, gender roles

were constantly being undermined and reinscribed. During the Second
World War, the munitions-plant worker—a woman in overalls with hands
dirty from physical labor—became an acceptable, even cherished, image
of the American woman. After the war, however, women were sent back
into the home; their work became the home with all its appliances and
devices. The advertising image of the woman at work usually included a
glamorous model in high heels and a cocktail dress just barely touching
a sleek new Electrolux vacuum cleaner with one gloved hand. Curiously
enough, women's fashions in the late forties on into the fifties, following
the antiausterity New Look of Dior, replicated the archetypal antebellum shape of the Southern Belle: corseted waist, tight bodice, huge skirt
over crinoline. Evening dresses even had hoops. The socially conservative South held the line most vehemently on gender roles, as it did with
racial roles, yet people could not help but be aware that there were white
ladies (in full petticoats) aiding and abetting the Montgomery bus boycott.[9] Upper-class women such as Virginia Foster Durr and Lillian Smith
were speaking out on political issues, putting themselves at odds not only
with the dominant politics of white suprematism in the South but also
with the convention that women be silent and apolitical. No representation is ever solid or uncontradictory: Eula and Temple shift positions in
the range of possibilities for women in southern society. They are rewritten (rehabilitated?) as women struggling through to a painful acceptance
of the role of mother at great cost to their own desires and their own
selves.

Eula Varner and Temple Drake, sexually powerful in The Hamlet and Sanctuary, are encouraged by their communities, fearful of unregulated desire,
to repent of their "sins." Significantly, Gavin Stevens is involved in both
narratives of the suppression of the feminine, the disruptive self, in favor
of the child and the family, in The Town and Requiem for a Nun. He presides
over Eula's and Temple's confrontations of conventional motherhood
and, according to Moreland, witnesses—in Temple's case "therapeuti-
cally analyzing"—their struggles with voice and silence. As Adrienne Rich
points out: "Institutionalized motherhood demands of women maternal
'instinct' rather than intelligence, selflessness rather than self-realization,
relation to others rather than the creation of self" (42). Faulkner's fictions
are full of narratives wherein someone tries to contain a desiring woman:
sometimes she breaks free (like Caddy), sometimes she is destroyed (like
Charlotte). Sometimes she makes a bitter détente with her culture.

In *The Hamlet* Eula Varner is no masculinized woman but the unconscious, inexorably fertile feminine, a mock-heroic Venus comically married to the white trash Vulcan Flem Snopes. By the time we get to *The Town*, published seventeen years later, Eula is fast becoming a *mater dolorosa*, still beautiful as Helen, but as an object of desire, a contentious body. Her inarticulate sexuality disrupts Jefferson, threatening to harm her daughter. Eula's damaging beauty must be contained; in the end, she sacrifices herself to assure her place in "respectability," in the community sense of order, and the "correct" middle class family, sparing her daughter any "shame."

The Town's Eula is no longer a burlesque Aphrodite, though she is still the passive focus of erotic fantasy, especially for two of the most prominent citizens of Jefferson: the Byronic heir to an old plantation family, Manfred de Spain, who becomes her lover, and the over-verbal lawyer Gavin Stevens. The voices of the men in the novel construct Eula. Charles Mallison, Gavin Stevens, and V. K. Ratliff make her in turn a distant and tragic heroine, the embodiment of some female archetype, and a suffering mother caught in a male power game. Yet unlike *The Sound and the Fury*, where Caddy's voice manifests itself in the bisexual spaces of the novel, Eula is entirely contained by her "authors." To the young Charles she is "beauty" embodied: "too much of white, too much of female, too much of maybe just glory, I dont know: so that at first sight of her you felt a kind of shock of gratitude just for being alive and being male at the same instant with her in space and time" (6).

Eula is a wish fulfillment, an invention of testosterone, not a person. Her hyperfemininity defines and authenticates the masculine, making Charles (and all the other men) feel "grateful" for being male. She has no being on her own terms; she can exist only as men require her to complete a fantasy. First, she is the desired body, then she becomes the angelic mother: in her, as in Laverne Shumann, the apparent binaries of madonna and magdalen are collapsed, destroying both the opposition of chastity/sexuality *and* any sense of a discrete self, yet mysteriously reaffirmed at the same time. She is a born-again "good woman," even though she has to die to achieve this state.

Eula does not act—until her suicide—she is acted upon: her silence makes her seem even more an erotic fantasy. We are not allowed to know what she knows or even, except in rare instances, to hear her speak. The blooming sexuality she exudes is strangely detached from her: desire is

for others, not for her. She treats her own body not as an erotic instrument but a location of nurture, offering herself to Gavin Stevens as casually
and unnervously as if she suggested making him a cup of tea, because
she thinks it will make him happy. She thinks her body is all she has to
offer anyone. To Eula, sex is simply a part of being, her body is articulate
where her words are not: "Dont expect. You just are, and you need, and
you must, and so you do" (94).

Gavin makes all the (male) eloquent speeches about pity and honor
and love: like Faulkner's nympholepts from Januarius Jones onward, he
does not really desire physical union with the beloved but a kind of
courtly love that betrays a deep fear (and loathing) of the female body.
Eula does not concern herself with abstractions. She is a thoroughly un-
apologetic adulteress. It is as if moral choice were not involved in the
initial sexual encounter that produced her daughter and is not involved
in the eighteen-year affair with Manfred de Spain; it is simply a matter of
"old biology." Her body speaks her whole being: it is her life. She is a blank
page—or space—on which men's desires and aspirations are engraved:
"Beneath the extravagant worship of the sex goddess, we can hear the
echo of Otto Weininger's words: 'Woman is nothing" (Griffin 205). Eula is
a sex goddess. She has been compared to Marilyn Monroe, the ultimate
wish-fulfillment woman, the composite of all that male culture tells us
is beautiful.[10] Eula, like Marilyn Monroe, is made up of men's visions of
her. Susan Griffin says: "a woman angry with pornography's false image
of herself tries to destroy her own body. This is how a being in pain from
an imposed silence comes to finally strike out against herself" (206).

Is this why Eula kills herself? In The Mansion it is said that she was
"bored." But in The Town her suicide seems to be the only way out for a
woman whose cataclysmic sexual effect on others cannot be controlled,
indeed, must be eradicated in order to "save" her daughter. Initially,
she tries to get Gavin, her perpetual admirer, to marry Linda, to preserve her from the backlash of illegitimacy and the "shame" of her
mother's intended elopement with her lover. Eula wants to preserve
the respectability she perceives as central to a tolerable life in Jefferson.
Respectability never quite adheres to Eula herself: Gavin's sister Margaret
Mallison tries, out of kindness and for her brother's sake, to get the exquisite Mrs. Snopes accepted by Jefferson's "town ladies," but Eula is not
interested. How can Aphrodite crave the approval of the Jefferson Cotil-
lion Club?

Margaret Mallison is the overtly successful mother of the novel, exhibiting maternal behavior at every turn, mothering not only her son, Chick, but her husband, her father, and particularly her twin brother, Gavin. Her name, as well as her all-encompassing warmth, suggests she is Margaret Powers returned from Faulkner's first novel, an actual mother instead of a surrogate one. Margaret Mallison is Faulkner's first concession that the middle-class "church ladies" he used to travesty in novels like *Sanctuary* and *The Unvanquished* could be other than hypocritical. She mirrors the "angel mom" of the fifties, all-wise, ever-kind in her frilly apron, presiding with moral exactitude every night over the perfect dinner. Yet she provides a kind of conventional backdrop for Eula's more vexed and ambivalent response to being a woman and a mother in the postagrarian South.

Eula Varner is finally subsumed into the ideology of maternal sacrifice. Her last conversation with Gavin is, as we shall see, similar to conversations Gavin has in *Requiem for a Nun* with Temple Drake and Nancy Mannigoe, affirming the primacy of the patriarchal family. In *The Town*, Gavin promises to look after the abandoned Linda but says bitterly to Eula: "Change her name by marriage then she wont miss the name she will lose when you abandon her" (332). As Temple in *Requiem* is forced to give up her desire in favor of her remaining child, Eula decides not to run away with de Spain. Instead, she removes herself from the economy of sexuality; she annihilates her disruptive body and so is, according to the male voices of the novel, redeemed. In death the town-wrecking adulteress, the pagan goddess, turns into an ironic Christian saint, her gravestone engraved:

A Virtuous Wife Is a Crown to Her Husband
Her Children Rise and Call Her Blessed (355)

The fiction takes over and the woman who seemed once a walking paean to the womb is contained in the earth, her body now invisible forever.

In death Eula pays for her lifetime of overripe sexuality. She is not only contained but revised by maternal martyrdom, no longer mock-heroic but genuinely heroic, the *mater dolorosa* saved in the end, preserved forever in the myth-making memories of the men who saw her. From Mississippi Marilyn Monroe, turning a gun on her own body, her enemy, to madonna, Eula affirms the precedence of children over the mother herself. She is absolved from her woman's body at last, and motherhood is rehabilitated as a moral force.

Death is one way to silence the insistent female body. Faulkner has also explored the possibility of the repentant magdalen living out a renewed life as a self-abnegating mother in *Requiem for a Nun*. Temple Drake begins as a renegade from ladyhood, raped, imprisoned in a whorehouse: according to the masculine stories told in *Sanctuary*, a liar, nymphomaniac, and monster. In *Requiem*, published twenty years later (though begun in the early thirties) Faulkner reenvisions her past life and invents her post-*Sanctuary* career to understand her life anew in what Moreland calls a "revisionary repetition." Whether or not Temple is "redeemed," as many critics have insisted, or simply humiliated by Gavin Stevens, as Noel Polk suggests, is not a simple issue.[11] Temple's story is thrown against an historical exposition of Jefferson—her life appears in the context of a public, historical space. Moreland suggests that Temple's retelling of her story is part of a series of social crises provoked by her as well as Nancy Mannigoe and Cecilia Farmer, placing *Requiem* in a continuum of public and private morality. I agree that the "stage settings" in *Requiem* are not simple evocations of "one historical period but a transition from one social order (with its own characteristic ways of organizing both its internal and external boundaries) toward another" (Moreland 195–96).[12] But it is also significant that Temple herself is a transitional figure, spanning twenty years of Faulkner's fiction-writing career and representing both the breakdown of the icon of the southern white lady and her reinvention as a moral agent.

In *Sanctuary* Temple Drake's body is inscribed with masculine power— according to the masculine reading of the rape, the corncob "teaches" her to be a woman, not merely a lady. As we have seen, Ruby, a speaker for the symbolic order, begins her lesson at the Old Frenchman Place by penetrating "ladyhood" to reach toward the radical reality both of desire and women's sexual subordination in culture. By the end of the novel, Temple, having suffered "a fate worse than death," seems nearly dead herself, no more animated than the marble effigies of the dead queens in Paris. But her marriage to Gowan and her two children by him still do not teach her to eradicate her demanding self. It remains for Nancy Mannigoe, an exprostitute like Ruby, to administer Temple's second lesson. But this time, instead of showing her desire, Temple meets the necessity to sacrifice it, to accept her place in the symbolic order as lady, wife, and mother.[13]

Nancy Mannigoe predates Temple in Faulkner's fiction, first appearing in "That Evening Sun," a short story of 1930. There she is an intermittent streetwalker and sometime nursemaid to the Compson children. She is pregnant by some man, probably some white man, not her husband Jesus: " 'I can't hang around white man's kitchen,' Jesus said. 'But white man can hang around mine. White man can come in my house, but I can't stop him' " (*Collected Stories* 292). In "That Evening Sun" her sexuality, triggering the murderous jealousy of Jesus, destroys her. In *Requiem* she is resurrected and rewritten, defusing the power of desire in favor of self-immolating motherhood. This "Negress, quite black," this prostitute Nancy Mannigoe with her "worthless nigger life," redeems the fallen Temple Drake and salvages the white Stevens family with her death, in Gavin Stevens's moral scheme. As in *The Sound and the Fury* and *Absalom, Absalom!*, maternal, or at least caretaking, values reside in the black woman, who is, of course, officially "degraded" or low in southern culture. Yet, as we have seen, the white lady, the elevated, celebrated body in southern culture, is dependent upon the "low" black woman for her status and, in Faulkner's moral understanding of southern racism, her regeneration. For Temple to survive, she must in some way parallel Nancy's self-abnegation as she has paralleled Nancy's life in illicit sexuality and "sin." The defining hierarchies of white over black, lady over whore, are in crisis as Temple and Nancy move toward each other. Nancy is the "only animal in Jefferson that spoke Temple Drake's language" (158).

The "language" Nancy speaks is of a self Temple feels she has to hide. It is her past, her sexual self, her "shame," perhaps even the argot of the whorehouse, which Nancy, being "out of the gutter," can appreciate. Nancy speaks the body as Temple wishes to speak the body. Temple's affair with her Memphis whorehouse lover's brother is a bid for freedom from the nice middle-class home in which Gowan has installed her, another confining space like her father's house, the dormitory, the Old Frenchman Place, and Miss Reba's, where she has been imprisoned.

Nancy's and Temple's rebellions are incomplete and finally inadequate: the class, race, and gender edifices of the South are not shaken to the point of collapse. Yet in their secret language, in their talks in the kitchen, in their friendship itself, Nancy and Temple expose some of the fissures and gaps in the southern social order. "Friendship"—or some sort of bond—between white women and their black maids helped solidify the Montgomery bus boycott. I am not suggesting any overt connection between Nancy and Temple and the civil rights movement, but Faulkner was certainly aware that the South was confronting a social revolution, at the center of which were women and blacks.

The secret language of the novel, of women, is desire: the pornographic letters Temple wrote to her lover Red while locked in the brothel ("good letters . . . you would have wondered how anybody just seventeen and not even through freshman in college could have learned the—right words").[14] Yet desire is ultimately negated in favor of sacrifice. Nancy foils Temple's plan to "steal" her own money and jewels to run off with Pete the blackmailer; she confronts Temple with the consequences of acting on her desire, constantly preaching the obligation of a mother to her children. Nancy now overtly recalls Dilsey, who offered up her body to be beaten by Jason in place of Quentin II:

> "Hit me. Light you a cigarette, too. I told you and him both I brought my foot. Here it is." (She raises her foot slightly)
> "I've tried everything else; I reckon I can try that too." (186)

In a weird inversion of ethics that, frankly, is impossible to swallow as any kind of moral act, Nancy murders Temple's baby to shock her out of self-gratification into selfless maternal duty, "so good can come out of evil," evil being, in Temple's case, desire. The prostitute redeems Temple from sex. Nancy's humility and moral authority force Temple into recognizing her "selfishness"; she asks the reason for "trying to hold us together in a household, a family that anybody should have known all the time couldn't possibly hold together? even in decency let alone happiness?" while Nancy replies, "I reckon I'm ignorant. I dont know that yet. Besides, I ain't talking about any household or happiness neither. . . . I'm talking about two little children—" (188–89). Moreland interestingly reads the murder as Nancy's need to "have" the six-month-old fetus she lost as well as a revisionary repetition of the abortions and infanticides in The Wild Palms and Absalom, Absalom! (236–37). While this explains Faulkner's sense of recurrent narratives in history, it does not solve the ethical problem of why a dead child is supposed to redeem her mother. Perhaps Nancy is insane; perhaps, like God, she moves in mysterious ways unfathomable to mere white folks like Gavin, Gowan, and Temple.

For all her subversiveness as the repository of a higher moral mandate, Nancy serves middle-class conformity dedicated to the suppression of female sexuality. A mysterious (and finally inexplicable) distinction arises between Temple's possible murder of her baby through desertion and neglect and Nancy's actual murder of the child through "love." The ultimate goal is a martyrdom of the self so that another might see the "truth."

Nancy is going to be executed for murder. According to the racist Christianity operating in the novel, Nancy's sacrifice renders her "poor crazed lost and worthless life" the most worthy of all. Christlike, she dies so that Temple might live under the terms of "decency," a Faulknerian virtue almost as high as endurance, which, for women, means the renunciation of desire. *Sanctuary* is rewritten by Temple and Gavin in the course of *Requiem*; Temple claims to have discovered she "liked evil," but in the terrorized, nearly deranged, gin-soaked teenager of that novel, there is little evidence of culpability. Why does Temple insist on her guilt? Why is she the focus of this "corrective" narrative? Gavin co-opts and reconstructs her past to insist that her degradation was her own fault, that she introduced sin into her marriage, that Gowan has every right to be angry at her for not being a virgin (though her trip to the Old Frenchman Place was because of his drunkenness). Given this revised text of her life, Nancy's violence forces her to abdicate her own identity and give herself up, as at the end of *Sanctuary*, to a world controlled by the conventional story of what the family is, what a mother is, what a woman is—Mrs. Gowan Stevens.

Temple is duped into turning her soul inside out, for her own good, according to Gavin. She has always listened too well to men's stories about her. In *Sanctuary* her father and her brothers made her believe they would always protect her, while Gowan pretended he knew what he was doing out at the Old Frenchman Place. Here Gavin, Gowan, and the governor (a trinity of Gs) know that Nancy will be executed no matter what Temple says. Temple knows it, too. The elaborate scheme, the midnight sneaking, and sleeping pills that do not get taken, are a hoax "to give Temple Drake a good honest chance to suffer" (133). Temple is victim of a conspiracy to force her into "Christian" altruism: first she must forgive the murderer of her child, begging for mercy on Nancy's behalf, then she must expiate her own "crimes." The triumvirate make Temple tell her story again— she told one version before to another lawyer, Horace Benbow, in the Memphis brothel, then another version in a Jefferson court room. Do the multiple tellings and confessions make Temple powerful or weak: Is her body being expressed here or erased?

Desire is on trial in *Requiem for a Nun*: on her knees in act 2, scene 3 before the Great Seal of the state in Jackson, before both the governor and her husband as the representatives of God, the Law of the Father reasserts itself. Temple's sentence is to suffer, her body and soul condemned for the crime of sexuality. Class and race save her from Nancy's, the designated sacrifice's, fate of physical destruction, but in rewriting the story of her degradation, she will be erased, subsumed into another role. She makes her narrative with even more verbose glosses and revisions from Gavin, and interruptions as well. This "chivalric" inquisitor modifies her words, always pushing her to tell what she'd rather not. Gavin's version of Temple's story ventures into the abstract and the theoretical, especially about women, demanding of the governor, "Don't you know anything at all about women?" Temple's story, on the other hand, slips between first and third person (167). Names become important: sometimes Nancy is abused as a "nigger dopefiend whore" and other times she is Temple's only friend. The governor remarks that she has an "old Charleston name," *Manigault*, corrected by Gavin who says it is a Norman name, *Maingault* (122). It is interesting Faulkner should choose a "corruption" of this "Norman patronym"; the Manigaults were South Carolina rice-plantation aristocrats with a reputation for being highly conservative even during slavery. After Emancipation, Charles Manigault pulled together his family lands and began to reassert the plantation order somewhat repressively. In a sense, Nancy inherits the still-unresolved enslavement of blacks in the South. She has a mangled plantation name and nominal freedom in a New South that also has laws to restrict her every movement. Temple Drake is also a product of the New South. Nancy carries the mark of her culture—her blackness—on her, proclaiming her low status, sexual availability, and maternal proficiency; Temple is marked with white ladyhood, alternately evoking it and rejecting it. Nancy cannot escape the master's name; Temple cannot escape her "sacred" name. Insisting that "Temple Drake is dead," hiding herself in "Mrs. Gowan Stevens" does not free her or exonerate her (92). No one, especially a woman, escapes history in *Requiem for a Nun*.

The world of *Requiem for a Nun* does not necessarily make good moral sense. It is hard to see how the death of one baby (the daughter, not the son: Gowan is not left without an heir) justifiably redeems the other child and Temple. As in *Pylon*, the movement of the novel is toward conformity. Laverne, her man, and her coming child must form a family; Temple, Gowan, and their remaining child must become a family bonded together in an orderly, even if painful, relationship. The story of Temple Drake's dark night of the soul is thrown against the historical pageant of Yoknapatawpha County as if to point out both the particularity and commonplaceness of tragedy. Gavin says: "The past is never dead it's not even past." The contrapuntal sections of the novel, one historical and social, the other theatrical and personal, complement each other, rather like the alternating plots of The Wild Palms. We are meant to see the tragedy of Nancy and the guilt of Temple in context, products of a gradual disintegration of the cohesive community now becoming suburbanized and ethically barren. From Mohataha's dispossession to Cecilia Farmer's inscription of her self on the window to Nancy's singing, women are associated with imprisonment, exile, pain; they are traces of history, emblems of the aspirations and anxieties of their time.

Temple lays herself on the maternal altar in the end: the claims of the child are absolute. Gavin tells Temple: "You came here to affirm the very thing which Nancy is going to die tomorrow morning to postulate: that little children, as long as they are little children, shall be intact, unanguished, untorn, unterrified" (211). Acceptance of this will save Temple Drake's soul, "if there is a God to save it—a God who wants it" (212). The historical chapters of the novel underline the sense of community continuity. The final scenes of the novel, in the jail from which Nancy is to be taken to be executed, emphasize the immensity of self-immolation: "Just believe," says Nancy. Just believe in the sanctity of motherhood and fall mute into that selfless role. Temple has told her story but has not understood it. She fails to see that the villain of the piece is not she but her father and brothers and Gowan and Gavin, who cannot imagine or will not countenance a feminine desire outside the maternal. Temple's voice, given her temporarily both to insist on her self and to tell a story against herself, is taken from her again. If she "believes" she will be dumb. Her old life, her history, are supposed to be cleansed by her long confession; actually, they are eradicated. Temple Drake is truly "dead": the perfect mother, the perfect woman, is invisible without language to speak her story, without a body to disrupt the world. And yet Temple and Nancy, marked by history, also mark. Nancy sings in the jail, Temple refuses to feel the need for revenge. In the end, a white woman and a black woman have experienced love. Though Temple returns to her last sanctuary, her family, and Nancy goes forth to the death of the sacrificing black woman, Faulkner allows a glimpse of a revolution in the South's history, the changes that will insist on being known and heard. Requiem for a Nun, its title evoking death and female virtue, the erasure of the feminine body and its elevation as the Virgin, allows the roles offered women by the South to collapse in on each other, slipping into something finally unlimitable. Both Nancy and Temple are represented by the nun—and neither is. The categories are bankrupt, the kitchen and the pedestal both now empty.

Notes

Introduction

1. See Minrose Gwin, *The Feminine and Faulkner*; John T. Matthews, *The Play of Faulkner's Language*; James Snead, *Figures of Division: William Faulkner's Major Novels*; John N. Duvall, *Faulkner's Marginal Couple: Invisible, Outlaw, and Unspeakable Communities*; Gail Mortimer, *Faulkner's Rhetoric of Loss: A Study in Perception and Meaning*; Karen Ramsay Johnson, "Gender, Sexuality, and the Artist in Faulkner's Novels"; Deborah Clarke, "Gender, Race, and Language in *Light in August*"; Marsha Warren, "Time, Space, and Semiotic Discourse in the Feminization/Disintegration of Quentin Compson"; Frann Michel, "William Faulkner as a Lesbian Author."

Chapter 1   The Confederate Woman

1. See especially Anne Goodwyn Jones, *Tomorrow Is Another Day: The Woman Writer in the South, 1859–1936*, chap. 1; Minrose C. Gwin, *Black and White Women of the Old South: The Peculiar Sisterhood in American Literature*, chaps. 1 and 2; Elizabeth Fox-Genovese, *Within the Plantation Household: Black and White Women of the Old South*, chaps. 1, 2, 4, and 5; Louise Westling, *Sacred Groves and Ravaged Gardens: The Fiction of Eudora Welty, Carson McCullers, and Flannery O'Connor*, chap. 1; and Kathryn Lee Seidel, *The Southern Belle in the American Novel*, chap. 1.

2. See Seidel, *Southern Belle*. See also Bertram Wyatt-Brown, *Southern Honor: Ethics and Behavior in the Old South*; and Catherine Clinton, *The Plantation Mistress*.

3. The South was seen as "oriental" by both southerners and northerners. In Harriet Beecher Stowe's *Uncle Tom's Cabin*, New Orleans is described in particularly lush orientalist terms, conflating Africa, Spain, and the tropics (see chap. 15). Mary Chesnut speaks of white slaveholders having black harems, as do Frances Kemble and Frances Trollope. See Hortense Spillers, "Changing the Letter: The Yokes, the Jokes of Discourse, or, Mrs. Stowe, Mr. Reed," in *Slavery and the Literary Imagination*, ed. Deborah McDowell and Arnold Rampersad.

4.   See Drew Gilpin Faust, *James Henry Hammond and the Old South: A Design for Mastery.*

5.   See also Mary Ann Loughborough, *My Cave Life in Vicksburg with Letters of Trial and Travel,* New York: 1864; Belle Boyd, *Belle Boyd in Camp and Prison:* 1865; *Diary of a Southern Refugee During the War by a Lady of Virginia, Our Women in the War: The Lives They Lived, the Deaths They Died, A Confederate Girl's Diary;* T. C. De Leon, *Belles, Beaux, and Brains of the '60s,* New York: 1909; Grace King, *Memories of a Southern Woman of Letters,* New York: 1932.

6.   Chesnut rewrote her own work during the 1880s, and her "diary" was first published in 1905, but only in 1981 were the journal and diary integrated by C. Vann Woodward in *Mary Chesnut's Civil War.* She did keep a considerable Civil War journal, but her manuscripts date mainly from 1881 to 1884. The journal is much looser, and somewhat franker, than what she intended for publication.

7.   See Fox-Genovese, *Within the Plantation Household,* 339–65. Fox-Genovese disagrees that Mary Chesnut seriously challenged her society, seeing her instead as a woman dissatisfied with her possibilities and power within it.

8.   See also Thomas Nelson Page's "Meh Lady," in *Marse Chan and Other Stories;* and *Red Rock.*

9.   See Annette Kolodny, *The Lay of the Land: Metaphor as Experience and History in American Life and Letters,* on the historical connection of the southern land with the female body.

10. Kathleen Blee's book *Women of the Klan: Racism and Gender in the 1920s* details the history of the WKKK and related groups called things like Hooded Ladies of the Mystic Den, the Kamelia, Ladies of the Golden Mask, and Puritan Daughters of America, pointing out most interestingly that while white men had based the KKK on "messages of female vulnerability" to black rapists and preached the fragile purity of white womanhood, the WKKK defined women as powerful and interested itself in racial and religious privilege and women's rights.

11. For the usual antifeminist line on Drusilla, see Lynn Levins, *Faulkner's Heroic Design in the Yoknapatawpha Novels,* 120. Cleanth Brooks, *William Faulkner: Toward Yoknapatawpha and Beyond,* 335; and *The Yoknapatawpha Country,* 82–83.

12. Dean Faulkner Wells, Faulkner's niece, said that Faulkner made up Judith as a story for the children but also "believed in her." See *The Ghosts of Rowan Oak,* 61.

13. See Elisabeth Muhlenfeld, ed., *William Faulkner's "Absalom, Absalom!": A Critical Casebook* on the origins of the novel, its revisions, and its relationship to the shorter fiction that carries some stories later used in the novel.

14. See Leslie Fiedler, *Love and Death in the American Novel,* 382–84, 436–36; David Punter, *The Literature of Terror,* chaps. 2 and 14.

15. Judith is more than Judith here to Quentin. As John T. Irwin remarks in *Doubling and Incest/Repetition and Revenge: A Speculative Reading of Faulkner,* "Quentin reconstructs the story of Bon, Henry and Judith in light of his own experiences with Candace and Dalton Ames" (74).

16. In Mississippi in 1948, Davis Knight was sentenced to five years in jail for breaking the miscegenation law. He claimed he was white, but the state proved he had a slave great-grandmother. See F. James Davis, *Who Is Black? One Nation's Definition,* 9–10.

17. Faulkner showed some ambivalence over a Mississippi case in 1951 where a black

man, Willie McGee, was accused of raping a white woman. Faulkner spoke against the death penalty since no apparent "violence" was used (indeed, there was not conclusive proof of rape) but also dismissed more radical criticism of the whole incident, arguing against women from the Civil Rights Congress. See Frederick Karl, *William Faulkner, American Writer*, 822n.; Joseph Blotner, *Faulkner: A Biography*, 1377–38.

Chapter 2   Mammy

1. See Cathy Campbell, "A Battered Woman Rises," on the familiar food icon Aunt Jemima. The original models for the Quaker Oats supercooks, Nancy Green and later Ethel Ernestine Harper, became community activists. But the shiny representation of the "nurturing" old black cook, however "corporatized" in the 1980s, remains an astonishingly racist image.
2. Other novels of the twenties and thirties that either celebrate or debunk the plantation Eden with notable mammies include T. S. Stribling's *Forge* trilogy, Allen Tate's *The Fathers* (1938), Caroline Gordon's *None Shall Look Back* (1937), Edith Everett Taylor Pope's *Not Magnolia* (1928) and *Old Lady Esteroy* (1934), and Stark Young's *So Red the Rose* (1934).
3. Five states made Davis's birthday a legal holiday; Mississippi was not among them. But Mississippi did not make Lee's birthday a holiday either, perhaps having a resistance to bureaucratic mandates. Mississippi did not lag behind other former Confederate states in chapters of the United Daughters of the Confederacy and the United Confederate Veterans, or in monuments and commemorative events. See Gaines M. Foster, *Ghosts of the Confederacy: Defeat, the Lost Cause, and the Emergence of the New South, 1865–1913*.
4. Snead points out that Benjy's "censored actual name, 'Maury,' " comes from the Latin Maurus, "a Moor" (*Figures of Division*, 36). This "suppressed name" becomes a sort of password to the "underworld" of black language in the fourth section.
5. Dilsey's own name probably comes from "Dulcie," meaning sweet. I don't see, however, that this gets us very far—except ironically.

Chapter 3   The Tragic Mulatta

1. I am indebted to Jonathan Dollimore of Sussex University for his illumination of the fear of sameness and the interdependence of apparent oppositions, in the lecture "The Cultural Politics of Perversion: St. Augustine, Shakespeare, Freud, Foucault," delivered at the University of Alabama, 9 April 1990.
2. See Neil R. McMillen, *Dark Journey: Black Mississippians in the Age of Jim Crow*, 99–106 (especially on Tougaloo University, which by 1930 had granted one thousand degrees) and 177 on black newspapers in Jackson.
3. Chesnut's "beastly negress beauties" are commented on by a number of observers of the southern scene. Frederick Law Olmsted's *The Cotton Kingdom* details the Louisiana *plaçage* system (which Faulkner writes about in *Absalom, Absalom!*), Frances Kemble's *Journal of a Residence on a Georgian Plantation in 1838–1839* tells horrific stories

of slave women raped by overseers. The sexual availability of black women to white men was assumed on into the twentieth century. See John Dollard's *Caste and Class in a Southern Town*, 135, 334.

4.   See Herbert G. Gutman, "Marital Norms Among Slave Women," in *A Heritage of Her Own: Toward a New Social History of American Women*, ed. Nancy F. Cott and Elizabeth Pleck, 298–308.

5.   See Joel Williamson, *New People: Miscegenation and Mulattoes in the United States*, 43, on the historical likelihood of this.

6.   Dion Boucicault, *The Octoroon*. The London production had a happy ending: see R. G. Hogan, *Dion Boucicault*, 74.

7.   See also *Cane* (1923) by Jean Toomer; Nella Larsen, *Passing* (1929); and Zora Neale Hurston, *Their Eyes Were Watching God* (1937).

8.   See also Edna Ferber, *Show Boat* (1926); Erskine Caldwell, *A Place Called Estherville* (1949); Robert Penn Warren, *Band of Angels* (1955); and Shirley Ann Grau, *The Keepers of the House* (1964).

9.   John Matthews (*Play*, 224) remarks that the colors of the cards—red, white, and black—signify the intermingled races that form the background of the characters in *Go Down, Moses*.

10.   Admittedly these are also the tasks of a wife in conventional American society. But the importance of washing and cooking as racial markers in the South is, I think, Faulkner's point.

11.   I take these terms from Joel Williamson's book *The Crucible of Race: Black/White Relations in the American South Since Emancipation*. When John Spencer Bassett of Trinity College (later Duke University) in North Carolina wrote a piece for the *South Atlantic Quarterly Review* called "Stirring Up the Fires of Racial Antipathy" in 1903, he was hauled before the college administration to explain his apparent view that social equality could happen. Bassett allowed as how he didn't think it would happen in his lifetime but perhaps in five or six hundred years. See Williamson, *Crucible*, 262–67.

12.   Eric J. Sundquist in *Faulkner: The House Divided* discusses *The Sins of the Father* and its relation to *Absalom, Absalom!* and *Go Down, Moses*; see 72, 143–44.

13.   See Joel Williamson, "How Black Was Rhett Butler?" 91–93; and Darden Asbury Pyron, *Southern Daughter: The Life of Margaret Mitchell*, 215–17, on the history of this story.

14.   Thadious M. Davis feels that Dilsey is more "successful" and "more imposing" than Clytie. See *Faulkner's "Negro": Art and the Southern Context*, 199.

Chapter 4   The New Belle

1.   I take my use of the word *story*, meaning cultural discourse, from Alan Sinfield, whose work is the most lucid account I have come across of how and why societies believe what they believe about themselves. See Alan Sinfield, *Literature, Politics and Culture in Postwar Britain*; and Jonathan Dollimore and Alan Sinfield, "History and Ideology: The Instance of Henry V" in *Alternative Shakespeares*, ed. John Drakakis (London: Routledge, 1988).

2.   Cabell's ersatz medievalism influenced *Mayday*, a hand-illustrated, hand-bound

allegory made by Faulkner in 1926 as a gift for Helen Baird. See William Faulkner, *Mayday*.

3. For a fuller explication of the novel and how it fits into the Southern Belle canon, see Seidel, *Southern Belle*, 154–56.

4. As with all of Quentin's section, it is possible that he imagined or made up what he reports his mother saying.

5. Sundquist reads Quentin-Ophelia as joining the water, "his bodily self falling to meet the enchanted corpse living always beneath the shadowy surface of the prose" (*Faulkner*, 18).

6. Snead makes an intriguing connection along these lines in *Figures of Division*: "The division Quentin insists upon seems about a racial and sexual mixing he both desires and fears. Whether Quentin likes it or not, people consider him at times 'black' and at times a 'woman.' . . . Caddy names a daughter after him, so that not even his name, 'Quentin,' is unequivocably male" (26).

7. Critics who "blame the victim" include Sally R. Page, Lawrence S. Kubie, Leslie A. Fiedler, David Williams, James Cypher, William R. Brown, George Monteiro, Olga Vickery, and Robert R. Moore. Two comments by Page and Williams will suffice to give the gist of this sort of anti-Templeism. First Page: "The disasters that envelop Temple are the result of a combination of her cruelly selfish lust which makes her completely disregard the well-being of any other person, and her childish naïveté which makes her incapable of anticipating the extent of the evils in which she is involved" (*Faulkner's Women: Characterization and Meaning*, 81); now Williams: "[Temple is] carried off into virtual prostitution, meanwhile discovering that she has all along consented to it, even enjoyed it, and that her affinity for evil is absolute" (*Women in Faulkner: The Myth and the Muse*, 142). Some critics, while allowing that Temple is somewhat victimized, posit a masculine reader who participates in her rape; for example, Moore: "If she demands our sympathy and protective impulses, she is also fair game for our sexual fantasies" ("Desire and Despair: Temple Drake's Self-Victimization," 114). This "our" seems to exclude the female reader.

8. See *Marionettes* (1920), Faulkner's *symboliste* drama, in which Marietta, a Narcissa Benbow–like denizen of a walled garden, is forced into the "dance" of sexuality by an intruding Pierrot; see also the images of rape in *The Sound and the Fury* in Quentin's holding the knife at Caddy's throat and Jason's erotically charged violence against Quentin II, Januarius Jones's fantasies of rape in *Soldiers' Pay*, and in *Mosquitoes* the artist Gordon's rape urges toward Patricia (who is raped, in a sense, by the mosquitoes that pierce her flesh and leave her bleeding).

9. See John T. Matthews's essay "The Elliptical Nature of *Sanctuary*," in which he points out the parallel between the Drake family—the Judge, Temple, and her four brothers—and the bootlegger family at the Old Frenchman Place: Pap, Ruby, and the four "brothers," Popeye, Lee, Van, and Tommy. The linkage of perverse families is carried on in the Memphis sporting house with Miss Reba as mother and Popeye as "Daddy." Duvall, in his chapter on *Sanctuary*, "Man Enough to Call You Whore," in *Faulkner's Marginal Couple*, also discusses what he calls "deviant" families in *Sanctuary*.

10. Duvall (*Faulkner's Marginal Couple*, 73–74) and Noel Polk (in "The Space Between *Sanc-*

tuary," 20) see Horace as both rapist and victim, noting the slippage of pronoun from masculine to feminine, and the shift from Horace's vomiting coffee to the black substance rushing out of the female body (*Sanctuary, Corrected* 234–35).

11. See Duvall, *Faulkner's Marginal Couple*, 75.

12. *Kohl* not only sounds appropriately alien and "Jewish," but is a dark substance used as eye makeup in the Middle East. It could be that there is an association with *blackness* that underscores both Barton Kohl's and, perhaps, Linda's otherness: an intersection of a metaphoric kind with the black Other of the South.

13. Autherine Lucy was denied dormitory space at the University of Alabama and had to attend class under guard. A mob formed in front of the library where she was sitting and shouted, "Kill her!" and "Hey, hey, ho, where in the hell did Autherine go? Hey, hey, ho, where in the hell did that nigger go?" There were riots and Klan-sponsored rallies. As Howell Raines puts it, "In the two weeks following her first day in class, the [White] Citizens Council enrolled forty thousand new members." See Raines, *My Soul Is Rested: The Story of the Civil Rights Movement in the Deep South*, 325–27.

14. However, in his (moderate) "If I Were a Negro" letter to *Ebony* magazine, he says if he were black he *would* be a member of the NAACP since there's nothing else.

15. See Minter 239 and Blotner, *Faulkner*, 1612, on the connections between Faulkner's affairs and Linda.

16. Hee Kang's discussion of Linda as the new feminine voice in Faulkner is compelling and convincing ("The Snopes Trilogy: (Re)reading Faulkner's Masculine and Feminine). I am indebted to her for pointing out the importance of the ivory pad in *The Mansion*.

Chapter 5   The Night Sister

1. Louisa May Alcott, *Little Women*, 385. See her novel *Work* (1873) for a celebration of the single life without condescension.

2. In 1931 the Scottsboro alleged-rape case crystalized the fear and hatred. Nine young black men were accused of raping two white women on a train. Eight were condemned to die in the electric chair. Evidence was later introduced that suggested their innocence, but the importance of the case was the way in which a community myth was being enacted. See Dan Carter, *Scottsboro: A Tragedy of the American South* (Baton Rouge: Louisiana State University Press, 1969).

3. The way Faulkner portrays Miss Habersham's success in helping prevent the lynching of Lucas Beauchamp probably owes something to Jessie Daniel Ames and the Association of Southern Women for the Prevention of Lynching, a movement begun in 1930 to "liberate" white women from chivalry and black men from violence. See Jacquelyn Dowd Hall, *Revolt Against Chivalry: Jessie Daniel Ames and the Women's Campaign Against Lynching*.

4. Among the works of the late twenties and early thirties by Faulkner that deal with repressed sexuality in middle- to upper-class white women are "Miss Zilphia Gant," written in 1928 (which eventually appeared in a Book Club of Texas special edition of three hundred copies, introduced by Henry Nash Smith, on 27 June 1932); *The Sound and the Fury*; "The Big Shot"; "Dull Tale," a reworking of "The Big Shot"; "Elly"; "Dr. Martino"; "The Brooch"; "Dry September"; and *Sanctuary*.

5. See Duvall, *Faulkner's Marginal Couple*, 34, for a useful discussion of this.
6. Quoted in Hall, *Revolt Against Chivalry*, 78. The *Memphis Press Scimitar* responded by calling for the lynching of the "man" who "utters these calumnies." The offices of the *Free Speech* were destroyed, and Wells herself was unable to return to the South from New York.
7. See Duvall, *Faulkner's Marginal Couple*, 35, for a discussion that suggests Lena and Byron beat the system: "[Byron's] loving Lena undercuts the foundation of the patriarchy—the name of the father; Byron accepts the role of husband and father while the biological father escapes." See also Snead, *Figures of Division*, 92–93, which intriguingly suggests that Lucas Burch is "Christmas' darker double" who names Joe as "nigger" to divert suspicion from himself. Burch is actually the mulatto, and Lena's child is a mulatto, thus perpetuating the line of mixed-race children (and the mulatto realm of the narrative).

Chapter 6   Mothers and Motherhood

1. See Thomas Laqueur, "Orgasm, Generation, and the Politics of Reproductive Biology."
2. See Johnson's intelligent discussion in her article "Gender." She suggests that "the simultaneous activity and passivity of artistic creation" requires that "traditional male and female sex roles must be confused and conflated as the writer (and reader) rejects stable categories of self-definition to participate in the re-creative process of narration" (1).
3. Maud Butler, William Faulkner's mother, was, as Judith L. Sensibar points out, "a witty but distant and cold person" (*The Origins of Faulkner's Art*, 52). The mother in an affluent white family of Faulkner's day was encouraged to be a distant exemplar and moral standard; the mammy, on the other hand, dealt with the less sanctified aspects of child-rearing: the diapering, feeding, washing, discipline, and comfort. Sensibar traces the contradictory views Faulkner had of women to his "double mother," Maud Butler and Caroline Barr: "Faulkner *really* had two antithetical mothers, hence the ease with which he and his characters see their 'mothers' as antithetical doubles" (237 n. 34).
4. Maud Butler Falkner made William Faulkner wear a back brace from the time he was thirteen until he was sixteen to make him stand up straight. See Sensibar, *Origins*, 51, 236 n. 30. See also Michael Grimwood, *Heart in Conflict: Faulkner's Struggles with Vocation*, 37, on Maud's corset and its influence on Faulkner's life.
5. See Elaine Showalter and English Showalter, "Victorian Women and Menstruation," in *Suffer and Be Still: Women in the Victorian Age*, ed. Martha Vicinus, 38–44.
6. Joan Williams, "In Defense of Caroline Compson," in *Critical Essays on William Faulkner: The Compson Family*, ed. Arthur E. Kinney, 402–7.
7. Daisy Mae in the comic strip "Lil' Abner" is one example. Others include Ellie Mae in the television series "The Beverly Hillbillies" and the (sanitized) Tammy in the films of that name, originally starring Debbie Reynolds. A more contemporary example is Daisy (Catherine Bach) the short-shorted buxom accessory to the racing car in "The Dukes of Hazzard."
8. The situation was based on the opening of Shushan Airport in New Orleans, Febru-

ary 1934. See Minter 146. There was a woman parachute jumper called Eris Davies at the opening as well as a crash in Lake Pontchartrain. See Michael Millgate, *The Achievement of William Faulkner*, 139–40.

9. See Raines, *My Soul Is Rested*, 37–70, on the boycott and Virginia Foster Durr, *Outside the Magic Circle*, 241–321, about white women's participation in the civil rights movement.

10. See Lewis J. Hilliard, "A View of Faulkner's Women" (M.A. thesis, Southern Illinois University, 1957), on Eula and Marilyn Monroe.

11. I am indebted to Noel Polk's "corrective" reading in *Faulkner's "Requiem,"* though I depart from his conclusions in a number of significant ways.

12. Richard Moreland's interesting and serious reading of *Requiem* places much emphasis on Faulkner's historical contextualizing and characterizes Nancy as a "sorceress" and Temple as an "hysteric," women who cause a narrative about "imprisonment, rape and abortion." See *Faulkner and Modernism: Rereading and Rewriting*, 195.

13. I agree with Polk in *Faulkner's "Requiem"* that Temple does struggle to escape the past in trying hard to become "Mrs. Gowan Stevens," the "matron," but I think she also rebels against her (well understood) place as a southern lady, even as Gavin Stevens works to torture her back into it. See Polk 65, 94, 147.

14. Narcissa Benbow in "There Was a Queen" is also blackmailed over sexually suggestive letters by a man who eventually becomes her lover, but they are letters written to her, whereas Temple's are written by her. Still, it is as if the *text* of the belle's sexuality is so potent, such explosive evidence, that in the process of containing her body, the very language of sexuality must also be suppressed.

Bibliography

Primary Sources

Alcott, Louisa May. *Little Women*. New York: Dutton, 1948.

Anderson, Sherwood. *Dark Laughter*. London: Jerrolds, 1926.

Andrews, Eliza Frances. *The War-time Journal of a Georgia Girl, 1864–1865*. New York: D. Appleton, 1908.

Andrews, Matthew Page, ed. *Women of the South in War Times*. Baltimore: Norman, Remington, 1923.

Bacon, Francis. *The New Atlantis*. London: University Tutorial Press, 1937.

Baldwin, James. *Notes of a Native Son*. Boston: Dial, 1955.

Benet, Stephen Vincent. *John Brown's Body*. London: Heinemann, 1928.

Bilbo, Theodore G. *Take Your Choice: Separation or Mongrelization*. Poplarville, Miss.: Dream House, 1947.

Boucicault, Dion. *The Octoroon*. London: Dick's Standard Plays, 1884.

Boyd, Belle. *Belle Boyd in Camp and Prison*. New York: Blelock, 1865.

Brown, William Wells. *Clotel; or, The President's Daughter*. London: Partridge and Oakey, 1853.

Cabell, James Branch. *The Cream of the Jest*. London: John Lane, 1923.

———. *Domnei: A Comedy of Woman-Worship*. New York: Robert McBride, 1921.

———. *Jurgen: A Comedy of Justice*. New York: McBride, 1919.

Cable, George Washington. *Madame Delphine and Other Tales*. London: F. Warne, 1881.

Cash, Wilbur J. *The Mind of the South*. New York: Knopf, 1941.

Chesnut, Mary Boykin Miller. *Mary Chesnut's Civil War*. Edited by C. Vann Woodward. New Haven, Conn.: Yale University Press, 1981.

Chesnutt, Charles Waddell. *The House Behind the Cedars*. 1900. Reprint. Ridgewood, N.J.: Gregg Press, 1968.

———. *The Marrow of Tradition*. 1901. Reprint. New York: AMS Press, 1972.

Child, Lydia Maria. *Fact and Fiction: A Collection of Stories*. London: n.p., 1847.

Chopin, Kate. *Complete Works*. 2 vols. Edited by Per Seyersted. Baton Rouge: Louisiana State University Press, 1969.

Clay-Clopton, Virginia. *A Belle of the Fifties*. Edited by Ada Sterling. New York: Appleton, 1904.

Cooper, James Fenimore. *The Last of the Mohicans*. New York: Washington Square, 1960.

Dawson, Francis W., ed. *Our Women in the War*. Charleston, S.C.: n.p., 1885.

De Leon, T. C. *Belles, Beaux, and Brains of the '60s*. New York: Dillingham, 1909.

Dew, Thomas R. *The Pro-slavery Argument*. 1852. Reprint. New York: Negro Universities Press, 1968.

Dickens, Charles. *Great Expectations*. London: Penguin, 1983.

Dixon, Thomas Jr. *The Clansman: An Historical Romance of the Ku Klux Klan*. New York: Doubleday, 1905.

——— . *The Leopard's Spots: A Romance of the White Man's Burden, 1865–1900*. London: Doubleday, Page, 1902.

——— . *The Sins of the Father*. New York: Doubleday, Page, 1912.

——— . *The Traitor: A Story of the Fall of the Invisible Empire*. New York: Doubleday, Page, 1907.

Durr, Virginia Foster. *Outside the Magic Circle*. Tuscaloosa: University of Alabama Press, 1988.

Eastman, Mary H. *Aunt Phillis' Cabin; or, Southern Life As It Is*. Philadelphia: Lippincott, Grambo, 1852.

Evans, Augusta Jane. *Beulah*. London: n.p., 1860.

——— . *Macaria; or, Altars of Sacrifice*. 3 vols. London: n.p., 1864.

——— . *St. Elmo*. New York: Carleton, 1867.

Falkner, M. C. *The Falkners of Mississippi*. Baton Rouge: Louisiana State University Press, 1967.

Falkner, William C. *The Spanish Heroine: A Tale of Love and War Scenes Laid in Mexico*. Cincinnati: J. Hart, 1851.

——— . *The White Rose of Memphis*. Introduction by Robert Cantwell. New York: Coley Taylor, 1953.

Faulkner, John. *Dollar Cotton*. Oxford, Miss.: Yoknapatawpha Press, 1970.

Faulkner, William. *Absalom, Absalom!* 1936. New York: Vintage, n.d.

——— . *As I Lay Dying*. New York: Vintage, 1964.

——— . *Collected Stories of William Faulkner*. 1950. New York: Viking, 1977.

——— . *Essays, Speeches, Public Letters*. Edited by James B. Meriwether. New York: Random House, 1965.

——— . *Flags in the Dust*. Edited by Douglas Day. New York: Random House, 1973.

——— . *Go Down, Moses*. New York: Random House, 1942.

——— . *The Hamlet*. New York: Random House, 1940.

——— . *Intruder in the Dust*. New York: Random House, 1948.

——— . *Knight's Gambit*. New York: Random House, 1949.

——— . *Light in August*. Corrected Text. 1932. New York: Vintage, 1987.

——— . *The Mansion*. 1959. New York: Vintage, 1965.

——— . *The Marionettes: A Play in One Act*. Edited by Noel Polk. Charlottesville: University Press of Virginia, 1977.

——— . *Mayday*. Introduction by Carvel Collins. South Bend, Ind.: University of Notre Dame Press, 1978.

——— . *Mosquitoes*. New York: Boni and Liveright, 1927.

————. *Pylon.* New York: Harrison Smith and Robert Haas, 1935.

————. *Requiem for a Nun.* New York: Random House, 1951.

————. *Sanctuary.* Corrected Text. 1931. New York: Vintage, 1987.

————. *Sanctuary.* Original Text. Edited by Noel Polk. New York: Random House, 1981.

————. *Soldiers' Pay.* New York: Boni and Liveright, 1926.

————. *The Sound and the Fury.* 1929. New York: Norton, 1987.

————. *The Town.* 1957. New York: Vintage, 1961.

————. *Uncollected Stories.* Edited by Joseph Blotner. New York: Random House, 1979.

————. *The Unvanquished.* New York: Random House, 1938.

————. *The Wild Palms.* New York: Random House, 1939.

Fitzgerald, F. Scott. *Ledger: A Facsimile.* Introduction by M. J. Bruccoli. Washington, D.C.: NCR Microcards, 1972.

————. *This Side of Paradise.* London: W. Collins, 1921.

Fitzgerald, Zelda Sayre. *Save Me the Waltz.* London: Jonathan Cape, 1968.

Fitzhugh, George. *Sociology for the South; or the Failure of Free Society.* 1859. Reprint. New York: Burt Franklin, n.d.

Gilman, Caroline. *Recollections of a Southern Matron.* New York: Harper and Bros., 1838.

Glasgow, Ellen. *The Miller of Old Church.* Garden City, N.Y.: Doubleday, Page, 1911.

————. *Virginia.* 1913. London: Virago, 1983.

Glenn, Isa. *Southern Charm.* New York: Knopf, 1928.

Gordon, Caroline. *None Shall Look Back.* New York: Charles Scribner's Sons, 1937.

Greenhow, Rose O'Neal. *My Imprisonment and the First Year of Abolition Rule at Washington.* London: n.p., 1863.

Haardt, Sara. *Southern Album.* Garden City, N.Y.: Doubleday Doran, 1936.

Henry, Evelyn Whitfield. "The May Party." *Apalachee* (Tallahassee Historical Society) (1946): 35–45.

Hentz, Caroline Lee. *The Planter's Northern Bride.* 2 vols. Philadelphia: T. B. Peterson, 1854.

Hildreth, Richard. *The White Slave.* London: W. Scott, 1890.

Hughes, Henry. *Treatise on Sociology.* Philadelphia: Lippincott, 1854.

Ingraham, J. H. *The Quadroone.* London: Richard Bentley, 1840.

Jacobs, Harriet. *Incidents in the Life of a Slave Girl.* 1861. New York: Oxford University Press, 1988.

Kemble, Frances Anne. *Journal of a Residence on a Georgian Plantation in 1838–1839.* London: Longman, 1863.

Kennedy, John Pendleton. *Swallow Barn.* 1832. Introduction by William Osborne. New York: Harper's, 1971.

King, Grace. *Memories of a Southern Woman of Letters.* New York: Macmillan, 1932.

LeConte, Emma. *The Day the World Ended: The Diary of Emma LeConte.* Edited by E. S. Miers. New York: Oxford University Press, 1957.

Loughborough, Mary Ann. *My Cave Life in Vicksburg with Letters of Trial and Travel.* New York: D. Appleton and Co., 1864.

Martineau, Harriet. *Society in America.* New York: Sander and Otley, 1837.

Mitchell, Margaret. *Gone with the Wind.* New York: Macmillan, 1936.

Newman, Frances. *The Hard-boiled Virgin.* 1926. Reprint. New York: Arno Press, 1977.

Olmsted, Frederick Law. *The Cotton Kingdom.* 1861. New York: Knopf, 1953.

Page, Thomas Nelson. *Bred in the Bone*. New York: Charles Scribner's Sons, 1904.
———. *In Ole Virginia*. New York: Charles Scribner's Sons, 1912.
———. *Marse Chan and Other Stories*. New York: Charles Scribner's Sons, 1887.
———. *The Old Dominion: Her Making and Manners*. New York: Charles Scribner's Sons, 1908.
———. *The Old South: Essays Social and Political*. New York: Charles Scribner's Sons, 1892.
———. *Red Rock*. New York: Charles Scribner's Sons, 1898.
———. *Social Life in Old Virginia Before the War*. Illustrated by the Misses Cowles. New York: Charles Scribner's Sons, 1897.
Ruskin, John. *Sesame and Lilies*. New York: Mershon, 1871.
Russell, William Howard. *My Diary North and South*. 2 vols. London: Bradbury and Evans, 1863.
Schoolcraft, Mrs. Henry R. [Mary]. *The Black Gauntlet: A Tale of Plantation Life in South Carolina*. 1861. New York: Negro Universities Press, 1969.
Scott, Sir Walter. *The Abbot*. 3 vols. Edinburgh: A. Constable, 1820.
———. *The Monastery*. 3 vols. Edinburgh: A. Constable, 1820.
———. *Redgauntlet*. 3 vols. Edinburgh: A. Constable, 1824.
———. *Rob Roy*. 3 vols. Edinburgh: A. Constable, 1818.
———. *Waverley; or, 'Tis Sixty Years Since*. Edinburgh: A. Constable, 1814.
Simms, William Gilmore. *The Forayers; or, The Raid of the Dog Days*. New York: Redfield, 1855.
Smedes, Susan Dabney. *Memorials of a Southern Planter*. Edited by Fletcher M. Green. New York: Knopf, 1965.
Smith, Lillian. *Killers of the Dream*. New York: W. W. Norton, 1949.
———. *Strange Fruit*. New York: Reynal and Hitchcock, 1944.
Stowe, Harriet Beecher. *Uncle Tom's Cabin*. 1852. London: Penguin, 1984.
Stribling, T. S. *Birthright*. New York: Century, 1922.
———. *The Forge*. London: Heinemann, 1931.
———. *The Store*. London: Heinemann, 1932.
———. *Unfinished Cathedral*. London: Heinemann, 1934.
Surghnor, Mrs. M. F. *Uncle Tom of the Old South: A Story of the South in Reconstruction Days*. 1896. Reprint. Freeport, N.Y.: Books for Libraries Press, 1972.
Tate, Allen. *The Fathers*. New York: G. P. Putnam's Sons, 1938.
Twain, Mark [Samuel Langhorne Clemens]. *Pudd'nhead Wilson*. New York: Harper, 1899.
———. *Life on the Mississippi*. New York: Harper and Bros., 1923.
Van Evrie, J. H. *White Supremacy and Negro Subordination*. New York: Van Evrie, Horton, 1868.
Victor, Mrs. Metta V. *Maum Guinea and Her Plantation Children: A Story of Christmas Week with the American Slaves*. London: n.p., 1861.
Warren, Robert Penn. *Band of Angels*. New York: Random House, 1955.
Wells, Dean Faulkner. *The Ghosts of Rowan Oak*. Oxford, Miss.: Yoknapatawpha Press, 1980.
Young, Stark. *So Red the Rose*. New York: Charles Scribner's Sons, 1934.

Secondary Sources

Bakhtin, M. M. *Rabelais and His World*. Bloomington: Indiana University Press, 1984.
Beauchamp, Fay E. "William Faulkner's Use of the Tragic Mulatto Myth." Ph.D. dissertation, University of Pennsylvania, 1974.

Berlant, Lauren. "National Brands/National Bodies: *Imitation of Life*." In *Comparative American Identities*, edited by Hortense Spillers. New York: Routledge, 1991.

Berzon, Judith R. *Neither White nor Black: The Mulatto Character in American Fiction*. New York: New York University Press, 1978.

Blee, Kathleen. *Women of the Klan: Racism and Gender in the 1920s*. Berkeley and Los Angeles: University of California Press, 1991.

Bleikasten, André. *Faulkner's "As I Lay Dying."* Translated by Roger Little. Rev. ed. Bloomington: Indiana University Press, 1973.

Blotner, Joseph. *Faulkner: A Biography*. 2 vols. New York: Random House, 1974.

Brodsky, Louis Daniel, and Robert W. Hamblin, eds. *A Comprehensive Guide to the Brodsky Collection*. Jackson: University Press of Mississippi, 1982–85.

Brooke-Rose, Christine. "Woman as Semiotic Object." In *The Female Body in Western Culture*, edited by Susan Rubin Suleiman. Cambridge: Harvard University Press, 1986.

Brooks, Cleanth. *William Faulkner: Toward Yoknapatawpha and Beyond*. New Haven, Conn.: Yale University Press, 1978.

———. *The Yoknapatawpha Country*. New Haven, Conn.: Yale University Press, 1963.

Brown, Sterling. *The Negro in American Fiction*. Washington, D.C.: Associates in Negro Folk Education, 1937.

Campbell, Cathy. "A Battered Woman Rises." *Village Voice*, 7 November 1989, 44–46.

Carby, Hazel. *Reconstructing Womanhood: The Emergence of the Afro-American Woman Novelist*. New York: Oxford University Press, 1987.

Carter, Dan. *Scottsboro: A Tragedy of the American South*. Baton Rouge: Louisiana State University Press, 1969.

Christian, Barbara. *Black Feminist Criticism*. New York: Pergamon, 1985.

———. "Shadows Uplifted." In *Feminist Criticism and Social Change*, edited by Judith Newton and Deborah Rosenfelt. London: Methuen, 1985.

Cixous, Hélène. "Castration or Decapitation?" Translated by Annette Kuhn. *Signs* 74 (Autumn 1981): 41–55.

———. "The Laugh of the Medusa." In *New French Feminisms*, edited by Elaine Marks and Isabelle de Courtivron. Amherst: University of Massachusetts Press, 1980.

———. "Sorties." In *The Newly-Born Woman*. Translated by Betsy Wing, Minneapolis: University of Minnesota Press, 1986.

Clarke, Deborah. "Gender, Race, and Language in *Light in August*." *American Literature* 61, no. 3 (October 1989): 398–413.

Clinton, Catherine. *The Plantation Mistress*. New York: Pantheon, 1982.

Cott, Nancy F., and Elizabeth Pleck, eds. *A Heritage of Her Own: Toward a New Social History of American Women*. New York: Simon and Schuster, 1979.

Cowley, Malcolm. *The Faulkner-Cowley File: Letters and Memories, 1944–1962*. New York: Viking Press, 1966.

Cypher, James. "The Tangled Sexuality of Temple Drake." *American Imago* 19 (1962): 243–52.

Davis, F. James. *Who Is Black? One Nation's Definition*. University Park: Pennsylvania State University Press, 1991.

Davis, Thadious M. *Faulkner's "Negro": Art and the Southern Context*. Baton Rouge: Louisiana State University Press, 1983.

Degler, Carl N. *At Odds: Women and the Family in America from the Revolution to the Present*. New York: Oxford University Press, 1980.

Derrida, Jacques. "Le facteur de la vérité." In *The Post Card: From Socrates to Freud and Beyond*. Translated by Alan Bass. Chicago: University of Chicago Press, 1987.

Dollard, John. *Caste and Class in a Southern Town*. Garden City, N.Y.: Doubleday, 1957.

Dollimore, Jonathan. *Radical Tragedy: Religion, Ideology, and Power in the Drama of Shakespeare and His Contemporaries*. Chicago: University of Chicago Press, 1984.

Douglas, Margaret Mary. *Purity and Danger: An Analysis of the Concepts of Pollution and Taboo*. London: Routledge and Kegan Paul, 1978.

Duberman, Lucile. *Gender and Sex in Society*. New York: Praeger, 1975.

Duvall, John N. *Faulkner's Marginal Couple: Invisible, Outlaw, and Unspeakable Communities*. Austin: University of Texas Press, 1990.

Faust, Drew Gilpin. *James Henry Hammond and the Old South: A Design for Mastery*. Chapel Hill: University of North Carolina Press, 1982.

Ferguson, Mary Anne, ed. *Images of Women in Fiction*. Boston: Houghton Mifflin, 1981.

Fiedler, Leslie A. *Love and Death in the American Novel*. Rev. ed. New York: Stein and Day, 1966.

———. *No! In Thunder: Essays on Myth and Literature*. Boston: Beacon Press, 1960.

Foster, Gaines M. *Ghosts of the Confederacy: Defeat, the Lost Cause, and the Emergence of the New South, 1865–1913*. New York: Oxford University Press, 1987.

Fowler, Doreen, and Ann J. Abadie, eds. *"A Cosmos of My Own": Faulkner and Yoknapatawpha 1980*. Jackson: University Press of Mississippi, 1981.

———. *Faulkner and Women: Faulkner and Yoknapatawpha 1985*. Jackson: University Press of Mississippi, 1986.

Fox-Genovese, Elizabeth. *Within the Plantation Household: Black and White Women of the Old South*. Chapel Hill: University of North Carolina Press, 1988.

Fraser, John. *America and the Patterns of Chivalry*. New York: Cambridge University Press, 1982.

Friedan, Betty. *The Feminine Mystique*. London: Victor Gollancz, 1963.

Gaines, Francis Pendleton. *The Southern Plantation: A Study in the Development and the Accuracy of a Tradition*. New York: Columbia University Press, 1924.

Garber, Marjorie. *Vested Interests: Cross-Dressing and Cultural Anxiety*. New York: Routledge, 1992.

Gilbert, Sandra, and Susan Gubar. *The Madwoman in the Attic: The Woman Writer and the Nineteenth-Century Literary Imagination*. New Haven: Yale University Press, 1979.

Godwin, Gail. "The Southern Belle." *Ms.* 4 (July 1975): 49–52, 84–85.

Gresset, Michel, and Noel Polk, eds. *Intertextuality in Faulkner*. Jackson: University Press of Mississippi, 1985.

Griffin, Susan. *Pornography and Silence: Culture's Revenge Against Nature*. New York: Harper and Row, 1981.

Grimwood, Michael. *Heart in Conflict: Faulkner's Struggles with Vocation*. Athens: University of Georgia Press, 1987.

Guerard, Albert J. *The Triumph of the Novel: Dickens, Dostoevsky, Faulkner*. New York: Oxford University Press, 1976.

Gwin, Minrose C. *Black and White Women of the Old South: The Peculiar Sisterhood in American Literature*. Knoxville: University of Tennessee Press, 1985.

———. *The Feminine and Faulkner: Reading (Beyond) Sexual Difference.* Knoxville: University of Tennessee Press, 1990.

Gwynn, Frederick L., and Joseph Blotner, eds. *Faulkner in the University: Class Conferences at the University of Virginia, 1957–1958.* Charlottesville: University Press of Virginia, 1959.

Hall, Jacquelyn Dowd. *Revolt Against Chivalry: Jessie Daniel Ames and the Women's Campaign Against Lynching.* New York: Columbia University Press, 1979.

Harris, Trudier. *From Mammies to Militants: Domestics in Black American Literature.* Philadelphia: Temple University Press, 1982.

Hart, James. *The Popular Book.* Berkeley and Los Angeles: University of California Press, 1961.

Hilliard, Lewis J. "A View of Faulkner's Women." Master's thesis, Southern Illinois University, 1957.

Hogan, Robert Goode. *Dion Boucicault.* New York: Twayne, 1969.

Howard, Jean E. "Crossdressing, the Theatre, and Gender Struggle in Early Modern England." *Shakespeare Quarterly* 39 (1988): 418–40.

Irigaray, Luce. *Speculum of the Other Woman.* Translated by Gillian C. Gill. Ithaca, N.Y.: Cornell University Press, 1985.

———. *This Sex Which Is Not One.* Translated by Catherine Potter with Carolyn Burke. Ithaca, N.Y.: Cornell University Press, 1985.

Irwin, John T. *Doubling and Incest/Repetition and Revenge: A Speculative Reading of Faulkner.* Baltimore: Johns Hopkins University Press, 1975.

Jehlen, Myra. *Class and Character in Faulkner's South.* New York: Columbia University Press, 1976.

Jenkins, Lee. *Faulkner and Black-White Relations: A Psychoanalytic Approach.* New York: Columbia University Press, 1981.

Johnson, Karen Ramsay. "Gender, Sexuality, and the Artist in Faulkner's Novels." *American Literature* 61 (1989): 1–15.

Jones, Anne Goodwyn. *Tomorrow Is Another Day: The Woman Writer in the South, 1859–1936.* Baton Rouge: Louisiana State University Press, 1981.

Jordan, Winthrop D. *The White Man's Burden: Historical Origins of Racism in the United States.* New York: Oxford University Press, 1974.

Kang, Hee. "The Snopes Trilogy: (Re)reading Faulkner's Masculine and Feminine." Ph.D. dissertation, University of Alabama, 1992.

Karl, Frederick. *William Faulkner, American Writer.* Boston: Faber, 1989.

Kent, George E. "The Black Woman in Faulkner's Works, with the Exclusion of Dilsey, Part I." *Phylon: The Atlanta Review of Race and Culture* 35, no. 4 (December 1974): 430–41.

———. "The Black Woman in Faulkner's Works, Part II." *Phylon* 36, no. 1 (March 1975): 55–67.

Kinney, Arthur, ed. *Critical Essays on William Faulkner: The Compson Family.* Boston: G. K. Hall, 1982.

Kolodny, Annette. *The Lay of the Land: Metaphor as Experience and History in American Life and Letters.* Chapel Hill: University of North Carolina Press, 1975.

Kristeva, Julia. "Stabat Mater." In *The Female Body in Western Culture,* edited by Susan Rubin Suleiman. Cambridge, Mass.: Harvard University Press, 1986.

Kubie, Lawrence. "William Faulkner's Sanctuary." In *Faulkner: A Collection of Critical Essays,* ed. Robert Penn Warren. Englewood Cliffs, N.J.: Prentice-Hall, 1966.

Lacan, Jacques. "Desire and the Interpretation of Desire in Hamlet." Translated by James Hulbert. In *Literature and Psychoanalysis*, edited by Shoshana Felman. Yale French Studies, no. 55/56. New Haven, Conn.: Yale University Press.

Laqueur, Thomas. "Orgasm, Generation, and the Politics of Reproductive Biology." *Representations* 14 (Spring 1986): 1–24.

Levin, Lynn Gartrell. *Faulkner's Heroic Design: The Yoknapatawpha Novels*. Athens: University of Georgia Press, 1976.

McDowell, Deborah and Arnold Rampersad, eds. *Slavery and the Literary Imagination*. Baltimore: Johns Hopkins University Press, 1989.

McGovern, James R. *Anatomy of a Lynching*. Baton Rouge: Louisiana State University Press, 1982.

McHaney, Thomas L. *William Faulkner's "The Wild Palms": A Study*. Jackson: University Press of Mississippi, 1975.

McMillen, Neil R. *Dark Journey: Black Mississippians in The Age of Jim Crow*. Urbana: University of Illinois Press, 1989.

Matthews, John T. "The Elliptical Nature of Sanctuary." *Novel* 17 (1984): 246–66.

———. *The Play of Faulkner's Language*. Ithaca, N.Y.: Cornell University Press, 1982.

———. *"The Sound and the Fury": Faulkner and the Lost Cause*. Boston: Twayne, 1991.

Meriwether, James B., and Michael Millgate, eds. *Lion in the Garden: Interviews with William Faulkner, 1926–1960*. 1968. Reprint. Lincoln: University of Nebraska Press, 1980.

Michel, Frann. "William Faulkner as a Lesbian Author." *Faulkner Journal* 4, nos. 1 and 2 (1988–89): 5–20.

Milford, Nancy. *Zelda Fitzgerald: A Biography*. London: Bodley Head, 1970.

Millgate, Michael. *The Achievement of William Faulkner*. London: Constable, 1966.

Mims, Edwin. *The Advancing South: Stories of Progress and Reaction*. Garden City, N.Y.: Doubleday, Page, 1927.

Minter, David. *William Faulkner: His Life and Work*. Baltimore: Johns Hopkins University Press, 1980.

Monteiro, George. "Initiation and the Moral Sense in Faulkner's Sanctuary." *Modern Language Notes* 73 (1958): 500–504.

Moore, Robert. "Desire and Despair: Temple Drake's Self-Victimization." In *Faulkner and Women*, edited by Doreen Fowler and Ann Abadie. Jackson: University Press of Mississippi, 1985.

Moreland, Richard. *Faulkner and Modernism: Rereading and Rewriting*. Madison: University of Wisconsin Press, 1990.

Mortimer, Gail. *Faulkner's Rhetoric of Loss: A Study in Perception and Meaning*. Austin: University of Texas Press, 1983.

Muhlenfeld, Elisabeth, ed. *William Faulkner's "Absalom, Absalom!": A Critical Casebook*. New York: Garland, 1984.

Newton, Judith Lowder. *Women, Power, and Subversion*. Athens: University of Georgia Press, 1981.

——— and Deborah Rosenfelt, eds. *Feminist Criticism and Social Change*. London: Methuen, 1985.

Nussbaum, Felicity, and Laura Brown, eds. *The New Eighteenth Century*. London: Methuen, 1987.

O'Donnell, George Marion. "Faulkner's Mythology." In *Faulkner: A Collection of Critical Essays*, edited by Robert Penn Warren. Englewood Cliffs, N.J.: Prentice-Hall, 1966.

Osterweis, Rollin G. *The Growth of Southern Nationalism*. New Haven, Conn.: Yale University Press, 1973.

——. *The Myth of the Lost Cause, 1865–1900*. Hamden, Conn.: Archon Books, 1973.

Page, Sally R. *Faulkner's Women: Characterization and Meaning*. Deland, Fla.: Everett/Edwards, 1972.

Parkhurst, Jessie W. "The Role of the Black Mammy in the Plantation Household." *Journal of Negro History* 23, no. 3 (July 1938): 349–69.

Peters, Erskine. *William Faulkner: The Yoknapatawpha World and Black Being*. Darby, Pa.: Norwood Editions, 1983.

Polk, Noel. *Faulkner's "Requiem for a Nun": A Critical Study*. Bloomington: Indiana University Press, 1981.

——. "The Space Between Sanctuary." In *Intertextuality in Faulkner*, edited by Michel Gresset and Noel Polk. Jackson: University Press of Mississippi, 1985.

Punter, David. *The Literature of Terror*. London: Longman, 1980.

Pyron, Darden Asbury. *Southern Daughter: The Life of Margaret Mitchell*. New York: Oxford University Press, 1991.

Raines, Howell. *My Soul Is Rested: The Story of the Civil Rights Movement in the Deep South*. 1977. London: Penguin, 1983.

Reed, Joseph W. *Faulkner's Narrative*. New Haven, Conn.: Yale University Press, 1973.

Reese, Judy. "Womb/Woman as Text." Paper presented at seminar, University of Alabama, 1990.

Rich, Adrienne. *Of Woman Born: Motherhood as Experience and Institution*. New York: Norton, 1976.

Rogers, K. M. *The Troublesome Helpmate: A History of Misogyny in Literature*. Seattle: University of Washington Press, 1966.

Rubin, Gayle. "The Traffic in Women: Notes on the 'Political Economy' of Sex." In *Toward an Anthropology of Women*, edited by R. R. Reiter. New York: New York Monthly Review Press, 1975.

Schopenhauer, Arthur. *Parerga and Paralipomena*. Translated by E. F. J. Page. Oxford: Clarendon Press, 1974.

Scott, Anne Firor. *Making the Invisible Woman Visible*. Urbana: University of Illinois Press, 1984.

Scott, Evelyn. "On William Faulkner's *The Sound and the Fury*." Pamphlet. New York: Cape and Smith, 1929.

Sedgwick, Eve Kosofsky. *Between Men: English Literature and Male Homosocial Desire*. New York: Columbia University Press, 1985.

Seidel, Kathryn Lee. *The Southern Belle in the American Novel*. Tampa: University of South Florida Press, 1985.

Sensibar, Judith L. *The Origins of Faulkner's Art*. Austin: University of Texas Press, 1984.

Showalter, Elaine. "Representing Ophelia: Women, Madness, and the Responsibilities of Feminist Criticism." In *The Woman's Part*. Urbana: University of Illinois Press, 1980.

Sinfield, Alan. *Literature, Politics and Culture in Postwar Britain*. Oxford: Basil Blackwell, 1989.

Slatoff, Walter J. *Quest for Failure: A Study of William Faulkner*. Ithaca, N.Y.: Cornell University Press, 1960.

Snead, James A. *Figures of Division: William Faulkner's Major Novels*. New York: Methuen, 1986.

Stallybrass, Peter, and Allon White. *The Politics and Poetics of Transgression*. London: Methuen, 1986.

Suleiman, Susan, ed. *The Female Body in Western Culture*. Cambridge, Mass.: Harvard University Press, 1986.

Sundquist, Eric J. *Faulkner: The House Divided*. Baltimore: Johns Hopkins University Press, 1983.

Taylor, William R. *Cavalier and Yankee: The Old South and American National Character*. New York: George Braziller, 1961.

Trudgill, Eric. *Madonnas and Magdalens: The Origins and Development of Victorian Sexual Attitudes*. London: Methuen, 1976.

Vicinus, Martha, ed. *Suffer and Be Still: Women in the Victorian Age*. 1972. Reprint. London: Methuen: 1980.

Vickery, Olga. *The Novels of William Faulkner*. Baton Rouge: Louisiana State University Press, 1964.

Waggoner, Hyatt H. *William Faulkner: From Jefferson to the World*. Lexington: University Press of Kentucky, 1959.

Warner, Marina. *Alone of All Her Sex: The Myth and Cult of the Virgin Mary*. London: Picador, 1985.

Warren, Marsha. "Time, Space, and Semiotic Discourse in the Feminization/Disintegration of Quentin Compson." *Faulkner Journal* 4, nos. 1 and 2 (1988–89): 99–112.

Westling, Louise. *Sacred Groves and Ravaged Gardens: The Fiction of Eudora Welty, Carson McCullers, and Flannery O'Connor*. Athens: University of Georgia Press, 1985.

Wilde, Meta Carpenter, and Orin Borsten. *A Loving Gentleman: The Love Story of William Faulkner and Meta Carpenter*. New York: Simon and Schuster, 1976.

Williams, David. *Women in Faulkner: The Myth and the Muse*. Montreal: McGill-Queen's Press, 1977.

Williamson, Joel. *The Crucible of Race: Black/White Relations in the American South Since Emancipation*. New York: Oxford University Press, 1984.

———. "How Black Was Rhett Butler?" In *The Evolution of Southern Culture*, edited by Numan V. Bartley. Athens: University of Georgia Press, 1988.

———. *New People: Miscegenation and Mulattoes in the United States*. New York: Free Press, 1980.

Woodward, C. Vann. *The Strange Career of Jim Crow*. New York: Oxford University Press, 1955.

Wyatt-Brown, Bertram. *Southern Honor: Ethics and Behavior in the Old South*. New York: Oxford University Press, 1982.

Zanger, Jules. "The 'Tragic Octoroon' in Pre–Civil War Fiction." *American Quarterly* 18 (Spring 1966): 63–70.

Index